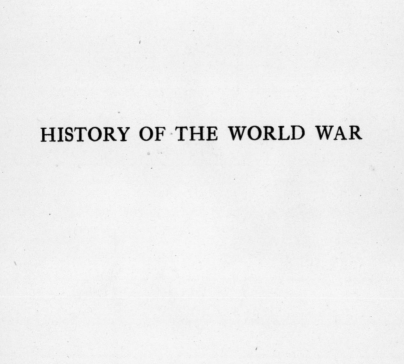

HISTORY OF THE WORLD WAR

HISTORY OF THE WORLD WAR

BY
FRANK H. SIMONDS
Author of "They Shall Not Pass"—Verdun

FULLY ILLUSTRATED

VOLUME FOUR
AMERICA AND RUSSIA

GARDEN CITY   NEW YORK
DOUBLEDAY, PAGE & COMPANY
1919

"CARRY ON!"

From the painting by Edwin Howland Blashfield

CONTENTS

PART I

CHAPTER I

THE FOURTH PHASE

CHAPTER II

THE AMERICAN PEOPLE AND THE WAR

CHAPTER III

THE PROGRESS OF EVENTS

CHAPTER IV

THE GREAT RETREAT

CHAPTER V

THE BATTLE OF ARRAS—BAGDAD

CHAPTER VI

THE FRENCH OFFENSIVE

CHAPTER IX

THE SUBMARINE

CHAPTER X

THE THIRD BATTLE OF YPRES—PASSCHENDAELE

CHAPTER XI

CAMBRAI—JERUSALEM

CHAPTER XII

CAPORETTO—AND PETAIN'S ACHIEVEMENT

CHAPTER XIII

POLITICAL EVENTS

CHAPTER XIV

BREST-LITOVSK—CONCLUSION

LIST OF ILLUSTRATIONS

xiii

LIST OF MAPS

DIAGRAM

HISTORY OF THE WORLD WAR

CHAPTER ONE

THE FOURTH PHASE

I
ON THE MILITARY SIDE

Between January, 1917, and March, 1918, that is, between the failure of the first German peace offensive in the west and the promulgation of the treaties of Brest-Litovsk and Bukharest in the east, the old Triple Entente of France, Great Britain, and Russia—which had in 1915 been reinforced by Italy—suffered disastrous defeat. While British, French, and Italian armies were checked or routed in the field, Russia collapsed and quit the war and her allies, and, but for the entrance of the United States into the struggle in April, 1917, before Russia had yet vanished, Germany would have won a measurable if not a decisive victory. She would at the very least have been able to preserve Mittel-Europa and the mastery of the East.

The period of fourteen months which we are now to examine began on the military side with that stupendous and terrible German retreat from the Somme to the Scheldt—from the battlefields of 1916 to the Hindenburg Line—which not alone defeated Allied strategy but transformed a thousand square miles of fertile fields and scores of busy industrial towns into the saddest and most terrible desert in all the world. This retreat, on the human side, was one of the most gigantic crimes in all the long list of German offences against civilization and humanity, but on the military side it was a success which postponed Allied victory in the west and allowed Germany time to transfer from the Dwina and the Vistula the divisions which in 1918 were to win the memorable battle of March 21st.

The German retreat began in February. When it was over in April the British army flung itself upon the new and the old German positions from Vimy Ridge to the Somme and Sensée, won a brief and brilliant victory and then, in the swamps and mud of Passchendaele, submitted to a grinding, gruelling struggle which broke the spirit and the heart of the finest and mightiest force that had ever assembled under the flag of Britain.   Day by day in the storm and carnage of the campaign, hopeless at the outset, a monument alike to stupidity and folly, in the mud and mire of the swamps—the man-made swamps that lie between Ypres and Passchendaele—British regiments and British divisions were flung ruthlessly and obstinately against German artillery and German entrenchments under conditions of weather which made movement almost impossible, until the British army lost confidence in its commanders, faith in victory, and declined in morale to that danger point which made the German triumph of the following spring not only possible, but inevitable.

Even more disastrous was the history of the French army.   Under its new commander, leaving its entrenchments at the Aisne in the third week of April, that army which had won the Marne and Verdun, which had demonstrated alike the qualities of brilliant offensive and tenacious defence unsurpassed in all its splendid history, went to heart-breaking defeat between the Aisne and the Vesle.   For the first time the morale of the *poilu* began to crumble.   Some of the best divisions in the French army refused to attack, and at the close of a few brief days of brilliant fighting on the Craonne Plateau, the offensive value of that army had temporarily disappeared.   Thenceforth for more than a year there was no hope of another Allied offensive which should include the French. Succeeding Nivelle, who had failed and disappeared, the single and gigantic task of Petain was to restore the confidence of the soldiers, at first, in their officers, and, then, in themselves.   For all practical purposes the French army disappeared from the calculations of offensive warfare from May to the following March.

While the British and the French armies thus endured defeats which, on the moral if not on the military side, were disasters, the Russian army, after a final despairing offensive, melted into flight on the field of victory and Russia as a military force disappeared; and to Russian desertion in June there was added Italian disaster in October.

At Caporetto an Austro-German offensive in one brief day swept away all the gains of the Italian armies in two years of desperate and sustained fighting, transferred the conflict from the banks of the Isonzo to the Piave, removed Trieste from Italian menace, and brought the Hapsburg shadow back over Venice. Almost half Venetia, after fifty years of deliverance, was once more in Austrian hands when this brief campaign ended. Under the threat of an impending ruin as great as that which had overtaken the Russian armies, the Italian forces rallied at the Piave, but escaped only with the aid of French and British divisions drawn from the western front where already Ludendorff was preparing the most gigantic assault in all human history.

Thus on the military side the French offensive was broken in Champagne, the British attack foundered in Flanders, the Russian army ceased to exist after a brief Galician operation, and the Italian army suffered the greatest disaster on the Allied side in four years of war. And with these defeats and disasters the hope of success practically disappeared from the minds of the soldiers, and of three nations, each of whose armies had won victories, earned glory and honour, and each of which now, at last, was convinced that all possibility of victory by offensives, directed at an enemy entrenched and provided with all the instruments of modern warfare and all the advantages of well-selected positions, had vanished. And while the Russian army disappeared in the east, the western Allies began dimly to perceive that with their own armies sadly lessened by the butcheries of Champagne and Passchendaele they had to expect a new attack made by opposing armies now reinforced by a full hundred divisions brought from the east.

Thus on the military side the period that we are to examine is the gloomiest and the most terrible of the whole war. While the armies of the nations allied against Germany, in Europe, were thus crumbling, America, the new ally, was incapable of sending men or armies to fill the gap. A few battalions marching through Paris, to rouse the enthusiasm of the people who were beginning to know the truth, was the sole military contribution of which the United States was capable in the campaign of 1917. Russia disappeared; Italy fell; the spirit of the French army was impaired, the confidence of the British army shaken; and, to balance this, there was on the military side only that hope for the future, still distant, supplied by the presence of a handful of American troops in Europe.

II. ON THE POLITICAL SIDE

In this same time, while the military fortunes of the Allies declined, what of the political circumstances?

In Russia, revolution marched in a few short months from the deliverance of the great Slav people from Romanoff tyranny to the complete destruction of national life and order in the Bolshevist terror of Lenin and Trotsky. In less than a year Russia disappeared from the number of nations in Europe and became a vast assemblage of chaotic fragments, as one after another the peoples of the western fringes who had been annexed as the Russian wave of expansion had swept westward, passed from the Russian to the German orbit or sank into a state of parochial anarchy which has no parallel in modern history.

In France, defeat at the front, the deflection of the morale of the army, coincided with an enormous expansion of treason and "defeatism" behind the line. While the soldiers flatly declined to advance against the impregnable positions of the enemy, politicians even more frankly demanded peace—negotiated, surrender-peace—with the Germans. Before this double menace became too great to check, Clemenceau came and Caillaux exchanged the rôle of traitor for the condition of prisoner. But neither Petain in the army nor Clemenceau in the Cabinet could promptly or utterly redeem France before the supreme test of 1918 came. France, tried beyond her resources of endurance, having made greater sacrifices than any other nation in all history, at last began visibly to crumble. She would be capable of one more renaissance which would save the war, but this last miracle was hidden from all eyes before the March offensive of Ludendorff.

As for England, her condition also had undergone a dangerous change. At the Somme and at Passchendaele a million casualties had failed to win a single substantial reward. The horror of the Somme and the butchery of Passchendaele had already begun to effect a lodgment in the minds of the people of the British Isles who were no longer to be deluded by promises of victory just beyond the horizon. And for the British there was one more circumstance more terrible than all others. When the Germans in February, 1917, opened their gigantic submarine campaign, all the illusions of sea power and impregnability, which had filled the English brain for five hundred years, fell away. Week by week the British saw their merchant marine decline and knew the approach, the actual approach, of famine. England was at last becoming beleaguered in her narrow islands, and it required but a simple calculation—the division of the tonnage of the world by the monthly harvest of the submarines—to indicate at what point she would be forced to surrender if the undersea warfare continued unchecked.

And from London, as from Paris, there was heard the voice of those who advised negotiations to close the horrors and the agonies of a war which no longer could be won; and these views gained new authority and new weight as the additional terror of Bolshevism burst forth in Russia and gave fresh apprehension to the conservatives of the world, who read in the excesses of Petrograd and the crimes of Moscow the lesson of what defeat following too-great national strain might bring even to western nations. The counsels of cowardice and weakness, disguising themselves as the voice of reason, called from London for that peace which the whispers of treason urged in Paris, while in Italy half a dozen influences, mysterious and strengthened by a supreme national disaster—itself procured by their intervention—demanded peace.

In sum, while the armies of the Allies for the first time faltered in the presence of the enemy, the politicians behind the lines lost heart.

In midsummer, 1917, Germany had already effected a moral conquest of Europe. Could she have followed that moral achievement by a military triumph, swift and sure; could Ludendorff have struck in August, 1917, instead of March, 1918, the war would infallibly have been lost. From this terrible catastrophe the world was saved—not by the skill, the courage, the foresight of the politicians or the generals of the Allied armies; not even by the entrance of the United States into the war; but by the unutterable folly of the Germans, who, intoxicated by the extent of the actual and the prospective gains of the war, wrote —at Brest-Litovsk and at Bukharest—treaties of peace which served notice upon all mankind that no tolerable arrangement would be made with the enemy, that nothing but death or national dismemberment awaited western Europe after German victory. And out of this realization was born a final resolution, a new and ultimate courage of desperation, which just availed to man the lines and delay, if not halt, the enemy until millions of American troops became available in Europe and the tide of hope, as of numbers, turned.

III. THREE CURRENTS

In the sombre period which we are now to examine we have, then, several clearly separate currents of events to analyze. We have to note the collapse of Allied hopes on the military side with the concomitant degeneration of public opinion and political courage behind the line. We have to study the entrance of America, reviewing not merely the history of American effort from the moment of her declaration of war, but also that long, slow process by which America was transformed from a neutral into a belligerent, and from a belligerent unarmed and untrained into the greatest single potential force in the alliance against Germany. Finally we have to examine, at least in passing, the rise and progress of revolution in Russia, the transition from an autocracy of tradition to the most stupendous and destructive anarchy of which there is any record. And we shall perceive that as Germanism—the German idea of conquest by force alone, directed by military dynasty—reaches its apex and takes decisions which foreshadow its ultimate collapse, there arises a new menace and a new enemy to Western civilization and democracy, a force which will challenge the conquerors of Germany in a future not distant, and before they have completed the formulation of their terms of peace to be served upon their fallen enemies.

For the period covered by the present volume, anarchy in Russia remains hidden behind the fogs of censorship, lost in the distance which separates Petrograd and Moscow from London, Paris, and Washington, and disguised by the natural but mistaken illusions of Western liberalism awake to the iniquity of the ancient Russian régime but blind to the fury of the new. In this period the Western world is conscious only of the desertion of a great ally, which has imperilled the whole future of the war. It is conscious of strange, incomprehensible words uttered by new and unknown Russian leaders—words seized upon by the radicals of the West as the first authentic sign of a new democratic gospel, seized upon by the leaders of Germany as the basis for propaganda and disintegrating manœuvres amidst the enemy publics.

Not even the immediate significance of the Russian Revolution was clear to mankind fighting above the Aisne and about Ypres, contemplating with horror German strategy which created a desert in Artois and Picardy, and beholding, with acute anxiety, that disaster which brought Italy almost to the edge of surrender. In 1917 military disasters and submarine terrors filled the minds of statesmen and soldiers of the west. The great new social and political problems presented by the Russian Revolution were seen only in terms of the loss to the Entente of their strongest ally. The alliance between Germanism and Bolshevism was recognized; the possibility of the victory of these combined forces was at least dimly perceived; but the chance that, after Germanism had fallen, Bolshevism might erect itself as a new and greater peril was undreamed of.

Between the rejection by the Allies of the German peace proposal of January, 1917, and the promulgation of the peace of Brest-Litovsk and that of Bukharest in 1918, the cause of that Western civilization which we call representative democracy marched from disaster to disaster until, with the coming of the spring of 1918, it stood on the brink of complete ruin, its one real chance of salvation depending upon effective American intervention. By the latter date Germany had destroyed the balance of power in Europe, eliminated Russia from the war, broken Italian military strength almost fatally, put England and France upon a defensive which was in itself doomed to failure and collapse unless American reinforcements could arrive in time. The European contestants had fought their war out, and Germany would have won it had she not, in the hour of victory, been guilty of two blunders, each of which in future history will rank with Napoleon's adventure to Moscow: the one, the submarine campaign, brought America to Europe with all the untouched resources of one hundred millions of people at last roused to the truth; the other, at Brest-Litovsk, gave to the people of France and England and Italy that courage of despair which only comes to those threatened with defeat who perceive that their enemy seeks to annihilate them, and that surrender will compel them to accept a condition so unbearable that death seems the more tolerable.

CHAPTER TWO

THE AMERICAN PEOPLE AND THE WAR

I
THE FIRST DAYS

On January 31, 1917, the German Ambassador at Washington presented to the United States Government formal notification that the Imperial German Government purposed on the following day to begin a ruthless submarine warfare directed against all ships—neutral and belligerent alike—found in European waters. On February 3rd, the United States severed diplomatic relations with Germany, recalling its own ambassador from Berlin and presenting the German Ambassador in Washington with, his passports. A little more than two months later, on April 6th, Congress declared that a state of war existed between the United States and the Imperial German Government.

We have now briefly to review the steps by which the United States, remote from the scene of the European struggle, its neutrality fortified alike by its oldest tradition and by the most earnest desire of the majority of its people, was dragged into a world war by a series of aggressions and injuries unparalleled in history. Such an examination necessarily divides itself into three distinct phases. It is essential to review the state of American feeling with respect to the European conflict from the outset to the moment when we entered the war; the progress of events themselves; and the meaning of American entrance immediate and eventual in view of the situation that then existed in Europe.

Even after the passage of so brief a time it is almost impossible to re-constitute the real emotion of America at the moment when the World War broke. For the millions there was almost literally no warning. The assassination of the Archduke in June claimed only a passing notice in the press. The suppressed tension and the surcharged atmosphere of European chancelleries revealed themselves only in curious stock-exchange variations, unnoted save in financial quarters and even there misunderstood.

When the Austro-Hungarian Government served its ultimatum upon the Serbian Government in the closing days of June, American public opinion became vaguely aware that Europe was entering into another one of those crises which had become familiar in the previous ten years, but neither then nor in the next few days was there any real belief in the United States that the events in Europe indicated anything more dangerous than another such crisis as that of Tangier or Agadir. While Europe marched inescapably to the catastrophe, America continued on its daily routine; in the press the events of the baseball field claimed equal attention with those of the European crisis, and more Americans were interested in the Caillaux murder trial than in the Austrian aggression against Serbia. To the very end the American public remained good-naturedly sceptical, unconquerably incredulous. For them the very idea of war seemed preposterous, and on the day before the first declaration of war—that of Germany against Russia which precipitated the deluge—the conviction that the storm would pass remained unshaken from New York to San Francisco.

When the war did break, the initial American emotion was one of mingled consternation and indignation. For the mass of the American people it seemed as if Europe had suddenly gone mad. No single one of the real causes of the war was in the slightest degree understood or appreciated. The very idea of war between civilized countries seemed to the Americans to convict those nations of essential barbarism. In the first hours, in the first weeks, the American people as a whole interpreted the war as a struggle for power and for plunder between nations equally guilty of sacrificing right and justice to ambition and selfishness. America as a whole, in the first phase, in the opening hours of the struggle, was not merely neutral. It felt a sense of moral superiority combined with a deep-seated satisfaction that not only the Atlantic but also American tradition separated the United States from Europe. Between the two forces arrayed against each other American public

AMERICA MOBILIZES

THE DECLARATION OF WAR

Signed by Champ Clark, Speaker of the House of Representatives, and by Thos. R. Marshall, President of the Senate; and approved 6th of April, 1917, by Woodrow Wilson, President of the United States.

PREPAREDNESS PARADES
PATRIOTIC DEMONSTRATIONS

THE PRESIDENT ADDRESSES CONGRESS

"The world must be made safe for democracy. . . . We have no selfish ends to serve. We desire no conquest, no dominion. . . . We are but one of the champions of the rights of mankind. We shall be satisfied when those rights have been made as secure as the faith and the freedom of the nations can make them."

A PREPAREDNESS PARADE

New York business men, one hundred and fifty thousand strong, march up Fifth Avenue, demonstrating for preparedness

TURNING CITIZENS INTO SOLDIERS

Above—The students of Princeton University, already in khaki, prepare for the call to the colors by vigorous calisthenics on the university campus.

Below—Candidates for commissions at Plattsburg, N. Y., take their first lesson in the "I.D.R." (Infantry Drill Regulations).

OFF FOR THE MOBILIZATION CAMP

Wisconsin infantry marching through Milwaukee on their way to the railroad station

PROVISIONING THE FLEET IN PREPARATION FOR ACTIVE SERVICE

THE CAMPAIGN FOR NAVAL RECRUITS

A dummy fleet consisting of battleship, submarine chaser, etc., was manœuvred over the tracks of Chicago's elevated railroad

CALLING LANDSMEN TO THE SEA

A recruiting rally around a wooden battleship "moored" near Broadway in Union Square, New York City

"THE AVENUE OF THE ALLIES"

Looking north from Forty-Second Street, along Fifth Avenue, New York City, during the campaign for the Fourth Liberty Loan. The "Haiti block" is in the foreground

opinion in the first hours neither could nor did discriminate. For the American the spectacle of Europe rushing to arms and to battle was a revelation of collective madness still incomprehensible, still inexplicable, and no single thought of American participation was roused anywhere. It would be difficult to describe for the future the paralysis alike of thought and of conscience which was the first resulting circumstance, in the United States, of the outbreak of the world explosion.

II. THE SPECTACLE

Thereafter, in the days while Europe was proceeding through mobilization to action, American attention was concentrated on two relatively trivial details: on the Atlantic seaboard, German ships—fleeing westward—arrived, landing their passengers at Bar Harbor and at Boston; excited ocean travellers related tales of imaginary adventures with phantom fleets, while from Europe came the ridiculous but absorbing reports of thousands of American tourists surprised at every watering place and at every tourist centre by the sudden outbreak of the conflict. The adventures and agonies of the rich and the locally famous, the tales of besieged embassies and stranded fellow-countrymen divided interest for the American public with the stupendous events which the censorship hid and American unfamiliarity with Europe made unfathomable. Even when there was a consciousness that millions of men were on the march the whole drama remained unreal, unbelievable, for the United States. It was like a gigantic nightmare, a nightmare in which all the inevitable horror was scarcely realized, a dream in which the sleeper, while perceiving a mirage of fantastic outlines, preserves a subconscious sense that it is a dream and not a reality.

Then suddenly the opening engagement of the war aroused a new emotion. While the newspapers day by day announced in enormous headlines incredible millions of men advancing to conflict, the people of the United States settled back to observe what was still for them little more than a spectacle. When Belgian neutrality was violated, when the French armies were broken in the first offensive, when the German hordes rushed downward on Paris, the press spoke little of

moral issues but continued day by day to forecast a Trafalgar at sea
and to expect a Waterloo on land not far indeed from the field where
Napoleon had fought his last battle.   The defence of Liége, the fall of
Brussels, the invasion of France; these were events which more and
more concentrated and absorbed the attention of the American people,
who awaited with an excitement hardly to be described the onrush of
the German wave as it engulfed northern France and approached Paris.

It was not until the Marne had been fought and won, it was not
until the German invasion had been turned back and the line began to
stabilize itself along the Aisne, that there crept into American comment
and arrived in the American mind and conscience a new sense of appreciation, vague but beginning, that moral issues were involved in what
had been hitherto, from the day of the declaration of war to that hour,
a wonderful, terrible, ineffaceable spectacle.   It was not until France
had saved herself and the world and it became clear that the decision
had been adjourned and the first German bid for victory had failed,
that the American people, getting their perspective, began slowly to
estimate, to consider, to appraise the meaning of the struggle—not in
terms of American self-interest, for not even then was American responsibility touched—but the meaning for the world of victory or defeat
for either group of nations involved.

Long after the event many public men protested that they had
favoured intervention in the war on the day that Belgium was invaded. The truth is otherwise. Long after the event men criticized the
President of the United States because he proclaimed American neutrality rather than announced American championship of Belgium.
But the fact is that neither the President of the United States, nor any
public men of prominence, nor any newspaper of influence, conceived
of American intervention then or for long months thereafter. America
at the outbreak of the World War was neutral. America as a nation
remained neutral—not alone in word, but in thought, for many, many
months. President Wilson in the opening phase merely spoke the will
of his country. It was not that Americans were essentially blind to
moral appeal, to justice or to right; it was that there existed in the

United States not the smallest conception of the truth of the European conflict.   For the mass of the people it was as if two groups of men in the public street had suddenly fallen into a terrific quarrel and begun to beat each other with fists and sticks.   What the origin of the quarrel was, the observers could not see.   If one is to understand American emotion between the Austrian ultimatum and the Battle of the Marne, it is essential to recognize that there was no comprehension of issues, no understanding of moral considerations involved—nothing but amazement, horror, and indignation, all of which were subordinated in a brief time to the realization that, from her remote point of observation, America was perceiving a conflict greater than the wars of Napoleon, more absorbing in its dramatic intensity than anything known in human experience.   Such was the first reaction of America in the World War.

III.   THE CLASH OF OPINION

With the arrival of that military deadlock which followed the Marne, the Aisne, and the Yser, Americans suddenly found themselves plunged into a battle of words, rival sympathies, and propaganda, unparalleled in all their history.   The mass of the American nation remained steadily neutral, obeying easily and loyally the advice of the President, but throughout the country three currents of opinion were nevertheless strongly developing.   The first was a thoroughly spontaneous national American view.   It was an opinion which interpreted events in Europe in the terms of American ideals.   It saw in the German invasion of Belgium, it saw in each German act which had been disclosed since the very opening of the struggle, the revelation of a spirit totally contrary to American conceptions.   The invasion of Belgium became, as week followed week, more and more a fatal comment on German purpose and German ambitions.

As between England and Germany in August, 1914, the sympathy of America was at least equally divided.   In point of fact, there was nowhere in America the same long-standing if ill-founded suspicion and dislike for the Germans which from the very time of the Revolution had survived in Eastern America with respect of the English. At the outset of the struggle not a few Americans were prepared to sympathize with Germany, recognizing, whatever else might be in the case, that Germany had become a great commercial rival of the English and that in past centuries a similar rise of any Continental State had been inevitably followed by the appearance of the English on the Continent as an ally of the enemies of the more prosperous State. Americans did not accept, and Americans were not as a mass profoundly impressed by the British assertions that their entrance into the war was an act of unparalleled devotion to the cause of justice and in defence of the sacred obligations of a treaty and the inalienable rights of a small people.

As between England and Germany the mass of the American people were prepared to be neutral, and had Germany neither attacked France nor invaded Belgium, American sympathy would never have been enlisted in any phase of the war. Even the invasion of Belgium was an act which only slowly appealed to the American conscience. Germany's explanation—that she was threatened, encircled, compelled to strike first to save herself, menaced primarily by the Russian peril— found sympathetic hearing in a country where Russia was the symbol of tyranny and the Jewish faction of the population influential and necessarily anti-Slav.

It was not until the first whispers of Louvain were heard in the world; it was not until men and women began dimly to be conscious of the fact that the German armies in invading Belgium had not merely transformed a solemn obligation into a scrap of paper, but had been guilty of crimes against women and children—had been guilty of deeds of wanton destruction unparalleled in a thousand years of European history, that there was a real if only a premonitory movement of American opinion; and this movement was stimulated by the German bombardment of Rheims Cathedral, which, in its turn, all over America stirred passionate protests from that relatively small but influential section of the population for whom beautiful things were sacred because they were beautiful.

IV. AMERICAN JUDGMENT

Thus, underneath the surface and following the first weeks of the war, the tide of American judgment almost imperceptibly, but no less surely, began to run against Germany and her allies. This tide was not influenced by the fact that one of the opponents of Germany spoke the language and held measurably the same political faith as America. It was not set in motion by any clear perception that one side was right and the other wrong in the war, which still remained for the mass of the American people primarily a contest between two commercial rivals. With the millions who were prepared to sympathize as much with Germany as with England, Germany lost a decided advantage when her armies, having invaded Belgium and northern France, added to the still debatable offence of unwarranted invasion, real and enduring wrongs of rapine and violence. Again; in America, divided on the question of England or Germany, the unanimity of sympathy with France was almost unbelievable. From the opening weeks of the war to the day of the armistice a renaissance of affection for France, an ever-mounting emphasis on the memories of Franco-American association in the Revolution, the glorification of successful French achievement in the war, more than any other circumstance influenced the American people in the direction of the alliance against Germany. The victory of the Marne, by its splendour, by its almost miraculous character, unloosed the tongues of thousands of those who loved France and believed in her, and silenced the slanders of those who misunderstood or despised her.

As time advanced, at first dozens, then scores, and at last hundreds of American boys crossed the ocean, following the example of Lafayette, and enlisted either in the armies or in the hospital service of France (although it is worth recording that there was a very considerable movement of the same sort in the direction of Canada and the Canadian Expeditionary Force, while not a few Americans entered the British army directly). The presence of France in the alliance against Germany more and more made impossible any thought of American entrance into the war save as an opponent of the Kaiser. Two forces even in this early time thus combined to lead American sympathies toward the Entente: (1) the German method and German manner in conducting the war, and (2) the glory and the peril of France which combined to re-awaken a friendship which was the oldest in American history and possessed a vitality which no one had suspected. Between the victory of the Marne and the sinking of the *Lusitania* even both these circumstances were, however, little perceived, and equally incapable of disturbing the resolute neutrality of the majority of Americans.

V. PROPAGANDA

Much more conspicuous and much more impressive in all this time was the battle fought between European propagandists upon American soil. At the first moment of the war, sympathy was silenced in both camps while American partisans of both alliances watched the fate of the world as it was being decided upon the battlefields of France and Belgium. Expression of sympathy with contesting forces was restrained by the very tenseness of the hour and by the magnitude of the events which were unrolled. But when it became clear that the circumstances of the Hundred Days and of 1870 were not to be repeated and that Europe was involved in a long struggle, not in a single, brief, decisive conflict, the American public suddenly beheld the outburst of a battle between the sympathizers of the two forces which left it bewildered, amazed, and in no small degree indignant.

The difference between the two camps of propaganda was day by day more clearly disclosed. While Englishmen, Frenchmen, and Belgians by individual word and letter, without organization, without even efficient method, laid before the American people the statement of the Allied case and found—fortunately for themselves and their cause— even abler advocates among Americans who knew or sympathized with the enemies of Germany, German propaganda more and more took on exactly the same character as German military attack in western Europe.

Of a sudden all the German-American press in America began to goose-step to the command of some unseen master. The same arguments, the same insinuations, the same charges were heard from Maine to California. The attack upon England was conducted by German agents in America with every possible appeal to ancient American prejudice and every conceivable incitation to Irish antipathies. In the nature of things this German-American outburst had to take the defensive as well as the offensive. It had to explain the invasion of Belgium, to deny with ever-increasing violence the charges and the evidence of German atrocities. And yet it was not unsuccessful in this first period. It was not without its sympathetic hearing. It might have availed to confuse American thinking and paralyze American conscience, had it been able to escape the constant necessity of explaining the inexplicable course of the German Government.

The American reaction to this sudden violent outburst of conflict of alien propaganda on American soil was on the whole clear in this period. There was a great and growing irritation alike with the champions of Germany and of England. The attacks of both conflicting forces upon American neutrality were equally resented and while along the Atlantic seaboard, where association and sympathy with England and with France was greatest, a slow but sure drift toward even more pronounced sympathies revealed itself, a compensating tide in the rest of the country disclosed alike an impatience with the propagandists of the opposing camps and with the growing partisanship of one section of the country for the Allied cause. The mass of the country resented at least equally, sectional American sympathy with the Allies and German-American championship of the German cause in America. All over the country there began to appear in offices and public places signs inviting the visitor in homely American phrase to avoid the discussion of the issues of the war and to refrain from support of a foreign cause at the expense of national peace of mind.

VI. THE WILL FOR NEUTRALITY

In the time between the Marne and the *Lusitania* Massacre, while the cause of the Allies rather than that of the Germans gained ground, that development was personal, not public, and the national will was unmistakably a will for neutrality. The Middle West viewed with contempt and hostility the patent sympathy of the Far East of America for the Allies. It did not itself indulge in profoundly pro-German sentiments but it continued to hold the balance even between the two, and more and more emphatically declared that real Americanism could only be expressed in neutrality—that the claims of the propagandists on either side of the firing line were equally unfounded. It refused to believe that Germans would commit atrocities; it declined to accept the eastern view of Allied moral superiority. It more and more gave itself up to an intense, if parochial, Americanism which asserted that, in the world in which two sets of European nations were fighting for old European aims and ambitions, America had alone remained faithful to the ideals of liberty and democracy and that the true American point of view could not be sympathetic with either of the camps but could only have unlimited condemnation for both.

Thus, during the first months of the war, American public opinion more and more firmly entrenched itself behind a breast-work of traditional isolation and more and more rigidly insisted upon unqualified neutrality. There was no chance then of American participation in the war on the German side. There was unmistakable and considerable sympathy with France; actual, if comparatively passive, condemnation of the German invasion of Belgium. But these latent currents were on the whole slight and there never was at any time the smallest possibility that the United States would, of its own volition and because of its approval of either of the alliances, enter the war.

The single problem posed on the day on which the war broke out and enduring long thereafter was whether one or the other of the alliances would, by its course, compel the United States to take up arms— not in the championship of a European cause but in the maintenance of American neutrality. But up to the sinking of the *Lusitania* there was nowhere in America any real conception that the United States could be involved in the struggle, just as there was nowhere any considerable

"LAFAYETTE, NOUS VOICI!"

Soon after the arrival of the American troops in France, General Pershing was invited to speak at the grave of Lafayette. The gallant Frenchman had fought to win freedom for America, and the Americans now were come to repay the debt by standing shoulder to shoulder with the men of France in the hour of their need. The delight of Marshal Joffre, Pershing's most conspicuous auditor, is very evident.

The laconic phrase, "Lafayette, we are here!" which the occasion spontaneously evoked, was uttered some say by General Pershing, some say by Colonel Stanton, and some say by neither speaker.

or influential body of opinion—that is, of purely American opinion—which advocated such an entrance.

Sympathy on the whole tended in the Allied direction, but the resolution to remain outside the area of struggle gained ground much more rapidly. By the time the war had been in progress for six months the neutrality of America seemed to be founded upon a rock, and there can be no more astonishing or impressive page in history than that which reveals the manner in which the Imperial German Government, by its folly, its essential blindness, its total surrender to the gospel of Force, literally drove a hundred millions of people—almost unanimous in their desire for neutrality—into an active and decisive participation in the European struggle.

Realizing that the United States did ultimately become a participant in the war on the Allied side, it is no less essential to recognize that, on the outbreak of the war, before and after the Battle of the Marne, up to the time of the sinking of the *Lusitania*, and even for a long period thereafter, public opinion in America remained faithful to the tradition that the United States should avoid entanglement in a European conflict; and the majority of Americans refused to believe that there was a preponderance of right on one side rather than on the other sufficient to demand American intervention. Like the President the mass of his countrymen refused to believe that America could have any other rôle than that of precise neutrality until such time as she was able to act as the peace-maker, and intervene, not as a belligerent but as an arbitrator, to restore peace—not to expand the area of conflict or the number of combatants by sending Americans to the fighting line. When German folly sank the *Lusitania* on the 7th of May, 1915, such was the state of American opinion and purpose and so strongly entrenched was American neutrality that it required a supreme madness on the part of German leadership to dislodge it.

VII. INCIDENTS

Between January and May the exasperation of the Government and of the people of the United States over unwarranted interference with

American commerce both by British and German sea power aroused emotions strangely reminiscent of American public opinion in the Napoleonic wars. The English blockade, not alone of German ports but of neutral harbours; the English refusal to accept the principles laid down in the Declaration of London largely by British representatives, led the Government to protest after protest which were only in part answered by British citation of Northern precedents during the Civil War. On the other hand, proclamation by the Germans of their submarine blockade—illegal from every point of view, and, in addition, indefensibly inhuman—aroused similar indignation. In this time the American Government essayed, as a great and powerful neutral, to compel both contesting alliances to live under international law, and this rôle seemed, to the larger part of intelligent Americans, the proper one for their own government.

In fact, the English, as the dominating sea power of the Entente, and the Germans, as the similar element among the Central Powers—both faced with new necessities and new conditions—imitated the precedents of a century before and tore up all existing guarantees of international law. Each blamed the other; each pointed to the illegal acts of the other as the justification of its own transgressions; yet each continued in a course disastrous to American interests, with a persistence only limited by a certain degree of caution.

But it is essential to recognize that in this period there was a clear governmental policy in the United States and that this policy had the substantial and adequate support of the American people. The United States Government undertook by moral suasion to compel the nations at war to conduct their struggle within the limits of international law. It spoke for the rights of its own citizens but it no less plainly spoke as the one great neutral for the rights of all the smaller neutral powers—rights which were equally unjustifiably violated by the Entente and by the Central Powers. Without considering yet the possibility of armed interference on behalf of the principles championed by official declaration, the United States began to build up for itself a position which, could it have been maintained to the end, would have been fatal to the Entente.

The state of international law at the moment of the outbreak of the war was such that, had it been observed, Germany would have continued to receive that food and those raw materials necessary to her, and in the very nature of things American championship of the principles of neutrality led to a defence of the right to trade with Germany. Ineluctably, if imperceptibly, American policy prior to the 7th of May, 1915, was drifting in the direction of the use of the most powerful weapon in American hands to enforce neutral rights on the sea against all who challenged it. It is not difficult to believe that an embargo upon the export of food and material alike to England and to France, on the one hand, and to Germany, on the other, would have followed British persistence in interfering with American trade with Germany through neutral ports and in non-contraband had Germany permitted the dispute with Great Britain, which was becoming steadily more acrimonious, to continue uninterrupted.

For the United States to have employed the embargo in 1915, or in any other year of the war, would have been in effect to give Germany the victory. For the Allies to have permitted the United States to trade with Germany in the exercise of its indisputable rights under international law would have been almost as certain to give Germany the victory. That the United States would have pursued a policy based upon the assertion and defence of these rights by the embargo seems almost certain. That we should have gone to war with Great Britain was always unlikely, just as it was equally unlikely that anything but slaughter of Americans would lead us into conflict with Germany. But that we should have employed the embargo at no distant date seems a reasonable and sound conclusion.

VIII. THE "LUSITANIA" MASSACRE

But while these discussions of interference with American sea-borne trade were more and more exasperating the American people, and more and more profoundly stirring resentment against Europe, without regard to the war or the alliances, there came suddenly the news of the supreme tragedy of the *Lusitania*, which must be reckoned as the turning point in American opinion in the World War.

Only a few years before the whole civilized world had waited and watched while the first fugitive splutters of the wireless told the story of the sinking of the *Titanic*. Hundreds of millions of people waited and watched for the final truth of the sinking of the greatest ship in the world, and the memory of that horror in the American mind still survived the reports of more recent battles. But the *Titanic* was an accident. Now, all the circumstances of the earlier tragedy were repeated as the result of a wanton act of man.

Few of the people who were alive in America on the day and night when the first reports of the *Lusitania* Massacre began to arrive will ever forget the horror, the indignation, the stupefaction produced by that crime. For twenty-four hours the country refused to believe that a civilized nation, presumably holding to the same ideals and the same conceptions of humanity, could permit its sailors to launch against a passenger ship, laden with women and children and carrying neutrals as well as belligerents, a torpedo which would inevitably result in the slaughter of innocent and helpless human beings.

When the truth was no longer to be doubted there swept from one end of the United States to the other an emotion which destroyed sympathy with Germany everywhere except among people of German origin or politicians dependent upon hyphenated votes for their political existence. The cause of Germany, so far as it had an appeal to the sympathy, the intelligence, and the conscience of the United States, went down with the *Lusitania*. Thereafter there could be but one issue: Should the United States remain neutral?—or should she enter the war on the Allied side? The brand on Cain's forehead was not more conspicuous or more fatal than the mark left upon the German cause by the *Lusitania* Massacre.

On the morrow of this massacre it would have been possible for the President of the United States to have carried a majority of his fellow-countrymen into the war against Germany. But it is not less certain that, even after this crime, a majority of the American people still believed that the duty of America was still to remain outside the conflict. It was clear instantly that, unless Germany renounced a policy of murder, the American people would demand of their government a declaration of war. It was no less clear that the inherent, the traditional antipathy to participation in a European struggle endured. American public opinion demanded that, once and for all—emphatically, definitively—the President should warn Germany. Even at this hour, in the presence of their dead, the American people faintly hoped that the German Government would disavow the act of a German officer—so naïvely did they still cling to the notion of German humanity.

The summer of the *Lusitania* Massacre sees the beginning of that national sentiment which pushed the Government into ultimate conflict with Germany. When Germany, instead of disavowing, quibbled, evaded, dodged; when the President of the United States, instead of speaking firmly, blundered in his "too-proud-to-fight" speech and argued in his long-continued notes, American restiveness increased with every hour. Still determined to remain neutral if possible there was not—except amongst those controlled by their sympathy with that foreign country from which they had come—the smallest willingness permanently to bow before German terrorism. The country asked of its government that, either by firmness in policy or by force in action, it should compel Germany to abandon murder.

IX. THE FIRST RESULT

With the sinking of the *Lusitania*, too, all chance of the equal application of the principles of international law, to both alliances, perished. From that hour onward the factories, the fields, and the workmen of the United States and the vast industrial and agricultural machinery of the country were mobilized on the Allied side. The campaign to compel Great Britain to permit America to trade with Germany and Austria died. We became in fact, on the days following the tragedy off the Old Head of Kinsale, the economic ally of the Entente. With ever-increasing volume our machines and our arms, our food and our raw material, flowed to western Europe, depriving Germany of the advantages of superior preparation and better organization.

This aid was not to prove adequate without the addition of American soldiers, but between May 7, 1915, and the spring of 1918, it was an indispensable contribution to Allied survival. Between the sinking of the *Lusitania* and the promulgation of the final German campaign of submarine ruthlessness, almost two years later, American public opinion marched surely to an acceptation of the Allied view of Germany; and the publication of the Bryce report upon the Belgian atrocities in Belgium, which almost coincided with the sinking of the *Lusitania*, reached a people at last prepared to believe those German crimes which hitherto had passed the credulity of a civilized nation. Retrospectively, and in the light of a crime which could not be denied, the American people interpreted the invasion of Belgium, the burning of Louvain, the campaign of rape and violence, murder and destruction over all of Belgium and northern France.

While our government continued in its official documents to talk of German regard for humanity; while the President pursued a policy founded on a determination to remain neutral, and buttressed on the faith that words could have power unsupported by arms in dealing with a nation which had given itself over utterly to a gospel of force; the American people, with ever-growing clarity, grasped the real meaning of Germany in the world. Morally, materially, in all ways that it is possible to measure, the German cause was lost in America with the sinking of the *Lusitania*, and the single question that remained to be answered was whether Germany would renounce a policy of which the *Lusitania* was an everlasting evidence, or accept an inevitable war with the greatest of the neutrals.

Between May 7, 1915, and January, 1917, Germany hesitated. For a long time she pursued a course of modified defiance. New "incidents", new attacks, came with relative frequency. The series culminated with the attack upon the *Sussex* in February, 1916, which would have led to war had it not been promptly followed by a German surrender in the matter of submarine warfare. Thereafter, so long as Germany observed her obligations, American neutrality endured; but while that neutrality endured, American abhorrence of German methods increased so that it was inevitable that if Germany ever departed from her pledges American entrance into the war would become almost automatic.

The *Lusitania* Massacre is one of the great landmarks in history, not alone in American history but in human history, because it ensured German defeat in the World War.   Looking to the terrible crisis of 1918 it is unmistakable that, had America been neutral in that hour, the victory of the alliance against Germany would have been unthinkable, nor is it less probable that Allied consent to peace by negotiation would have followed the defeats of the year which we are now to examine, had not the entrance of the United States served to create new hopes and restore shaken confidence.   American decision in the World War was finally made on the basis of the *Lusitania*.   Between the *Lusitania* Massacre and the entrance of American troops into the line at Château-Thierry a little more than three years were to elapse; but while, on the surface, America continued long after the earlier event to seem blind to the truth, deaf to the appeals of honour and safety alike, the forces released by this crime continued to march—continued to extend the area of their influence—until a united country ultimately entered the European war.   And, as a final detail, it is at least one of the most striking coincidences of which we have any knowledge that those terms of peace which imposed the sentence of the victorious nations upon a defeated Germany were delivered into German hands on the fourth anniversary of the sinking of the *Lusitania*.

X. THEODORE ROOSEVELT

No discussion of the development of American opinion in respect of the war would be complete without a mention of the contribution of Theodore Roosevelt to the illumination of the minds of his fellow-countrymen.

There was no American who saw more promptly the fundamental issues and principles involved in the German assault upon our Western civilization than Colonel Roosevelt, nor was there any other American who displayed so much force or exerted so great an influence in awakening people of the nation to the facts of the situation.

The war found Colonel Roosevelt at the close of a brilliant political career which had ended summarily. The break with his own party in 1912 was not healed. The campaign for the nomination of 1916 revealed the enormous popularity still retained by Colonel Roosevelt, but it was not sufficient to win for him the nomination, and that last defeat ended all hope of a return to public office. Physically a broken man, politically without a future, separated from most of those conspicuous figures of his own party who had been his associates and his subordinates in his own Administration, a lonely figure, he was yet able, by the sheer force of his personality, to rouse thousands and even millions of his countrymen to a perception of the meaning in America of the colossal crime in Europe.

Speaking; writing; constantly brushing aside, with impatient energy, theories, emotions, parochial and utopian conceptions; taking his stand firmly on that platform of virile Americanism of which he had been the greatest exponent in his own generation, Colonel Roosevelt inveighed against each German aggression, each German crime, with ever-growing force and effect.

Without Colonel Roosevelt it is conceivable that American neutrality might have been maintained to the end, with all its terrible consequences—first to Europe and ultimately to this country. Certainly no other man did so much to arouse his countrymen—to prepare them intellectually and morally for the great strain that was coming—as the man who, having twice occupied the White House and having been the conspicuous figure of his own generation in American public life, sat now almost in exile from his party councils and from his public associates.

Historians of the future will find it difficult to estimate and to appraise exactly the extent of the influence exerted by Theodore Roosevelt in a time of confused counsels, national blindness, political expediency. He saw the war as it was. He saw the Belgian crime in its full meaning. He saw the cause of the western Allies as the cause

THE AMERICAN DRAFT

THE RAW MATERIAL

Black and white, fat and lean, jolly and sober was the grist drawn into the draft-hopper. But Negro and Latin and Slav and Anglo-Saxon were Americans all, and gave a good account of themselves on the battle-fields of France

FIFTY-TWO TONGUES REGISTERED FOR THE DRAFT

This is a group of Spaniards. The interpreter is a young Spaniard who is already in khaki

DRAWING THE FIRST NUMBER

Copyright by Committee on Public Information

After he had been blindfolded, Mr. Baker, Secretary of War, plunged his hand into the large glass jar containing the 10,500 numbers inclosed in capsules. He drew one forth and passed it to a clerk who opened it and announced the number "258." Thus the drawing began. The date was July 20, 1917

DRAFT REGISTRATION AT HONOLULU

In the far islands of the Pacific long lines of yellow and brown Americans awaited their turn to register

DRAFT REGISTRATION IN CHINATOWN, NEW YORK CITY

It would have been a hopeless task, but for the help of the keen young civilian interpreter

EVEN THE TENDERLOIN FURNISHED ITS QUOTA

Registrars at work in the Tenderloin district, New York City

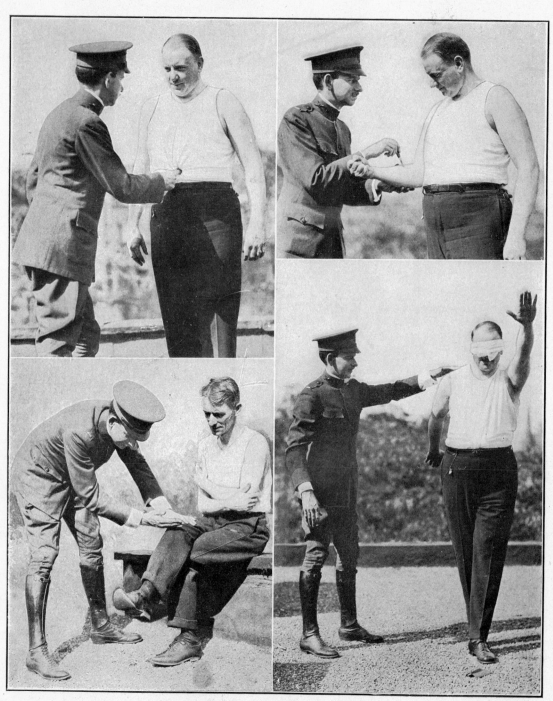

IT WAS A *SELECTIVE* DRAFT:

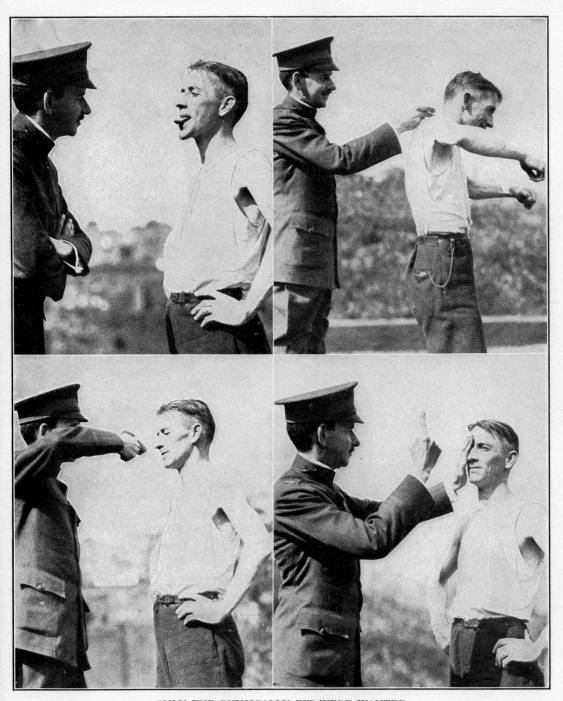

ONLY THE PHYSICALLY FIT WERE WANTED

PHILADELPHIA DRAFT ARMY PARADE

Twenty-five thousand men were drafted in Philadelphia. Before leaving for the training camp they paraded before a cheering crowd of relatives and friends

of the United States, and he saw plainly that there could be no escape from American entrance—that each halting, conciliating action, in the face of German menace, invited new aggression. He understood force. He understood the German conception. He saw that a victorious Germany would set its foot triumphantly upon that whole democratic doctrine which represented the political faith of the western powers.

Upon his head, during the long controversial period which preceded the actual entrance of the United States into the war, there burst a passion of denunciation. He carried in his body the bullet of a would-be assassin who bore a German name. Democratic politicians combined with German propagandists to assail the man whose services to his country should have placed him outside of the range of such attack. When at last his fight had roused an American public opinion which met the final German menace with a declaration of war, Colonel Roosevelt was denied the opportunity to lead troops against the enemy. His physical condition probably warranted the decision of the Government, but no one who knew him in those days could mistake the fact that this was the crowning disappointment of a life equally replete with great successes and corroding defeats. He lived to see three of his sons wounded in the firing line. He lived to give one of his boys to his country upon the battlefield. He did not die until the German had surrendered. At the very time when death came suddenly to him his voice was powerfully heard attacking, as a policy for making peace, precisely those conceptions which he had fought when they pointed the way to American neutrality. No living American of that time—with the possible exception of Elihu Root—knew his Europe, his world, or his history as did Theodore Roosevelt. Had he lived he would have been a potent foe of precisely those principles which were championed by the United States at the Paris Conference. What his influence might have been no man can say, but one thing is clear beyond all question, and that is, that from the outbreak of the war until the entrance of the United States into it, Colonel Roosevelt fought his last, his greatest, and on the whole his most successful battle. When he began to appeal to his fellow-countrymen they were alike blind and deaf to the truth.   Without the support of a political party, of a friendly press, of an organized body of adherents, single-handed, physically broken, he waged war in defence of the Americanism of which he had ever been the embodiment, and in the end his country adopted the ideas which he had championed and took that action which he had advocated almost from the beginning of the war.

When the United States at last entered the world conflict, the press of events, the magnitude of the effort, the tenseness of the interest, combined to efface from contemporary memory appreciation of the rôle which had been played by Colonel Roosevelt in arousing the conscience and the patriotism of the nation in days which every American will strive to forget.   That this period of national humiliation proved to be but the prelude to a national awakening of unrivalled splendour, was due more to Roosevelt than to any other living man.   Whatever he might have accomplished had he been in the White House, it is hard to believe that he could have exercised a more potent or a more valuable influence than that which he exerted as a private citizen—as an American who, seeing his country's duty and seeing it clearly, did not rest until he had communicated his vision to millions.

CHAPTER THREE

THE PROGRESS OF EVENTS

To trace in detail the progress of events between August 1, 1914, and April, 1917, could be no part of the present work, which is concerned with the narrative of the struggle itself. It is essential, however, to review, at least in a cursory fashion, the several phases which marked the transition of the United States from a remote and unconcerned witness to a united and powerful participant in the conflict. Nowhere else can the true meaning of German policy and German method be more perfectly grasped than by a brief examination of Germany's course with respect to the American people. Nowhere else can one see as simply and as clearly the essential fallacy which underlay the whole German conception of the world and of other peoples as in the story of how by use of force, by the resort to one illegal and immoral act after another, Germany destroyed such friendship as existed in America, aroused in its stead an indignation and a determination not surpassed in nations which had long recognized her as their hereditary enemy, and in the end brought two millions of American soldiers to Europe at the moment when their presence was a decisive factor in German defeat.

The morality or the immorality of German principles and German methods may perhaps be long debated. They may find champions in later generations, but what defence could ever be possible on the practical side for the policy which persuaded the greatest single neutral power in the world to lay aside a neutrality satisfactory to the mass of its people and, in exchange, adopt a hostility which endured even after Germany's arms had been struck from her hand and she lay prostrate before her conquerors

The phases in the education of the American people to the meaning of Germany in the world may be comprehended in three periods extending from August, 1914, to April, 1917, the first of which ran from the outbreak of the war to the *Lusitania* Massacre; the second, from the *Lusitania* Massacre to the German compliance with that ultimatum which followed the sinking of the *Sussex;* and the third, from that acceptance to the moment when the Germans gave public warnings of their purpose to reverse their policy and return to unrestricted sinking.

I. THE FIRST PHASE—"INCIDENTS"

President Wilson's proclamation of neutrality in the opening hours of the war was followed slowly by an ever-increasing interference with American commerce, both by British and by German sea power. The parallel with the course of France and Great Britain during the Napoleonic wars, which led to our war with Great Britain in 1812, must impress every student of history; nor is it less plain, from any examination of the evidence, that, during the first months of the war, it was toward a conflict with Great Britain and not with Germany that events were shaping. Admiral Mahan had written that in the next war the dominant sea power would make sea law to suit itself. The course of Great Britain in the early days of the war clearly demonstrated the accuracy of this prophecy. The British did not instantly take full and effective measure of the possibilities of the use of their historic weapon. Little by little, however, deliberately experimenting with American patience, they invaded one right after another and more and more abandoned the observation of the principles expressed in the Declaration of London of 1909, which was, to be sure, voluntary since that code of naval warfare had never been officially accepted by the British Government. The detention of American ships; the interference with American cargoes consigned to neutral states because those neutral states had not forbidden the re-export of articles contained in those cargoes; the ultimate prohibition of the export of food stuffs, consigned not merely to German ports but to neutral ports, constituted grievances which led as early as December, 1914, to a formal protest by the United States.

To this and other protests the British Government made answers, beginning on January 7, 1915, which could not be considered by any fair-minded observer as satisfactory or candid.

These interferences with American interests and rights, naturally seized upon by every German agent and sympathizer in America, culminated on March 1st in a declaration on the part of Great Britain and of France that they held themselves free to detain, and take into port, ships carrying goods of presumed enemy destination, which amounted to a declaration of purpose to prevent commodities of any sort from reaching the Germans.

It is true that this course was explained as retaliation for a German proclamation of a war zone about Great Britain and the first relatively restricted but no less unmistakable use of the submarine to sink on sight not neutral but belligerent ships. A further pretext was furnished the Allied Governments by the fact that on January 31st the German Government undertook something approaching a seizure of grain stocks; not primarily, as the events proved, for military purposes, but to regulate the supplies of the nation and thus early make preparation against waste and famine. Moreover, a third shadow of warrant for the Allied purpose, frankly asserted to be one of reprisal, was found in the policy of the German Government in indiscriminately sowing mines in the high seas. But the Germans on their part could as vehemently defend their war-zone policy as retaliation for the illegal acts of Great Britain and her allies, culminating in that proposed blockade, accepted and described by the Germans as an effort to starve them into submission.

On February 20th the American Secretary of State had addressed an Identic Note suggesting agreement on some reasonable basis which would restrict naval warfare within limits that would prevent injury to neutrals. In this Note it was advocated that mines should not be sown in the open seas, or submarines used to attack merchantmen, save in the old-fashioned way of exercising the right of visit and search; and that use of neutral flags, to which the British had frequently resorted, should be abandoned. Great Britain was called upon to abandon her purpose of making food and food-stuffs absolute contraband, provided that America ensured that these commodities should not be delivered in Germany for military use; and Germany was asked to give satisfactory guarantees.

On this basis Germany was willing to talk, as her reply of February 28th indicated, but the Allied Note of March 1st destroyed all chance of compromise and further exchanges elicited from the Allied Governments only a polite but unmistakable declaration that, in view of German practices, the British purposed to proceed with their blockade. Meantime the Germans had already complicated the situation by sinking, wantonly, in the Pacific, an American ship carrying wheat consigned to Liverpool.

The result of these several exchanges and debates between the United States Government and the belligerents left the situation utterly unsatisfactory. American exports were subjected to every sort of illegal interference and restraint. Because the Germans had resorted to inhuman and barbarous methods of making war at sea, the British and the French justified a policy which invaded American rights. Because the British and the French had resorted to illegal methods, and the United States had not taken up arms to defend those rights, Germany asserted her freedom to employ a weapon new to war which could only be effective in so far as it not merely interfered with the rights of neutrals but also involved the destruction of their property and even of their lives.

The British on their part were more fortunate in the fact that, in the nature of things, they could limit the extent of their interference with abstract rights. They could, as they purposed to do, stop neutral ships without destroying them, take their cargoes, pay for them, and thus avoid inflicting any financial loss upon neutral owners. The German with his submarine could only sink the neutral ship with its cargo and its crew. His weapon was obviously bound to be of utmost importance to him, his sole answer to superior sea power, but the use of it was fraught with incalculable peril because, while neutrals might submit indefinitely to interference with their rights, particularly if this interference carried with it no property injury, it was inconceivable that any neutral as powerful as was the United States would consent to suffer its citizens to be murdered while they used the seas in accordance with international law and with principles which had never before been challenged.

German statesmanship in this time was faced with an obvious dilemma.

It had either to pursue the policy enunciated in its proclamation of February 18th, wherein it proclaimed a war-zone and a policy of sinking on sight—which had been promptly answered by an American assertion of an intention to hold the Imperial German Government to strict accountability if American ships or citizens were the victims of this policy—or to refrain from any pursuance of the policy which could conceivably arouse the United States Government and await a time when the multiplication of British interferences with American ships and rights would lead, if not to hostilities between the United States and the enemies of Germany, at least to the proclamation of an embargo which would prevent the export of war materials to Great Britain and France, and thus almost inevitably ensure their defeat.

The Germans chose the former course. As early as February 28th a German cruiser sank the *William P. Frye* in the Pacific. On March 28th the British passenger ship *Falaba* was torpedoed and sunk, and among others an American citizen lost his life. Conversations between the United States and the German Government over the *Frye* and the *Falaba* led to nothing. On April 28th the American S.S. *Cushing* was bombed by a German airplane, while on the 1st of May the American *Gulflight* was sunk off the Scilly Islands, and as a consequence the captain and ten of the crew lost their lives.

This campaign culminated on May 7th when the *Lusitania* was sunk off the Old Head of Kinsale and 1,153 of the 1,918 people on board were drowned, including 114 men, women, and children of American citizenship. This crime had been preceded by the insertion in American newspapers of the following warning:

NOTICE!

Travellers intending to embark on the Atlantic voyage are reminded that a state of war exists between Germany and her allies and Great Britain and her allies; that the zone of war includes the waters adjacent to the British Isles; that, in accordance with formal notice given by the Imperial German Government, vessels flying the flag of Great Britain, or of any of her allies, are liable to destruction in those waters, and that travellers sailing in the war zone on ships of Great Britain or her allies do so at their own risk.

IMPERIAL GERMAN EMBASSY.

WASHINGTON, D. C., APRIL 22, 1915.

With the sinking of the *Lusitania* the policy of the United States—
manifestly based upon a purpose to endeavour to constrain both belligerents to conduct their naval operations, if not in accordance with international law, as written before the days of the submarine, at least to
follow such a course as would obviate intolerable interference with neutral
commerce—fell to the ground. The United States had been arguing
with the Germans against murder, with the British against forcible invasion of liberties and rights. While the discussion was proceeding
the Germans had resorted to a murder which startled and horrified the
American people. Until the policy of murder was abandoned by the
Germans there could no longer be any possibility of further debates
with the British. If the Germans hoped, by resorting to assassination,
to drive the United States into a forcible vindication of those rights
which had been invaded by the British, this infantile conception was
promptly abolished. German agents, German sympathizers, the
German-American press, might and did continue to assail England as
responsible, but whatever was the American resentment over British
policy at this time, now and henceforth the first business and the first
concern of the American people must be to persuade or to compel the
German Government alike to abandon a policy of murder and to disavow
a crime committed in defiance of all the laws of humanity as well as of
nations and at the expense of the lives of its citizens. '

II. SECOND PHASE—NOTES

On the morning following the *Lusitania* Massacre there was in every
American mind the recollection that the Secretary of State had warned
the Imperial German Government that it would be held to "strict
accountability" for any use of the submarine weapon which might result in the loss of American lives. The nation expected the President of
the United States to fulfil the obligation implied in this warning. There
had been and there remained a division of opinion as to the extent of
responsibility incurred by American citizens who embarked upon a
British ship in the hour of war. The very fact that the *Lusitania* was
a British ship, built for auxiliary service, complicated the question,

and the record was further obscured by the false charges made by the Germans that the *Lusitania* had carried ammunition and had sunk as a consequence of the explosives in her cargo. Even amidst the horror over the crime there were not lacking those who felt, however intolerable a stain the *Lusitania* Massacre was upon German honour, it was not of itself a sufficient basis to enter the war.

The expectation of a clear-cut statement on the part of the President of the United States was not fulfilled. At first retiring to his study when the news of the deed reached him, and separating himself from all his associates, the President finally broke a silence, which had become almost intolerable for his fellow-countrymen, in a speech delivered on May 10th, in Philadelphia, which contained no direct reference to Germany or to the *Lusitania* but which derived its subsequent importance from the following paragraph:

> The example of America must be a special example. The example of America must be an example, not of peace because it will not fight, but of peace because peace is the healing and elevating influence of the world, and strife is not. There is such a thing as a man being too proud to fight. There is such a thing as a man being so right that he does not need to convince others by force that he is right.

Three days later the State Department published the first of that series of notes addressed to the Imperial German Government which were all written by the President of the United States and were the continuing expression of that spirit expressed in the Philadelphia utterance. The United States, said this first note, had "observed with growing concern, distress, and amazement" that series of events of which the *Lusitania* was a culmination. It was "loath to believe—it cannot now bring itself to believe—that these acts so contrary" to the rules, practice, and spirit of modern warfare could be sanctioned or approved by the German Government. There followed a recitation of the facts; a biting reference to the irregularity incident to the publication in the American press by the German Embassy of that warning to the passengers of the *Lusitania*, and the final statement: "The Imperial German Government will not expect the Government of the United States to omit any word or any act necessary to the performance of its sacred duty to maintain the rights of the United States and its citizens and of safeguarding their free exercise and enjoyment." Throughout the country it was felt that this note was an anticlimax, after the "strict-accountability" warning, while abroad the note itself attracted only minor interest while the major attention was reserved for the "too-proud-to-fight" speech. In Germany and out of it this was assumed to be the assertion of a purpose to adhere to a policy of "peace at any price." As a consequence there was small occasion for surprise when the *Nebraskan*, an American steamer, was torpedoed off Fastnet on May 23rd. Public indignation, aroused at this new outrage, was intensified by the reception, one week later, of the German answer to the *Lusitania* note, which, instead of disavowing the act or repudiating the policy, quibbled, argued, attacked British policy, and fixed upon the British Government the responsibility for the whole episode, since it had "attempted deliberately to use the lives of American citizens as protection for the ammunition aboard, and acted against the clear provisions of the American law which expressly prohibits the forwarding of passengers on ships carrying ammunition, and provides a penalty therefor. The company, therefore, is wantonly guilty of the death of so many passengers." There could be no doubt that the quick sinking of the *Lusitania* was "primarily attributable to the explosion of the ammunition shipment caused by the torpedo. The *Lusitania's* passengers would otherwise in all probability have been saved."

The German response in no sense satisfying American demands, a new note was framed, but, in the drafting of it, Mr. Wilson and his Secretary of State, Mr. Bryan, came at last to open disagreement. Mr. Bryan was a frank advocate of a peace-at-any-price policy. The President was not. Mr. Bryan believed that a continuation of notes would lead to an ever-worsening situation, with war as the logical result. Mr. Wilson believed that by notes he could ultimately persuade the German Government and the German people. The President did not regard war as a possibility. Mr. Bryan saw clearly that it was inevitable unless the American Government were prepared to tolerate the murder of its fellow-citizens. His horror of war would permit him such toleration. Accordingly, Mr. Bryan resigned, was succeeded by Mr. Lansing, and in the meantime the exchange of notes progressed.

The new Secretary of State demolished the several German arguments presented in their reply and took position on the unassailable ground that the question of the *Lusitania* was not one of law but of humanity and that the United States was contending for nothing less high and sacred than the "rights of humanity which every government honours itself in respecting and which no government is justified in resigning on behalf of those under its care and authority." The final words of this second note were as follows: "The Government of the United States, therefore, deems it reasonable to expect that the Imperial German Government will adopt the measures necessary to put these principles into practice in respect of the safeguarding of American lives and American ships, and asks for assurances that this will be done."

But between asking for assurances and asserting a determination to hold Germany to "strict accountability" and to "omit no word or act . . ." it was plain that there was a wide gulf. The country felt very clearly that, with the massacre still lacking a German disavowal and a policy of assassination unrepudiated by the Germans, the United States Government was rapidly allowing itself to drift into dialectics. Impatience was everywhere on the increase, and this impatience was not lessened when the next German note, instead of giving the required assurances, shifted the discussion to a suggestion that American citizens should travel only on neutral ships, and further offered the impudent intimation that these neutral ships should be conspicuously marked and their sailing advertised to the German Government. Once more a German outrage contributed to aggravating the situation. On July 9th the *Orduna*, like the *Lusitania*, a British passenger ship in the Atlantic service, was attacked by a German submarine, not far from the scene of the *Lusitania* Massacre, and followed by the submarine, which shelled her until she was out of range.

Still once more the President had recourse to a note in which he rejected the preposterous German suggestion as to restricting American travel to neutral ships, and this time warned Germany yet again in the following words: "Friendship itself prompts the United States to say to the Imperial German Government that repetition, by the commanders of German naval vessels, of acts in contravention of those rights must be regarded by the Government of the United States, when they affect American citizens, as deliberately unfriendly." Four days later a German submarine sank the American ship *Leelaw*, but this time the crew was allowed time to quit the ship; and the cargo was contraband. Any thought that the Germans had changed their policy was destroyed on August 30th, when a German submarine attacked and sank the *Arabic*, again near the scene of the *Lusitania* Massacre. Of the 423 persons on the *Arabic*, 44, including two Americans, lost their lives. This was the "deliberately unfriendly" action which the President had indicated in his last note.

What could be left to discuss? What further use was there of discussing the question with the German Government? This was the demand of the American press and a large fraction of the American people. The German Government itself seemed to understand the gravity of the new crisis, because, through its ambassador at Washington, it asked that the United States Government should take no action until it was able to investigate the *Arabic* incident, and asserted that if it should be proved that Americans had actually lost their lives, this would be something contrary to German intentions. On August 26th the German Ambassador, following a conversation with the President, gave him the following pledge on behalf of the German Government: "Liners will not be sunk by our submarines without warning and without safety of the rights of non-combatants, provided the liners do not try to escape or offer resistance." This looked like a victory for the American contention, but three days later the *Hesperian*, with 650 passengers and crew aboard, was torpedoed off Fastnet. As there were Canadian soldiers aboard, and the ship mounted at least one gun, there was a general agreement to suffer this incident to pass without challenge.

Meantime, the activity in the Mediterranean of submarines, flying the Austrian flag but widely believed to be German, precipitated new complications. On November 7th the Italian passenger ship *Ancona* was torpedoed off the coast of Tunis by submarines which flew first the German and then the Austrian flag. On December 6th the American State Department demanded disavowal and reparation in terms more explicit and emphatic than had yet been employed in any previous note. To this the Austrian Government replied, after long delay, in tones which were insolent and contemptuous, refusing to comply with the American demand. The State Department responded to this with a somewhat curt repetition of the demand for disavowal and reparation and to this second note the Austrian Government yielded. One day after the Austrian surrender became known, the British S.S. *Persia* was torpedoed in the eastern Mediterranean and 392 passengers and crew were lost. Among these was an American consul on his way to his post. When the Austrian Government was approached in this matter it suggested that the crime might have been the work of a Turkish submarine.

The controversy continued to drag with no further grave incidents for two months more, during the course of which Germany, in a further communication, offered to modify its submarine campaign provided that the British would disarm their merchant ships. An enquiry, by the American Secretary of State, of the Allies as to their position in this question was met with a courteous but emphatic refusal.

Finally, on March 24th, a French channel boat plying between Folkestone and Dieppe was torpedoed, and although the vessel remained afloat, some 80 persons were wounded, including Americans.

The sinking of the *Sussex* was the last straw. Utterly derisory German justification was brushed aside, and on April 19th the President of the United States laid before Congress the whole history of the submarine debate, having on the day previously addressed to the German Government yet one more note, which closed with the following sentence: "Unless the Imperial Government should now immediately declare and effect an abandonment of its present method of submarine warfare against passenger- and freight-carrying vessels, the Government of the United States can have no other choice but to sever diplomatic relations with the German Empire altogether." On May 4th the German Government responded in a long note reviewing all the counter-charges against the British, plainly intimating that the United States Government was not pursuing, in respect of the British, the same course as in the case of Germany, but containing the all-important statement: "German naval forces have received the following orders: 'In accordance with the general principles of visit and search and destruction of merchant vessels, recognized by international law, such vessels, both within and without the area declared as naval war zone, shall not be sunk without warning and without saving human life unless those ships attempt to escape or offer resistance'."

This was all the United States had contended for. So far it was a complete victory for Mr. Wilson's method. There was, however, appended to the note this following minatory condition: "But neutrals cannot expect that Germany, forced to fight for her existence, shall, for the sake of neutral interests, restrict the use of an effective weapon if her enemy is permitted to apply at will methods of warfare violating the rights of international law." The German Government further expressed its confidence that the United States should now resume its debates with Great Britain and force that nation to comply with its contentions. Should the United States fail to do this the German note indicated that "the German Government would then be facing a new situation in which it must reserve to itself complete liberty of decision." This was no more than Bernstorff, the German Ambassador, had already promised on behalf of his government before the *Sussex* episode, but a subsequent German statement conceded Germany's failure to fulfil its promises in the matter of the *Sussex*, and expressed its sincere regret therefor and its readiness to meet claims for reparation.

So ended the great submarine debate. When, a little less than a year later, Germany withdrew her pledge and announced her intention to resume unrestricted sinking, the United States promptly severed diplomatic relations and shortly thereafter entered the war. Doubtless it would have entered it a year earlier but for the German surrender. That the episode itself injured American prestige abroad, humiliated

American pride at home, was and is unmistakable.   Mr. Wilson's notes
were the topic of derisory humour in the press and on the stages of all
the European capitals.   Europe did not derive the impression that
Americans were in fact "too proud to fight"—but too cowardly.   Such
unworthy and inaccurate suspicions were dissipated when America did
come into the war and the character of her participation forever
destroyed the misunderstanding due to the incidents of 1915.

In point of fact, Germany did not cease her submarine warfare until
Mr. Wilson laid aside arguments and resorted to the familiar ultimatum.
Had he consented to continue his notes Germany unquestionably would
have continued her sinkings.   She was neither convinced by his logic
nor impressed by his idealism, but in April, 1916, she confronted a situation in which she lacked the necessary submarines to make her campaign
effective and was at last aware that to continue the campaign meant to
ensure American belligerence.   Mr. Wilson and his fellow-countrymen
were not alone in misunderstanding the German surrender.   The
English Government and the English navy, like the American Government and the American people, believed Germany had abandoned the
submarine, and in this colossal misapprehension both failed to make
those preparations against a resumption of ruthless sinking for which
Germany was already preparing.   For the moment German surrender
was of material advantage to the Allies, but in the end it was of question-
able profit since it lulled them to sleep while the greatest danger which
was to threaten the Allied cause in the whole war slowly matured.

While the State Department and the President had been occupied
for nearly two years with the conduct of negotiations growing out of
submarine outrages there had been conducted in Congress—ostensibly
with the purpose of keeping the United States out of the war, but in
many instances by Congressmen whose sympathies with Germany or
whose truckling to constituencies in which the German-American vote
was large—campaigns which sought in the first instance to place an
embargo on the exportation of arms to the Allies, and subsequently,
when the submarine debate had reached its most acute stage, to forbid
Americans to travel upon armed merchantmen, and to deny clearance

papers to such vessels. Since the British and the French had now adopted the practice of arming all their merchantmen against the submarine, this latter course would in effect have paralyzed Allied transport, while an embargo would unquestionably have deprived the Allies of precisely those materials and weapons essential to defend themselves against the German assault.

In the matter of the embargo, the course of the President from the beginning was clear, definite, and correct. The United States, having always pursued a policy of unpreparedness for war, depended more than any other country upon its ability to import arms and war materials from other countries in case of conflict. To set up a precedent now in the matter of an embargo would be to establish a rule which might prove fatal to the United States at some future crisis. In the days of the Civil War the Union armies had been equipped almost exclusively from British and French sources and without such assistance the Confederacy would almost unquestionably have won the war. To put an embargo on the export, not merely of arms, but of food and food stuffs and raw materials generally, would have been not merely to break with American policy in the past and establish a precedent of incalculable peril to the country itself, but it would also have been a clear breach of neutrality, a deliberate change of the rules of war during the progress of the struggle, which could only inure to the benefit of one of the parties contesting. Moreover, the beneficiary of such a policy—Germany—had herself employed the unquestioned right of export of arms in the period of the Boer War and to the advantage of the opponents of Great Britain.

There were not a few Americans, whose sincerity and unselfishness were above question, who saw with disgust and humiliation a vast tide of wealth rolling in upon their nation as a consequence of its contributions of arms and munitions to a struggle in which its own sons did not participate. To grow rich out of the agonies of other nations was a thing repugnant to them. Yet, with small exception, their ultimate judgment sustained the policy of the President.

Again, those for selfish reasons interested in an embargo, the producers of cotton and of such other commodities as were momentarily

THE "FIGHTING SIXTY-NINTH" OFF TO CAMP

A last good-bye to sweethearts and wives as the train pulls out of the station

THOSE WERE STIRRING DAYS

When even the President of the United States led the parade, through the flag-decked sunny streets of the nation's capital

"GOOD-BYE, DEAR OLD MANHATTAN ISLE!"

New York boys, waiting for the train which is to take them to Camp Upton

"ARE WE DOWNHEARTED? NO!"

Men of the second draft leaving Long Island City for Camp Upton. A big German drive was on just then, but these men do not seem to be afraid

PHILADELPHIA "DRAFTEES" ARRIVING AT CAMP MEADE

It's a strange, new life which lies before them, and they regard the men already wearing khaki with much curiosity and some awe

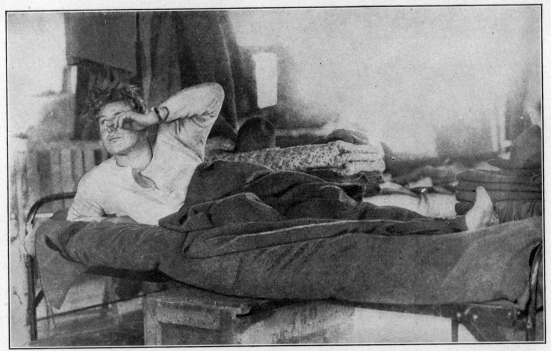

THE ROOKIE IS A BIT BEWILDERED WHEN REVEILLÉ SOUNDS

BUT HE ATTACKS HIS "CHOW" WITH GOOD APPETITE

FIRST STEPS IN MILITARY TRAINING

The day after their arrival at Camp Sherman these men settled down to work in a sober and determined spirit

THERE WAS TRAINING FOR BOTH MUSCLE AND BRAINS AT THE CANTONMENTS

WRITING LETTERS

After strenuous days, crammed with new experiences, there was much to tell the people at home

THE NEW UNIFORMS

Their apparel was neither neat nor gaudy, but the sidewalks of Fifth Avenue were packed with their friends as the New York conscripts marched along

affected by the closing of the German markets, were gradually appeased as the expansion of the Allied imports, consequent upon the ever-growing fraction of Allied population removed from industry to the firing line, absorbed their products. As the volume of the export trade of the United States grew to figures unprecedented in all past history the considerations which led to the advocacy of an embargo totally disappeared and were replaced by a far greater but not less selfish reason for opposing any embargo.

The question of forbidding Americans to travel upon belligerent ships, on the contrary, continued, during the whole period of the submarine warfare, to provoke protests and to attract legislative proposals. At the moment when the *Lusitania* was sunk there was throughout the Middle West a marked sentiment expressed in the statement that the American citizens who had embarked upon a British ship were themselves not alone responsible for the tragedy which overtook them but were also guilty of an unpatriotic act in risking the peace of their own country by their temerity. The right of Germany to commit murder was seldom asserted in any American quarter, but the duty of American citizens to refrain from travel upon British and French ships was often proclaimed.

When the British armed all their merchantmen against submarine attack, as they were entitled to do under international law, the controversy took a new shape. Many resolutions were introduced in Congress, the sum of all of which was to forbid Americans to travel on armed merchantmen and to prohibit the sailing of such armed merchantmen from American ports. Germany herself, at the height of the submarine controversy, offered to abandon ruthless attacks upon passenger ships provided the United States could procure from the British an abandonment of the policy of arming merchantmen. The Secretary of State, Mr. Lansing, made such a request to the British; the President himself for the moment wavered and seemed willing to accept the German suggestion.

Happily, however, Mr. Wilson's doubts were speedily cleared up. He recognized clearly that in arming their merchantmen the British were acting within international law. He perceived, as in the case of the embargo, that to undertake to change international law in the course of the conflict, in such way as to benefit but one of the contestants, would constitute a breach of neutrality and he squarely and courageously took his stand against such a course in the face of a campaign in Congress and in the public press which at moments seemed likely to overwhelm his policy but in the end came to nothing.

III.   THIRD PHASE—TREASON AND SEDITION

While there had been going forward, from the moment Germany proclaimed her submarine campaign to the agreement on a *modus vivendi* in April, 1916, a campaign of domestic agitation unparalleled in American history, it was only when this submarine peril seemed removed that the country at last appreciated clearly the extent to which its peace had been destroyed by the representatives of alien countries seeking to mobilize American public opinion against the Government of the United States and in support of the policies of other countries. Because President Wilson had declined to submit to a German policy of murder on the high seas, German agents and German sympathizers conducted against him and his Administration in the United States and through the medium of the press and certain public men, a campaign of utmost hostility.

Because the President and the Congress of the United States had declined to place an embargo upon the export of arms and munitions, both were assailed, and while the German influence still sought to force Congress to adopt an embargo, an ever-increasing campaign of ruthless violence was directed against the munition plants, the shipping, and the communications within the country. The investigations of this period and of these activities, conducted in New York State at a later time under the brilliant direction of a Deputy Attorney General, Mr. Alfred L. Becker, revealed the extent to which money had been employed in the purchase of American newspapers and in the corruption of men engaged in publicity work.

All this campaign centred in the German Embassy, where the German Ambassador, Count von Bernstorff, at one time conducted within the United States an ever-growing attack upon the President and the Government, and posed before the people of the United States as a friend of their country, seeking at all times to prevent his own government from taking extreme measures and precipitating a conflict.

Rarely, if ever, in history, has there been such a spectacle as Bernstorff presented. He knew the American press, its machinery, its weaknesses, and its strength. He made his embassy a gathering-place of newspaper correspondents; he talked to them frequently and with frankness. Through them he conducted a campaign of publicity of almost unrivalled extent. Day by day the German side of each controversy was set forth in all the papers of the United States, frequently in advance of any statement of the Government itself. He made war upon the President and he mobilized not alone the German-American press animated by sympathies with Germany; not alone that section of the American press, like the journals of Mr. William R. Hearst—whose hostility to Great Britain and sympathy with Germany led him to transform his vast and influential newspapers into organs and agents of the German cause; but also newspapers whose policy was unquestionably pro-Ally, since he provided their correspondents with news valuable to the paper and took his pay in the publicity his own views thereby acquired.

Nor did the German Ambassador stop with mere manipulation of the press. In his embassy the destruction of munition plants was plotted. A paralysis of American industry by strikes and disorders was prepared, and the murder of American citizens, alike in factories and on the high seas, was arranged. No single circumstance in all Mr. Wilson's policy of long-suffering, of patience in the hope of avoiding participation in the World War, was at once more striking, or for fractions of the American people, more humiliating than his toleration of Bernstorff, whose insolence knew no bounds, whose interference in American domestic affairs was beyond belief. In no other country in the world could Bernstorff have conducted a campaign against the Government and the peace of the nation to which he was accredited·

as the Ambassador of a friendly nation.   Evil he was, unscrupulous, an intriguer whose whole career in America was ultimately exposed but what all the country finally learned must have been long known to the Government which permitted him to continue his operations.

The Austrian Ambassador, by contrast a harmless and well-intentioned diplomat, was less fortunate and was obliged to leave the country at the request of the State Department after having been involved in the German campaign against munition plants.   Several of Bernstorff's agents shared a similar fate, after disclosures which rendered their stay in the United States impossible, but Bernstorff himself remained, until the action of his own government led to the severing of diplomatic relations, and in the period between the interruption and the resumption of unrestricted submarine warfare—that is, between April, 1916, and February, 1917—Bernstorff's activities rose to almost unbelievable heights.

In this same period President Wilson gave one more illustration of the fashion in which he held to the view that his own and his country's mission was to restore peace in the world.   When the German Chancellor, following the German victories in Roumania, made his first proffer of peace in December, 1916, President Wilson was himself preparing to make a gesture which might contribute to an ending of the conflict. He knew, moreover, that Germany contemplated a resumption of her unrestricted submarine warfare if the Allies did not accept this peace proposal, which was in its very nature unacceptable, since he had been directly warned by our Ambassador in Berlin.

It was unfortunate in the extreme that the President's own peace note followed so closely upon the German as to give it at least the colour of an attempt designed to strengthen Germany's hands; nor was it less humiliating to Americans in later times that this note had also the appearance of having been dictated by a desire to prevent a new submarine campaign.   In Paris and Berlin the President was held to have openly aided Germany.   In America it was felt that he had been coerced into uttering his peace note by a German threat to resume submarine warfare if he did not support Germany's peace movement.

The President's peace note was issued on December 18th. To the governments of the Central Powers the following communication was sent:

The suggestion which I am instructed to make, the President has long had it in mind to offer. He is somewhat embarrassed to offer it at this particular time because it may now seem to have been prompted by a desire to play a part in connection with the recent overtures of the Central Powers. It has, in fact, been in no way suggested by them in its origin, and the President would have delayed offering it until those overtures had been independently answered but for the fact that it also contains the question of peace and may best be considered in connection with other proposals which have the same end in view. The President can only beg that his suggestion be considered entirely on its own merits and as if it had been made in other circumstances.

The note to the Allies was slightly different in respect of the paragraph quoted above but otherwise similar. In both the President suggested a re-statement on the part of each contestant of its war aims and its peace terms, which, he pointed out—in language that excited heart-burnings alike in London and Paris—were identical in statement.

Each side desires to make the rights and privileges of weak peoples and small states as secure against aggression or denial in the future as the rights and privileges of the great and powerful states now at war.

Each wishes itself to be made secure in the future, along with all other nations and peoples, against the recurrence of wars like this and against aggressions of selfish interference of any kind. Each would be jealous of the formation of any more rival leagues to preserve an uncertain balance of power amid multiplying suspicions; but each is ready to consider the formation of a league of nations to ensure peace and justice throughout the world. Before that final step can be taken, however, each deems it necessary first to settle the issues of the present war upon terms which will certainly safeguard the independence, the territorial integrity, and the political and commercial freedom of the nations involved.

In the measures to be taken to secure the future peace of the world the people and Government of the United States are as vitally and as directly interested as the governments now at war. Their interest, moreover, in the means to be adopted to relieve the smaller and weaker peoples of the world of the peril of wrong and violence is as quick and ardent as that of any other people or government. They stand ready, and even eager, to coöperate in the accomplishment of these ends, when the war is over, with every influence and resource at their command. But the war must first be concluded. The terms upon which it is to be concluded they are not at liberty to suggest; but the President does feel that it is his right and his duty to point out their intimate interest in its conclusion, lest it should presently be too late to accomplish the greater things which lie beyond its conclusion; lest the situation of neutral nations, now exceedingly hard to endure, be rendered altogether intolerable; and lest, more than all, an injury be done civilization itself which can never be atoned for or repaired.

Short of such a re-statement of war aims, short of some composition of the differences

. . . the contest must continue to proceed toward undefined ends by slow attrition until one group of belligerents or the other is exhausted. If million after million of human lives must continue to be offered up until on the one side or the other there are no more to offer; if resentments must be kindled that can never cool and despairs engendered from which there can be no recovery, hopes of peace and of the willing concert of free peoples will be rendered vain and idle.

Coincident with this utterance of the President there was an interview with the Secretary of State, in which Mr. Lansing, in explaining the President's statement, said:

I mean by that that we are drawing nearer the verge of war ourselves, and, therefore, we are entitled to know exactly what each belligerent seeks in order that we may negotiate our conduct in the future.

The President's intervention, as we have seen in the previous volume, came to nothing, and a final German comment upon the failure contained the minatory declaration:

Germany and her allies have made an honest attempt to terminate the war and open the road for an understanding among the belligerents. The Imperial Government asserts the fact that it merely depended upon the decision of our adversaries whether the road toward peace should be entered upon or not. The hostile governments declined to accept this road. Upon them falls the full responsibility for the continuation of the bloodshed.

Most significant of all perhaps in the President's note, and in the discussions of this moment, was the first general publicity given to the idea of the League of Nations contained in an address before the Senate on January 22nd, which was at the moment memorable not because of its extended reference to the League-of-Nations idea but because it contained an astounding assertion that one of the prerequisites was "peace without victory." No single phrase—since "too proud to fight"—produced such an unfortunate impression abroad or created such far-reaching criticism at home. In London and in Paris it was once more felt that the President had failed utterly to discriminate between the moral status of the Allies and of their assailants; and, viewed in the light of this utterance, the President's whole action with respect to peace was wrongly and invariably interpreted as a championship of a German manœuvre which was at once dishonest and dangerous, while for the President's League of Nations there was little but derision to be heard at this time.

But whatever the President hoped or believed possible or probable in the world situation, he was called upon to lay aside both his hopes and his expectations when, on the last day of January, 1917, the Imperial German Government proclaimed a resumption of ruthless submarine warfare. This course was defended as the inevitable consequence of the British and French refusal to accept the German peace proffer. The "new situation," mentioned in the German pledge to the United States nearly a year before, had arrived, and Germany now resumed her freedom of action. She fixed barred zones about the British Isles and in the Mediterranean and announced that all ships, neutral and belligerent alike, found in those waters would be sunk. One regular American passenger ship a week was to be permitted to sail to and from Falmouth, provided that it complied with an intricate system of regulations as to course, cargo, and markings.

On February 3rd the President appeared before Congress and in an extended address containing a review of the whole history of the submarine campaign, closed with this momentous statement:

I think you will agree with me that, in view of this declaration, which suddenly and without prior intimation of any kind deliberately withdraws the solemn assurance given in the Imperial Government's note of the 4th of May, 1916, this Government has no alternative consistent with the dignity and honour of the United States but to take the course which, in its note of the 18th of April, 1916, it announced that it would take in the event that the German Government did not declare and effect an abandonment of the methods of submarine warfare which it was then employing and to which it now purposes again to resort.

I have, therefore, directed the Secretary of State to announce to his Excellency the German Ambassador that all diplomatic relations between the United States and the German Empire are severed, and that the American Ambassador at Berlin will immediately be withdrawn; and, in accordance with this decision, to hand to his Excellency his passports.

If the German Government should now be guilty of "an overt act" the President advised Congress that he would appear again before it to recommend further steps.

Severance of diplomatic relations did not, of itself, mean war; but in Europe, as in America, it was recognized as only a preliminary step. Meantime, whatever popular emotion was aroused anew against American participation in the war was definitively destroyed when, on the last day of February, the people of the United States learned from an official publication in their newspapers the astounding fact that, more than six weeks before, Germany had begun to prepare for war with the United States by seeking alliances with Japan and with Mexico, and that the German Foreign Minister, Zimmermann, had instructed the German Minister at Mexico City to undertake to procure an alliance with Mexico and induce Mexico to approach Japan with the same object. Mexico's reward for an attack upon the United States was to be the reconquest of her lost provinces of New Mexico, Texas, and Arizona. The full text of Zimmermann's note is as follows:

Berlin, Jan. 19, 1917.

On the 1st of February we intend to begin submarine warfare unrestricted. In spite of this, it is our intention to endeavour to keep neutral the United States of America.

If this attempt is not successful, we propose an alliance on the following basis with Mexico: That we shall make war together and together make peace. We shall give general financial support, and it is understood that Mexico is to reconquer the lost territory in New Mexico, Texas, and Arizona. The details are left to you for settlement.

You are instructed to inform the President of Mexico of the above in the greatest confidence as soon as it is certain that there will be an outbreak of war with the United States, and suggest that the President of Mexico, on his own initiative, should communicate with Japan suggesting adherence at once to his plan. At the same time, offer to mediate between Germany and Japan.

Please call to the attention of the President of Mexico that the employment of ruthless submarine warfare now promises to compel England to make peace in a few months.

ZIMMERMANN.

Since the *Lusitania* Massacre nothing had happened which had so profoundly aroused American indignation. The last possibility of effective opposition to American entrance into the war disappeared. A filibuster in the Senate in the closing days of the session—designed to prevent the passage of a resolution empowering the President to arm American merchant vessels—was in itself the last stand of the opponents of war, and while exciting momentary passion, was of minor importance. When President Wilson again took office on March 4th he had the support of the nation in a policy which was universally recognized as bound to lead to war with Germany within the briefest possible time. The Zimmermann note had demonstrated beyond all question the impossibility of avoiding conflict with a nation which, having asserted the right to bar our ships and citizens from the sea and to murder Americans who undertook to exercise their unquestioned right to travel on the ocean, was now inciting America's neighbours to attack her by promises of American territory if the United States ventured to protect the lives of its own citizens.

When, on April 2nd, Congress assembled in pursuance of a call of the President to Extraordinary Session, Mr. Wilson spoke to it the words for which the country was now waiting with impatience. This address reviewed at length the long list of injuries suffered by the American Government and people at the hands of the Germans and recognized at last that the German submarine warfare was a warfare against mankind and against all nations. If American ships had been sunk the challenge was after all not merely to America but to all mankind. The President advised Congress that in his judgment it should declare the recent course of the Imperial German Government to be war against the Government and people of the United States; that it accept it as such, and that it take steps to exert all the country's power and employ all its resources to bring the Government of the German Empire to terms.

Concerning American purpose the President said:

Our purpose now, as then, is to vindicate the principles of peace and justice in the life of the world against selfish and autocratic power and to set up among the really free and self-governed peoples of the world such a concert of purpose and action as will henceforth insure the observance of those principles. . . .

We have no quarrel with the German people. We have no feeling toward them but one of sympathy and friendship. It was not upon their impulse that their government acted in entering this war. It was not with their previous knowledge or approval.

It was a war determined upon as wars used to be determined upon in the old, unhappy days when peoples were nowhere consulted by their rulers and wars were provoked and waged in the interest of dynasties or of little groups of ambitious men who were accustomed to use their fellowmen as pawns and tools.

Commenting upon the recent experience of the Mexican intrigue, which he described as a challenge of hostile purpose which his own country was about to accept, he said:

We are now about to accept gauge of battle with this natural foe to liberty, and shall, if necessary, spend the whole force of the nation to check and nullify its pretentions and its power. We are glad, now that we see the facts with no veil of false pretense about them, to fight thus for the ultimate peace of the world and for the liberation of its peoples, the German people included; for the rights of nations great and small and the privilege of men everywhere to choose their way of life and of obedience. The world must be made safe for democracy. Its peace must be planted upon the tested foundations of political liberty.

We have no selfish ends to serve. We desire no conquest, no dominion. We seek no indemnities for ourselves, no material compensation for the sacrifices we shall freely make. We are but one of the champions of the rights of mankind. We shall be satisfied when those rights have been made as secure as the faith and the freedom of the nations can make them.

The President closed his address thus:

It is a distressing and oppressive duty, gentlemen of the Congress, which I have performed in thus addressing you. There are, it may be, many months of fiery trial and sacrifice ahead of us. It is a fearful thing to lead this great, peaceful people into war—into the most terrible and disastrous of all wars, civilization itself seeming to be in the balance.

But the Right is more precious than peace, and we shall fight for the things which we have always carried nearest our hearts—for democracy, for the right of those who submit to authority to have a voice in their own government, for the rights and liberties of small nations, for a universal dominion of right by such a concert of free peoples as shall bring peace and safety to all nations and make the world itself at last free.

To such a task we can dedicate our lives and our fortunes, everything that we are and everything that we have, with the pride of those who know that the day has come when America is privileged to spend her blood and her might for the principles that gave her birth and happiness and the peace which she has treasured. God helping her, she can do no other.

Following the President's address a resolution declaring that war existed with Germany was introduced both in the Senate and the House. On April 5th the resolution was adopted by the Senate and passed by the House by a vote of 373 to 50 and the following day the President issued a proclamation that a state of war existed between the Imperial German Government and the United States.

IV. THE EFFECT

The announcement that the United States had severed diplomatic relations with Germany reached London and Paris at the moment when the populations of both cities were suffering from the consequences of the most severe winter since the siege of Paris. The news was read to soldiers in the trenches, whose sufferings in this same tragic winter were almost indescribable. To the French and the British armies, still expecting a short and victorious campaign, the news of American participation was still one more evidence of the approach of victory.

The American declaration of war preceded by only three days the British offensive at Arras, and at least one American flag was carried by the victorious Canadian troops who climbed Vimy Ridge. When the British operation had ceased and the French attack had failed, when the morale of the Allied armies and Allied populations was beginning to decline dangerously, the arrival of General Pershing in Paris, with that small vanguard of the American hosts that were to come, served as a counter-weight to all the influences that made for pessimism and urged surrender. As the Russian Revolution continued to disorganize the great eastern ally until it fell first into chaos and then into a powerlessness which ended in the capitulation to Bolshevism, the coming of America served more and more to encourage those who saw, in the defection of Russia, Allied disaster and defeat.

Faithful to his ideal of preserving for his country, untarnished by any military effort, the rule of arbitrator and peacemaker, Mr. Wilson had kept America unarmed from August, 1914, to April, 1917. It was therefore impossible now for American divisions to march. It was necessary to arm the country. It was necessary first of all to invoke the draft and send the male population of the nation to training camps. If valuable service could be rendered by the Navy in combating the submarine peril, on the military side a full year must pass before anything was possible. The war became thus, as Mr. Lloyd George said at a later time, a race between the Kaiser and Wilson, although in 1917 the real gravity of the situation was not revealed. Still it was transparent to all the well-informed that America was the last hope of the Allies, and this in substance was the message brought by Balfour and Viviani, and by Marshal Joffre himself, when they came to the United States immediately after the declaration of war.

During 1917, save on the naval side, American contribution to the common cause was on the moral rather than on the military side. The German continued to believe, and certain portions of the Allied public still cherished the fear, that Germany would win before America could arrive. Both contending parties saw that if America could prepare before Germany attained a decisive victory, the latter's defeat was inevitable, and in that hope the Allied governments continued.

Meantime that gulf which had opened between the people of America and those of France and Britain was closed. For two years Englishmen and Frenchmen had seen with amazement American persistence in a neutrality which to both could but seem immoral selfishness, proof that the American democracy was in fact corrupt. More and more bitterly France and Great Britain criticized American blindness and inactivity in the presence of a moral duty. Had the war finished without American participation, even though the Allies had won, many years must have passed before America's course could have been forgotten. As it was, America's decision in a single hour abolished all misunderstandings. The hesitations, the haltings, the incomprehensible twistings and turnings of American policy were forgotten. Between the three great Western democracies not only was old friendship restored, but a new sense of nearness and association was aroused. The American flag flew over the Houses of Parliament, where no foreign flag had ever before waved, and General Pershing and his scanty companies of American troops were welcomed as no foreign troops had ever been welcomed in Great Britain or in France.

All this the German witnessed, not without misgivings. All through the summer of 1917 German and Austrian intrigues to procure peace went forward. They were thwarted by German military power, which was still confident of victory, and, with Russia in its grasp, was preparing to dispose of western armies before America arrived. Yet it is hardly too much to say that before America was able to put a single regiment or even a full company upon the firing line in France, American participation in the war had contributed decisively to repulsing the peace offensive of 1917, as American troops, in July of the following year, were to supply the necessary reserves to enable Foch to launch that counter-offensive which broke the "peace storm" of Ludendorff's hitherto unbeaten armies.

If America came late, came ill-prepared, came incapable immediately of more than a moral contribution, this contribution was hardly less decisive in averting a peace which must have preserved for Germany many of the fruits of her conquest than was the force of our man-power in ensuring German military defeat one year later. Had we lingered but a few more months; had the country, when it entered the war, continued a policy of hesitation and half measures, the campaign of 1918 would unquestionably have ended in a decisive German victory. The fact that, however late our entrance, we came as a united nation —prepared for every sacrifice, ready to make every effort—atoned in no small measure for previous delay and enabled us, by a very narrow margin, to perform a sufficient portion of the task which had devolved upon us to win the war. Napoleon's decision to go to Moscow and the Kaiser's resolution to resume ruthless submarine warfare must remain, in history, two of the most colossal mistakes of which there is any record, since each of them resulted in the fall of an empire and the ruin of a grandiose conception of world denomination.

CHAPTER FOUR

THE GREAT RETREAT

I
THE TWO STRATEGIC CONCEPTIONS

Allied strategy in the campaign of 1916 had been comprehended in a grand concentric attack upon the Central Powers in which British, French, Italian, and Russian armies, together with the Allied forces at Salonica and the British forces in Mesopotamia and Egypt, sought by coördinated and combined attack to exhaust the man-power of Germany and her allies, break through the circle of defences and win the war.

This plan had, on the whole, met with general failure despite local successes. The German offensive at Verdun, beginning in February, while unsuccessful in itself, had materially diminished French man-power and contributed to lessening the weight of the blow at the Somme. The Anglo-French offensive at the Somme had failed to achieve any immediate sweeping victory and had degenerated into a fight from trench to trench. Italy's blow at Gorizia had been no more successful, while the Russian offensive, after tremendous opening victories, had been beaten down.

Having thus checked her foes on all her fronts, Germany was able, in the closing months of 1916, to pass to the offensive, crush Roumania, and win a victory unquestioned on the military side and hardly to be exaggerated in its moral effect.

Nevertheless on all the fronts the Allies could point to local gains, to brilliant tactical achievements. Verdun had been saved, the British army had been trained on a battlefield on which material progress had been made, Russian armies had returned triumphantly to the scenes of their victories of 1914, even the Salonica army had reached Monastir. Therefore, though these results had been inconclusive in the larger sense, it was plain that Allied strategy for the campaign of 1917 would seek to follow that of the preceding year—to attempt, following the example of Grant in the Civil War, to exert pressure over the whole vast expanse of front until, if by no other means, at least by attrition, the enemy should be exhausted.

General Nivelle, when he succeeded Joffre in December, found awaiting him plans of his predecessor calling for an immediate and general offensive all along the line. The general scheme he adopted; the details of the attack he modified to suit his own peculiar conceptions. Under Nivelle, as under Joffre—at the beginning of 1917, as at the outset of the campaign of the previous year—Allied strategy was comprehended in the general attack of all the armies of the Allies. It was an essential condition to success that all the Allied armies should be ready to move at the same time, that the movement should be coördinated and that each of the greater Allies should be capable of as considerable an effort as that of the preceding year. The elimination of a single one of the great European Powers allied against Germany was bound to be fatal to the whole plan since it would give to Germany and her allies superiority in numbers, and since they occupied the central position, would enable them to beat down any attack swiftly and surely.

Allied strategy in 1917 was, therefore, conditioned upon the persistence of Russia. When Russia fell to revolution and chaos in the first months of the campaign, their entire conception fell also, and Germany was able to win considerable victories alike from France, Britain, and Italy. In point of fact, Russia was so nearly gone at the moment when the campaign opened that it seems impossible not to believe that history will deal severely with those who were responsible for sending French and British armies to inevitable defeat at the Craonne Plateau and Passchendaele against an enemy strongly entrenched and capable of matching division against division.

But Allied High Command—like Allied statesmanship—from the beginning to the end of the campaign of 1917, was blind to the truth so far as Russia was concerned. It continued to believe in effective Russian participation when there was no basis for such belief. It continued to hope when hope itself had become patently illusory. The result was that the campaign of 1917 developed into a series of fruitless separate attacks which successively exhausted the morale of the French, the British, and the Italian armies, and prepared the way for the Italian disaster of Caporetto and the crushing British defeat in the Battle of Picardy in the following year. To understand the campaign, however, it is essential to bear in mind the Allied conception of coördinated and concomitant attacks on all fronts, seeking victory as the result of equal pressure exerted at many points and putting a strain upon German man-power beyond its capacity.

German strategy, on the other hand, was solidly based upon an accurate knowledge of the facts. The German could calculate—and did—that the Russian conditions would, before the end of the year, practically, if not absolutely, eliminate the Russian foe. He could continue to follow the strategy of the past from which he had departed only in his attack upon Verdun and, holding fast in the west, finish with Russia. Thereafter, with his hands free, he would be able to concentrate his entire strength in a colossal and final effort to wrest a decision from the armies of France and Britain.

Therefore the German campaign of 1917 resolves itself into the story of a successful defensive in the west combined with such activity as was necessary in the east, activity of propaganda even more than of arms, to complete the destruction of the military power of Russia. The German at the opening of 1917 said: "This year I shall hold France and Britain, so far as my armies are concerned, while I dispose of Russia. But coincident with the defensive on land in the west I shall use my submarine warfare so to harry Allied commerce as to bring famine to Britain and exhaustion to the factories of France. Almost certainty in submarine campaign will bring Britain to surrender. Even if it does not I shall be able next year to dispose of both, and finally win the war."

The submarine was an essential element in the calculation. The German believed that relentless submarine warfare would effectively blockade Britain and equally effectively prevent the transport of Amer-

THE RETREAT TO THE HINDENBURG LINE

From a French Official Photograph

THE CATHEDRAL OF ARRAS AS THE GERMANS LEFT IT

ON THE BRITISH FRONT

Above—Cavalry resting near the Pol-Arras road.
Centre—Cavalry awaiting orders to advance.
Below—German prisoners helping to bring in the wounded to an advanced dressing-station.

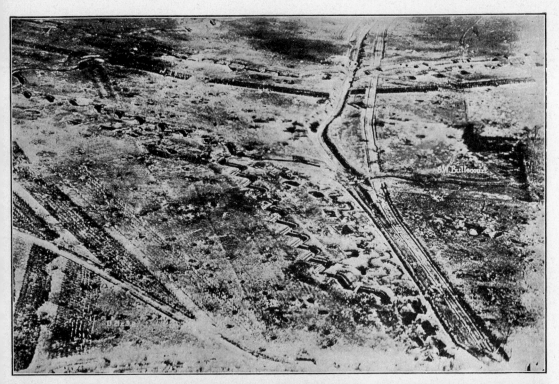

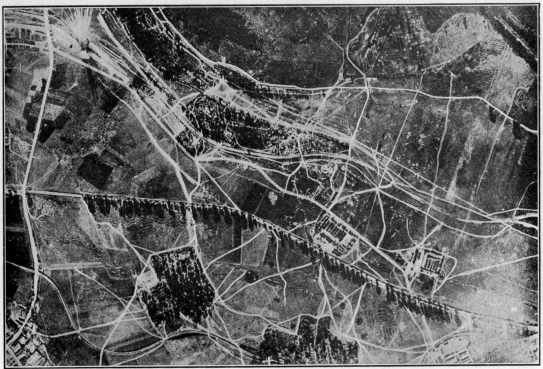

AIRPLANE PHOTOGRAPHS OF ROAD AND TRENCH SYSTEMS ON THE WESTERN FRONT

THE FIRST BRITISH SOLDIER WARILY ENTERS PERONNE

As the Germans evacuated the town they barricaded the streets and wrought all the damage which their hurried retreat permitted

From a British Official Photograph

A DISABLED GERMAN GUN NEAR BUISSY

A direct hit scored by the Canadian artillery put this gun out of commission. It had been in action beside the Arras-Cambrai road

A BRITISH WIRING PARTY

They are passing one of their own monster guns just outside Arras

SHELL-HOLES AS GUN EMPLACEMENTS

New Zealand artillery preparing to go into action in new positions

GENERAL MADOLON INSPECTS SOME NEW DUGOUTS WITH GENERAL WOOD

ican troops to the Continent. He did not reckon with America as a military force. He did not conceive of the possibility of the transport of vast American armies to Europe. He saw only the European factors in the game, and, seeing them alone, he saw victory. In this he reasoned not inaccurately, since only the arrival of American numbers ensured his ultimate defeat.

II. THE GERMAN PLAN

Having deliberately adopted the defensive on the western front, the German had to face immediate conditions which were unfavourable in the extreme. As a consequence of the Battle of the Somme, a broad, deep salient had been driven into his old line. At the outset, when the armies dug in between the Aisne and the Channel, he had had the advantage of time in the selection of his positions, and in the months that followed he had transformed these positions into a fortress. At the opening of the Battle of the Somme he held practically every vantage point from the Lys to Champagne.

But in the Battle of the Somme he had been pushed off the high ground; that portion of his force about Noyon nearest Paris found its rear and communications menaced by Allied gains from Péronne to Roye. The other section of his armies north of the Somme as far as Arras was equally menaced by the ever-growing British wedge driven toward Bapaume. British artillery had now gained the upper hand along the whole front and in inferior positions the German was compelled to take the medicine that had been the portion of the Allies for two years.

More than this, it was apparent from the beginning of the year that Allied attacks would be delivered from all the vantage points gained in the Battle of the Somme, and the enemy knew that during the winter British and French engineers had been busy constructing railroads and highways up to that new front and preparing for the attack of the coming campaign.

Given his experience at the Somme, given the advantage of the position the enemy now occupied, it was clear to the German that he was doomed to suffer at least considerable local defeats if he maintained the position in which he stood when the operations of the previous year terminated. He had therefore to choose between accepting battle on unfavourable ground, with the certainty of suffering local defeats, and of being compelled to make local retreats during the progress of the campaign, or solving all his difficulties by declining battle and retiring, in advance of attack, to new positions on more favourable ground.

On the military side the advantages of a general retirement were patent. The territory occupied had no value; it contained no cities of size, no industrial plants of value to the invader; much of it had been torn by shell fire, wasted by two and a half years of military occupation; the vantage points had been lost in the campaign of 1916, and were now securely in enemy hands. Allied success at the Somme had removed the chance of any push toward Paris from the Noyon salient. A retirement which would shorten and straighten his line, iron out the bulging and dangerous salients, releasing a certain number of troops, would be of obvious profit to the German.

On the other hand, a retreat, and a considerable retreat, the first in the west since the Marne campaign, would unquestionably bestow a great moral advantage upon the Allies. Following the repulse at Verdun and the considerable if gradual retirement at the Somme, it was bound to be interpreted in Allied quarters not merely as proof of victory in a past campaign but as the beginning of the end in the war itself. Coming at the opening of a new campaign it was bound to awaken new hopes and inspire greater efforts in Allied armies.

Notwithstanding the moral consequences of retreat, however, the German decision was quickly made. Hindenburg who, at the close of 1916 had risen to supreme command, had now come west and, what was of more importance, he had brought with him Ludendorff, henceforth the great figure on the German side and certainly one of the great figures in military history. The prestige of Hindenburg, now at its apex, was sufficient to deprive a retirement of any sting for the German public, while the confidence of the German people alike in their military idol and in their victorious prospects was sufficient to avoid any dangerous depression at home.

Therefore, by the 1st of January, German High Command had resolved upon the wide swinging retreat to new lines and by the first week in February this great operation began.

III. THE GREAT RETREAT

The German retirement in the late winter and early spring of 1917 is one of the great strategic conceptions of the whole war. It transformed the entire character of the campaign of 1917, it totally dislocated all Allied strategy in the west. By shortening the German line and by creating on nearly a hundred miles of front a desert without roads or communications it released many German divisions whose presence in Flanders and about the Aisne sufficed to defeat British and French offensives. At the moment when it developed, Allied plans and preparations were complete for a gigantic offensive extending from Arras to Soissons. By it all these plans and preparations were rendered useless and, instead of attacking on the ground they had chosen, the Allies were forced to decide between assault on narrow fronts, precisely where the enemy had made his great counter-preparations, and abandoning the offensive altogether.

It would be difficult to find in all history, certainly in all records of modern warfare, a more simple or more brutal policy than that which was expressed in the German retreat. Stripped of all disguise of euphemism German strategy was to turn a thousand square miles of fertile fields, smiling villages, busy towns into an absolute desert. Retiring to new positions selected in advance, prepared with every art of military science, the German willed to leave between himself and his enemies an indescribable region of bridgeless rivers, broken cities, destroyed railways. He reasoned—and he reasoned correctly—that with such a destruction any great Allied offensive on a wide front in the west would be impossible in 1917, and he calculated that in the respite gained he would be able to deal finally with Russia and then, turning westward, try again—as he had tried at the Marne and once more at Verdun—for decisive victory.

The story of German devastation between Arras and Soissons is one

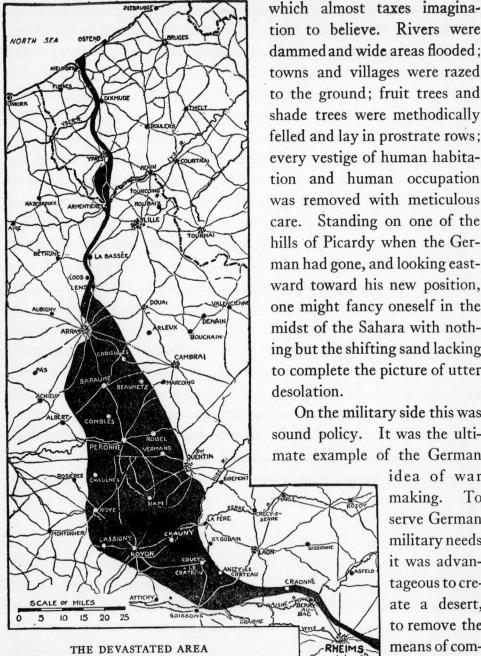

THE DEVASTATED AREA

The solid black from Lens to Craonne shows the country ravaged by the Germans in their great retreat to the Hindenburg Line or in the construction of this line. The small bit of black south of Ypres shows territory re-conquered by the British in the June attack on the Messines-"Whitesheet" Ridge.

which almost taxes imagination to believe. Rivers were dammed and wide areas flooded; towns and villages were razed to the ground; fruit trees and shade trees were methodically felled and lay in prostrate rows; every vestige of human habitation and human occupation was removed with meticulous care. Standing on one of the hills of Picardy when the German had gone, and looking eastward toward his new position, one might fancy oneself in the midst of the Sahara with nothing but the shifting sand lacking to complete the picture of utter desolation.

On the military side this was sound policy. It was the ultimate example of the German idea of war making. To serve German military needs it was advantageous to create a desert, to remove the means of communication by which the foe might approach his own lines, to remove the habitations in which this foe might find shelter in the coming winter. To make observation of his airmen easy, it was important to eliminate every possible means of cover. And since these were the facts the German did not hesitate. From the villages, from towns, he evicted the miserable remnant of the population which had failed to escape in the first weeks of the war and had lived in ever-growing wretchedness thereafter. Herding these people in a few scattered villages, sweeping off the able-bodied men and women to become his labourers or worse, he applied the torch, the bomb, the mine; for weeks after his retreat began the nights were lurid with the flames of burning villages and the earth shook with the explosions which destroyed towns and villages; while behind him he left every form of hellish device—delayed mine, booby trap—to slay his pursuers.

When he had completed his task of destruction and was within his own lines the German looked westward upon a waste hardly to be paralleled in Europe. Not a tree, not a wall, not a sign of human residence was to be seen from his front, and there were miles and miles of what had once been the garden land of France in which the only things left intact were those colossal cemeteries which the German had constructed on conquered territory and the huge, barbaric monuments he had erected to his own dead. And even as he honoured his own dead he dragged bodies of French men and women from their cemeteries, scattered their bones, defaced and defiled their monuments, as if to demonstrate that not even the dead themselves were to be spared in his rage of destruction.

IV. HOW IT WAS DONE

The actual details of the German retreat are simply told. The winter of 1917 was one of almost unprecedented cold. Much snow fell in northern France and for several weeks in January and February the temperature fell to zero Fahrenheit. The ground was frozen, military operations were impossible, aërial observations inaccurate and unsatisfactory, and in this time the German slowly and steadily moved his heavy artillery backward. In the words of Sir Douglas Haig—"The task of obtaining the amount of railway material to meet the demands of

our armies, and of carrying out the work of construction at the rate
rendered necessary by our plans, in addition to providing labour and
materials for the necessary repair of roads, was one of the very greatest
difficulty." On February 6th the British reported a German retirement out of Grandcourt on the arc facing Beaumont Hamel, the scene
of desperate fighting in the last campaign. Through February there
were multiplying reports of slight German retreats, retreats which

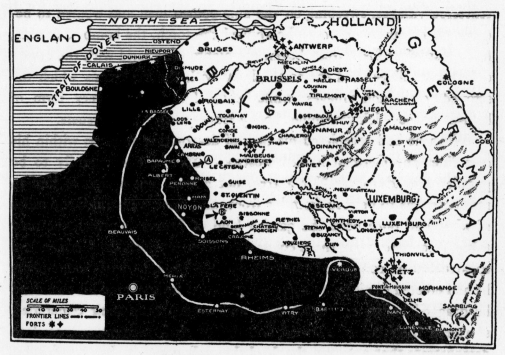

THE THREE FRONTS IN FRANCE

The solid black shows territory occupied by the Allies at the close of the Hindenburg
retreat in 1918. The white line from Arras to Soissons shows the front at the opening of the
Battle of the Somme in July, 1916. Both Arras and Soissons were then in Allied hands.
The white line from La Bassée through Beauvais, Meaux, Esternay, Vitry, to Verdun and south
of Verdun shows the limit of German advance in the Marne campaign of 1914.

seemed at the moment rather rectifications of the front, and this impression was confirmed by frequent German newspaper and official communications trumpeting the impregnability of the main German position while conceding and thus minimizing slight retirements.

It was not until the middle of March that the real movement began.
Then as the winter broke the weather became misty, the ground soft.

Of a sudden, on the whole front from Arras to Soissons, the German began to go back. Day by day the retirement spread and grew. Allied newspapers were filled with the account of the occupation of town after town and village after village which had been the unattained objectives of two years of fighting. Bapaume, Ham, Péronne, Noyon, were successively evacuated and occupied. Allied advance guards lost touch with the German rear guards and, for the first time in nearly three years of war, troops advanced in the open again and for the moment trenches disappeared.

It would be difficult to exaggerate the momentary burst of enthusiasm and joy which was evoked by the news of this German retreat. British and French publics alike, fired with the idea of the Somme as a decisive victory and Verdun as a colossal disaster, interpreted the German retirement as a confession of final defeat. The progress of the submarine campaign, the ever-deepening anxieties about Russia, were forgotten in the few days when Allied troops moved forward from the Scarpe to the Aisne over territory which had been lost since August, 1914.

Yet very early in the retreat it became patent that the German was drawing back deliberately, without disorder, in accordance with methodical, well-conceived plans. He left behind him neither prisoners nor guns. He took with him everything of the smallest value in all the country he had occupied, and what he did not move, he destroyed. Even the enthusiasm of the French soldiers pushing forward over a regained province could hardly dispel the agony of the whole French nation as it began to learn the extent of devastation and desolation which the German was leaving behind him.

At the moment when the retreat disclosed itself, Allied capitals were filled with speculation as to the extent of the withdrawal. Would it be to the frontier, as had long been forecast by military writers? If the German was actually hard pushed for numbers, if his man-power was in fact failing as the Allied critics asserted, no lesser retirement would suffice, and in the middle of March, Allied publics looked confidently forward to the swift arrival of French and British armies at the Belgian frontier from the Scheldt to the Meuse. The liberation of northern France, even the invasion of Germany, seemed at hand in that brief but joyous interlude between the hour when the German left his old battle-line and the moment when he was disclosed standing again behind those positions which henceforth for more than a year were to be known as the Hindenburg Line. That the German still felt himself victorious and certain to win the war was perhaps most clearly demonstrated by the ruthlessness of this retreat. Such destruction as he left behind him would have been unthinkable had he conceived for a single moment that he might lose the war and be compelled to restore the regions he had devastated, or had he thought that an hour might come when Allied armies would be able to enter German territory and, if they chose, imitate in the Rhine lands that policy which had turned so much of northern France into a waste.

On the merely statistical side the German destruction totally obliterated 264 villages, 225 churches, and more than 38,000 houses. On the artistic side, some of the most beautiful monuments of Europe were reduced to cinders; the splendid castle of Coucy-le-Château, hardly matched in the world, was transformed by dynamite into a shapeless pile; famous châteaux, churches, public buildings shared the same fate; the statues of the great Frenchmen of the past were torn from their pedestals; wells were filled or poisoned; the British army, entering the smoking ruins of Bapaume, saw before it a huge sign on which was painted the legend: "Show not wrath but wonder."

The German newspapers themselves frankly described the work of German hands. "All the country is but an immense and sad desert," said the *Berliner Tageblatt*, "without a tree, a bush, or a house. Our pioneers have sawed and cut the trees which for days have fallen until the whole surface of the earth is swept clear; the wells are filled up, the villages abolished. Dynamite cartridges explode on all sides; the atmosphere is obscured by dust and smoke."

Since the days of Attila, Europe has seen no such wanton and terrible waste of a country, and no modern people has ever accumulated such a debt as did the German people by this supreme offence against civilization.

V.   THE HINDENBURG LINE

It remains now to describe the line on which the German retired, which instantly became famous as the Hindenburg Line, while for its various ramifications it borrowed names from German legend.

The German retreat had swung inward from two fixed points, which were in a sense the hinges.   These fixed points were Vimy Ridge, north of Arras, and the Craonne Plateau, north of Soissons.   Each was a commanding position fortified by all the art of the German military engineers, each was regarded by the Germans as itself impregnable and as a guarantee against any flank attack.

Between these two anchorages the Hindenburg Line hung like a cable.   From Vimy Ridge it ran straight across the Douai Plain, covering Douai and Cambrai.   Thence it turned south on the high ground between the Scheldt and the Somme, covered St. Quentin, crossed to the Oise, and followed the east bank of the flooded river until it reached the enormous bulwark of St. Gobain Forest, which was like a central support, an impregnable barrier of forest and hill.   Beyond the St. Gobain Forest it passed south of Laon across the region between the Ailette and the Aisne, touched the Aisne east of Soissons, and then followed the course of the famous Craonne Plateau where Napoleon and Blücher had fought, crossing the famous Chemin-des-Dames which ran along the crest of the plateau.   Beyond Craonne it turned southward, following the old trace to those dismantled forts from which for more than two and a half years the German artillery had continued to pour shells into the city and cathedral of Rheims.

To defend this Hindenburg Line the German had constructed not one or several trench lines but a great fortified zone some ten or twelve miles deep in places.   This zone was lined with immense concrete machine-gun positions; it was covered by vast meshes of barbed wire.

Between the Scarpe below Vimy Ridge and the Oise south of St. Quentin, where it crossed open, rolling country, the German defence borrowed the swells, cunningly constructed dug-outs and concrete pill-boxes behind each upward curve of the ground; while behind the main fortified zone he constructed support or switch lines which served the purpose of compartments in an ocean liner and enabled him to hold the major part of his main fortified zone even though it were penetrated at some point.

To the eye the Hindenburg Line was not impressive, it was not a mass of great forts. It lacked those redoubts and "works" famous in the Battle of the Somme which offered such admirable targets to enemy artillery. It was organization in depth, and the German coined the phrase "elastic defence" to describe his tactics. Holding the outer fringe of the fortified zone lightly, but with picked troops and a wealth of machine guns, the German permitted his assailants to enmesh themselves and, when they advanced and became entangled in the outer series of lines, German reserves counter-attacked the exhausted and heavily punished troops.

The main elements in this new defence line were the concrete works so camouflaged as to escape the observation of the airmen, so spaced as to deliver deadly cross fire upon attacking troops, and sufficiently strong to offer protection to the three or four men who constituted the garrison, alike against artillery and against tanks. In this system positions such as had been contested in previous campaigns counted for little. Even when he had lost Vimy Ridge, the German retired to a switch line running across the plain and easily halted further advance of victorious British troops.

The natural obstacles in the pathway of the assailants of the Hindenburg Line were of two sorts. The Douai Plain is cut with many canals; the rivers are inconsiderable, but the canals, doubling the rivers in many places, constitute a protection against tanks and a difficult barrier for infantry to negotiate. Of these waterways the unfinished Canal du Nord, going northward from Péronne to the Douai Plain, and the Scheldt Canal going up from St. Quentin to Cambrai, played the most considerable part both in 1917 and 1918. The Oise River, from the point where the line touched it south of St. Quentin to La Fère, was transformed into an impassable lake. In addition to the water obstacles, Havrincourt Wood, where the Canal du Nord reaches the Douai Plain,

and Bourlon Woods looking down on Cambrai and the St. Gobain
Forest, were the most considerable; and the first two were scenes of
desperate fighting.

Yet in the main, from the Scarpe to the Oise the country was open,
rolling, a country of far views with hills little above the general level, a
country admirably suited for artillery, and, when the German had swept
it clear of villages and cover of every sort, a country in which every
movement of the Allies could be promptly discovered and every infantry attack terribly punished.

And German purpose expressed in this system of defence was not
to hold any given point but rather to exact such a price from the assail-
ant as to break the spirit of the army and exhaust the man-power of the
nation. The German calculated, and calculated correctly, that given
the devastation before his line and the long months of labour that must
ensue before the Allied troops could attack his new front, he could with
relatively restricted numbers hold out in the west until the task in the
east was completed. He further reasoned that by retiring from the old
front, now dominated by the enemy from positions which he had lost,
to a line of his own choosing, he would regain strategic freedom; and
if the hour arrived to return to the offensive he would be able to strike
with every advantage of position and communication in his own
favour.

In sum, then, the great German retreat resulted: first, in giving the
German a shorter front and thus releasing many divisions for service
at other points; secondly, the devastation, demonstrating as it did what
German tactics would be if German armies were compelled to make further retirement, insensibly but unmistakably affected French morale.
While French armies were still fresh, with the great offensive still in
preparation, a burning passion of anger fired the French nation; but when
the French army had broken against the Hindenburg Line, when the
spring offensive had come and failed, the effect of this terrible destruction was more and more potent for peace in a war-weary people. Thirdly,
by his retirement, the German totally disarranged the Allied plan of
attack. Instead of a colossal drive upon a great front the French and

the British were condemned to attack upon narrow fronts; and the German, immune from assault for many months along the whole stretch of his main front, was able to mass his reserves on those narrow sectors left to his enemy to attack.   Finally, as the German commentators affirmed at the time, thereby exciting Allied derision, the German regained strategic liberty of action.   The Hindenburg Line was not merely a defensive position; it was to prove a most admirable point of departure for that stupendous attack of the following year which so nearly won the war.

CHAPTER FIVE

THE BATTLE OF ARRAS—BAGDAD

I
VIMY RIDGE

The honour of opening the campaign in the west fell to the British. For the first time in the history of the war the British had consented to place their armies under the direction of a French generalissimo. Yielding to the representations of the French Government and of the new French Commander-in-Chief, the British had agreed that, for the period of the first great attack, British troops should obey the orders of General Nivelle, although it was carefully specified that it should be for Field Marshal Haig to determine when the opening battle had ended, and thus terminate the period in which he served as a subordinate.

Originally the British had expected to open the spring operations by a renewal of the Battle of the Somme, launching converging attacks upon the German troops in the salient between the Ancre and the Scarpe rivers, but their main stroke for the year was to be delivered in the region of Ypres and to have, for its larger purpose, piercing the German line on the Passchendaele Ridge, driving a wedge between the Kaiser's troops along the Belgian seacoast and in France, and compelling a withdrawal from that narrow strip of sea-front, become so important in the new German submarine operations.

The great German retreat eliminated the necessity of a new Battle of the Somme; but the weather was not suitable, nor were the preparations completed, for opening the Flanders campaign in April. Therefore, since the French scheme called for an immediate attack, it was necessary for the British to strike at once, and there was left to them as an available front only that narrow strip of German line between La Bassée and Arras where the German still stood in the positions he occupied from the moment when the western battle became stationary.

Moreover, on that portion of this front facing Arras, Haig had planned one of his two converging attacks before the general retreat and had made the necessary preparations.

The central feature of this available front was the great Vimy Ridge, the northern pivot or hinge of the recent German retreat, one of the commanding landmarks of the whole western front, which had already been the objective of two terrible but unsuccessful offensives. Like the Craonne Plateau to the south and the St. Gobain Forest east of the Oise, Vimy Ridge was one of the essential bulwarks in the German defensive plan.

Starting at the Straits of Dover, about Calais, there is a great chalk ridge which rises in gradual folds from the sea and breaks down abruptly into the northern plain of France and Belgium. Down its eastern slopes come all the little rivers tributary to the Scheldt, while the valley of the Somme marks its southern limit. When, in the fall of 1914, the German dug in after his failure to reach the Channel, he occupied the easternmost crests of this highland. Behind him the land sloped rapidly down to the plain. All the fighting of the various Allied offensives from Loos to the Somme had been attempts to drive the German off the high ground down into the plain. His retirement, under pressure, at the Somme and his great retreat had carried him down into the plain from the southern outskirts of Arras to the country south of Cambrai, but at Vimy he was still on high ground from which he commanded the country in all directions.

Vimy Ridge itself is a long isolated hill nearly five hundred feet above sea-level and more than two hundred feet above the plain. Approaching it from the westward the ascent is gradual and long, but on the eastern side it falls down abruptly into the plain. To the northward it is separated from the heights of Notre-Dame de Lorette and the plateau above Lens, on which the Battle of Loos was fought, by the little muddy brook of Carency, which at Lens takes on the name and dignity of the Souchez River. To the south it touches the Scarpe River just after that stream, also insignificant, emerges from the eastern suburbs of Arras.

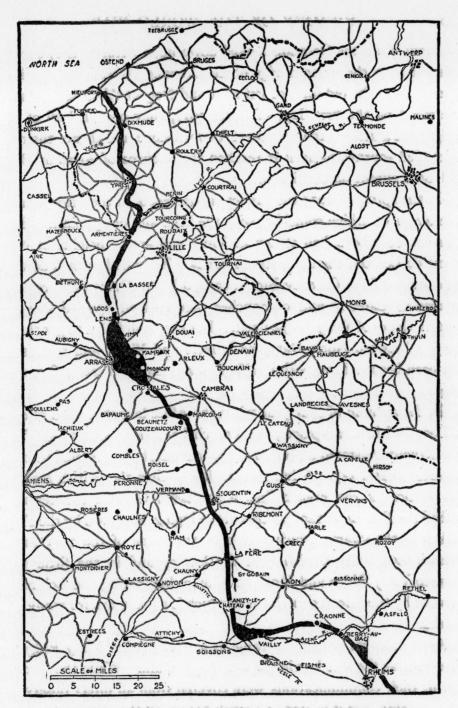

THE ANGLO-FRENCH OFFENSIVES OF APRIL AND MAY, 1917

The solid black from Lens to Croisilles shows the front of the British offensive of April 9th and the territory conquered between April 9th and May 5th in the Battle of Arras. The solid black north of Soissons and north of Rheims indicates the territory gained by the French in their offensive of April 16th and the front of attack extending from just north of Soissons to Rheims.

From Vimy the Germans looked down upon Arras as they surveyed Soissons from the western edge of the Craonne Plateau and dominated Rheims from the old forts of Brimont and Nogent-l'Abbesse. As their line stood on the first days of April, 1917, they occupied all of Vimy Ridge save a little of the northwest forward slope and thence their front descended southward until it reached the suburbs of Arras at Blangy and St. Laurent on the Scarpe.

In the spring of 1915 the French, under Foch, in their first considerable offensive, which coincided with the brief and disappointing British effort at Festubert, had struck at Vimy and at the heights of Notre-Dame de Lorette, then in German hands. They had pushed down the little valley of the Carency Brook, carried Notre-Dame de Lorette, the villages of Carency and of Souchez, and pushed upward along the western slopes of Vimy Ridge itself. But they had failed to get through the gap between Notre-Dame de Lorette and Vimy, and their attack had been beaten down with terrific losses along the western face of the ridge.

In the autumn of that year when the Allies launched their offensive at Loos and in Champagne, the French had tried again to get Vimy, had actually mastered a portion of the summit, but were unable to clear the crest of Hill 145. A few months later, when the British took over this portion of the French line, a successful German counter-attack pushed the British off that portion of the high ground won by the French back into the swamp which had been the scene of the 1915 battles. Thenceforward the British held the low ground in the little valley between Vimy Ridge and Mont St. Eloi, a dominating and isolated hill crowned by the ruined church tower which is a landmark for many miles around.

Apart from its immediate value as a strong point, Vimy Ridge was important as the last barrier to the Douai Plain. While the Germans held it, their communications were covered from all direct observation by the enemy. If it passed to British hands, all the country from Lens to Cambrai would be spread out like a map for British observers; Lens itself would be almost untenable, and the Germans at last would find themselves where the French and British had been for so long—in the low ground dominated by enemy positions on high. Moreover, once Vimy Ridge was in British hands, its steep eastern slopes would be an almost impregnable barrier to any new German offensive—wholly impregnable as the events of exactly a year later were to prove. Seated on Vimy, the German had been for more than two years reducing Arras to ruins as he had similarly destroyed Soissons and Rheims. Southward his lines actually touched the suburbs, but his real control of Arras lay in his occupation of Telegraph Hill, the southern crest of the ridge.

Vimy Ridge itself had been fortified with the utmost care. Here, as in all places where he occupied heights, the German had tunnelled; and vast galleries honeycombed the chalk cliff, giving his troops shelter, warm and dry cover from the elements, and equally complete protection against enemy artillery. On the whole extent of the western front no single position surpassed Vimy Ridge alike in natural strength and in the extent of its fortifications.

II. THE BRITISH ARMY

The armies that were selected to make the British attack upon Vimy Ridge were those of General Horne, who henceforth commanded the British First Army to the end of the war, and of General Allenby, who had won distinction as commander of the cavalry in the British retreat from Mons to the Marne and achieved justified reputation by his defence of the Messines Ridge in the critical days of the Ypres campaign. He was, moreover, at a later time to win still greater renown as the conqueror of Jerusalem and as the victor at Samaria.

The British army, as it entered the campaign of 1917, had reached a high point alike in training and in morale. It had suffered terrible losses at the Somme. The early expectations of swift victory had disappeared. It was comparable with the army of which Grant took command when he came East in 1864. It was no longer a civilian army but it was not yet merely a professional army. Despite the losses of the Somme it still contained much of the best of British manhood.

Moreover, the victories in the last phase of the Somme, the natural exultation excited by the recent German retreat, had created an atmosphere of confidence impossible to exaggerate, while, for the first time, the British troops found themselves, not only superior in artillery and all the other mechanical appliances of war as they had been at the Somme, but also saw all this machinery in the hands of men trained by battle experience to its use.

All through the long, hard winter the British army had felt with ever-growing certainty a sense of superiority over the enemy. They had seen him retire from the almost impregnable fortress of Bapaume Ridge; they had captured thousands of his best troops; during the winter months not a few deserters had come through the lines bringing stories of depression. In April, 1917, the British soldier felt himself to be "top dog," and for him the adequate proof of this superiority was found alike in the success at the Somme and the recent wide-swinging advance which had carried him over all the immediate objectives of the previous campaign.

Whatever doubts the High Command may have felt as they saw the Russian Revolution marching unmistakably toward the destruction of Russian military power—as they saw the German retreat, permitting a safe escape from the dangerous positions to new lines whose strength was suspected if not fully appraised—the British soldier had no misgiving. For him the campaign of victory was just beginning.

There can be no greater tragedy than the fashion in which this British army and this British spirit, closely rivalled by the French army, were to be shaken and all but broken by the terrible experiences that were now to come. Between the British army that marched to the victories of Arras, of Messines, and the terrible conflict of Passchendaele and the British armies that staggered and all but broke under the German offensive one year later, there can be no comparison. After those defeats of 1918 the British army rallied, reorganized, won great and far-shining victories; but after Passchendaele it was never again what it had been in the spring offensive which began at Vimy. During the winter the British army, which now numbered fifty-two divisions, as contrasted with thirty in the Somme time and seven during the First Battle of Ypres, had taken over a new sector of the front from the French, and their line was now nearly one hundred and twenty miles long as contrasted with less than twenty held in the first days of 1915. Under the efficient direction of Sir Eric Geddes the whole system of communications had been reorganized. Old local railroads had been rebuilt and double-tracked. Lines in England and even in Canada had been moved to France and the organization of the British rear had become, as it remained till the end the best on either side.

III. STRATEGIC AND TACTICAL PURPOSE

The British operation had for its main purpose occupying and attracting as large a number of German divisions as possible to the British sector. The main attack of the spring offensive was to be delivered by the French between the Somme and Rheims. In the larger conception the British offensive had no more considerable objective than that of occupying German reserves and placing a strain upon German man-power precisely at the moment when the main thrust was delivered by the French.

In this wholly subordinate operation the main British objective, geographically, was Vimy Ridge. It was remotely possible that having taken Vimy Ridge, the victorious British troops might be able to press eastward along the Douai road, southeastward along the Cambrai road, breaking the whole Hindenburg system of defences, and reach Douai and Cambrai—vital points in the enemy's railroad communications. But this was an utterly remote possibility. At the moment when the blow was delivered it was interpreted as an effort to break through, to penetrate the German defensive system and reach the great railroad bases; but this was inaccurate. Nivelle asked of Haig that he should keep German divisions occupied, thus lessening the resisting power of the Germans on the French front. This service Haig performed. In proportion as the French attack became more and more unsuccessful, greater and greater demands were made upon the British. The attack of April 9th reached its logical conclusion on April 14th. Because of the French situation, however, the British were asked to attack again, and still later a third time. Neither of these later attacks had any chance of larger success. They were costly in the extreme. Their explanation must be found in the French situation, not in any condition growing out of the original blow. As a battle, Arras was over on the 14th of April. The operations that followed were local.

In the initial attack only the British Third Army, commanded by Allenby, and the Canadian Corps of the First Army, were directly involved. The Fourth and Fifth armies to the south, under Rawlinson and Gough respectively, demonstrated during the first stages of the battle, and in the later phases participated to a certain extent; but the actual front of attack was not more than fifteen miles in width, more than half was covered by Vimy Ridge, and the Third Army and the Canadian Corps were alone engaged. In advance of the battle the British had concentrated some four thousand pieces of artillery on their front. The Germans, on their side, had massed not less than three thousand, and the artillery bombardment, which began on Easter Sunday, was one of the most terrific of the whole war. As usual, in the British offensives, the weather was bad. When the troops left the trenches on Easter Monday it was raining heavily. Before the day had advanced far, the rain turned into snow and the whole of the first day's operations went forward in weather inclement in the extreme, making aërial observation impossible.

Facing Vimy Ridge the main attack was delivered by the Canadians. For nearly a year they had held the sector opposite this barrier. Early in their tenancy they had been driven out of positions held by the French, from whom they had taken over, and this reverse had been a bitter blow to the pride of the troops who had won for Canada enduring fame at Ypres and were now to achieve the greatest success for them in the whole war. Southward of the Canadian front, Scottish troops also participated in the Vimy Ridge phase, while away down to the south, around the town of Bullecourt, henceforth to have almost as glorious and as bitter memories for Australia as Gallipoli—Anzac troops were in line. In the centre, where the English troops were brought up to the outskirts of Arras, they made use of a tunnel dug for the attack and passing under the city for more than a mile.

IV. THE ATTACK

After more than twenty-four hours of intense bombardment the attack was launched at 5.30 on the morning of Easter Monday. In the midst of rain and snow thousands and thousands of Canadian, Scottish, and English troops left their trenches and swept forward. The enemy was not surprised at the point of attack. It was clear that he had expected some effort on this front and had made a counter-concentration of guns and reserves. His surprise was, in the

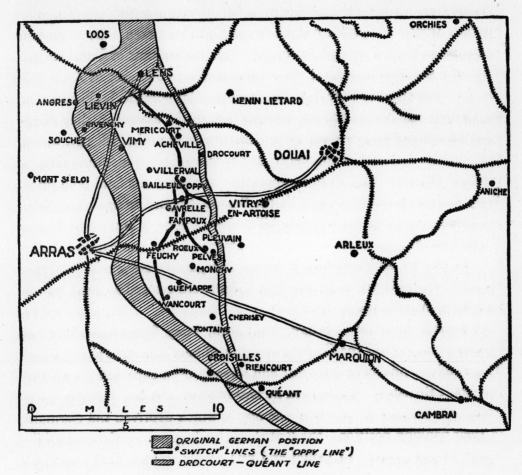

THE GERMAN DEFENCE SYSTEMS ATTACKED BY THE BRITISH ON APRIL 9TH

main, the result of the intensity and accuracy of the artillery preparation. At the Somme, the year before, French artillery preparation had been complete; British, largely a failure. In the offensive of 1917 the circumstances were now to be exactly reversed. The essential circumstance in the attack was an advance, to be carried out by a succession of comparatively short rushes, corresponding approximately with the enemy's various systems of defence; and this manœuvre required the closest sort of coördination between the infantry and their artillery barrages. In the first part of the attack the Canadians pushed up almost to the crest of Vimy Ridge, the Scottish and English troops to the southward broke out of the City of Arras, taking the suburbs of St. Laurent and Blangy. Within forty minutes of the "zero hour" practically the whole of the German front-line system had been stormed and taken. By noon the Canadians were in many places up and over the summit of Vimy Ridge. With the single exception of the railway triangle due east of Arras, all the second objectives were in British hands as far north as La Folie Farm on Vimy Ridge itself; and by three o'clock in the afternoon they occupied the entire crest, save for the northernmost summit, Hill 145, where the Germans maintained a desperate and successful resistance until late into the night, when they were compelled to abandon this final hold upon Vimy Ridge. Southward, astride the Scarpe, English troops were pushing through the gap between the hills where the river enters the Douai Plain, following the railroad and the highways which run parallel all the way to Douai; and still further south also gains were made. In this sector the Third German defence system had been crossed at many points and the gun positions reached.

By the morning of Tuesday, April 10th, Vimy Ridge was solidly in Canadian hands and the German troops had been driven into the plain. Thousands of prisoners and guns had already been captured, and up to this point British losses had been inconsiderable. On this Tuesday—following the Canadian success to the north, which deprived the Germans of their flanking position—the British centre began to push out rapidly along the Scarpe toward Douai and was as far east as Fampoux, and the whole of the enemy's third-line system south of the Scarpe was

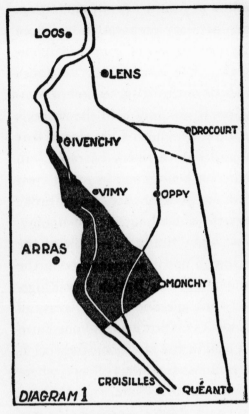

DIAGRAM 1

THE FIRST BLOW

Solid black indicates the territory gained by the British in the first days of their attack and shows how they penetrated the first German system and the Oppy Line.

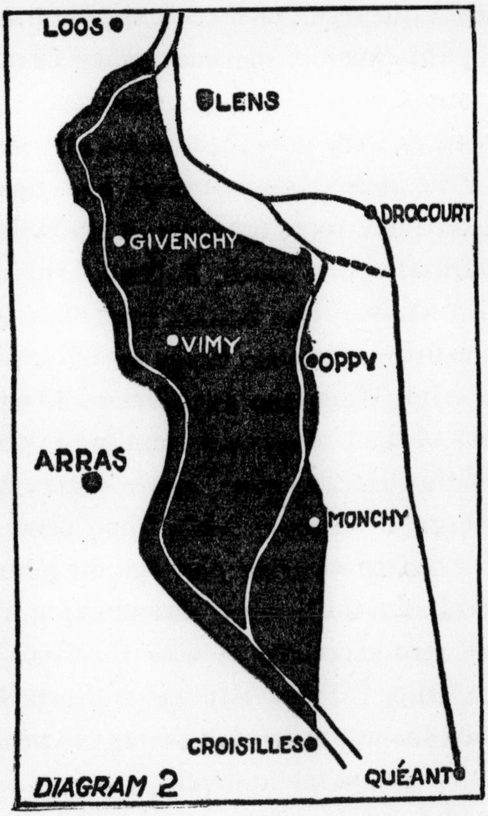

DIAGRAM 2

HOW THE LINE WAS STRAIGHTENED OUT

The solid black indicates the territory conquered between April 9th and May 5th and shows how the British were checked at or near the Oppy Line.

passed. On Wednesday, April 11th, Monchy-le-Preux, next to Vimy the most valuable position in this sector, was in British hands as the result of a daring cavalry charge; from the Souchez River straight south to the Arras-Cambrai road the Germans had been driven off the high ground; while still to the south, beyond the tiny Cojeul and Sensée rivers where they still clung to the heights, they were rapidly being enveloped from the north and the south alike.

The loss of Monchy was capital. Projecting out into the Douai Plain like a cape, this high ground not only commands a wide view eastward toward Douai, but northward and southward sweeps the country actually behind the lines on which the Germans were attempting to rally.

On Thursday, April 12th, the German had obviously abandoned all hope of regaining the ground which he had lost; northward and southward he was beginning his retirement to his new positions of defence. This gradual retirement continued all through Friday, the 13th; by Saturday, April 14th, British troops had passed Lievin, one of the suburbs of Lens, and were actually in the outskirts of the coal town itself; while farther to the south, Bailleul, Vimy, Givenchy, and Arleux were in British hands. The British front, which earlier in the week had been indicated by a convex bulge on either side of the Scarpe, now came down straight from the outskirts of Lens to the Scarpe, then southward to Croisilles. Fourteen thousand prisoners, including 285 officers and more than 200 guns, many of them of high calibre, were among the fruits of victory; while Vimy Ridge had passed permanently out of German possession and was to become a pillar in British hands when at last the Germans should come westward again.

But successful as were the British attacks, there had been no break through. There had never been the smallest chance of piercing the Hindenburg defensive system. At the very moment when Allied journals were incorrectly reporting the fall of Lens, the British advance had been definitely stayed on the first German "switch line," thenceforth notorious in the military reports of the day as the "Oppy switch." This line, constructed by the Germans against just such an emergency as had now come, ran down southward from Lens, crossed the Douai Plain, rejoining the old line near Bullecourt. On this line the first phase of the battle ended. German reserves, which were rushed up, counter-attacked and broke the weight of British pressure; and, moreover, halted at the "Oppy line," the British quickly learned that behind this defence was still a third and even more formidable barrier the Drocourt-Quéant "switch," which paralleled the "Oppy line" several miles to the east.

V. THE END OF THE BATTLE

Checked at the "Oppy line" after a week which was unmistakably the most successful in British military history during the whole war up to this point, the British reinforced and reorganized their front preparatory to a new attack. They had advanced rather more than four miles on a front of some twelve miles. They were on the outskirts of Lens. From Vimy Ridge and Monchy they looked out upon Douai and Cambrai, and between them and these cities, both of which were vital to the German communication system, there were no great natural obstacles.

Yet the experience of recent days had clearly demonstrated the practical impossibility of repeating the preliminary success, precisely as the history of the Champagne offensive in 1915 and the German attack on Verdun in 1916 had emphasized the same lesson. The British had advanced beyond the effective support of their heavy artillery and it was a matter of many days to move these guns forward. New communications had to be constructed over difficult country and, what was of even greater importance, the German was able to match division against division and his organization in depth had provided him with many more lines of defence. Moreover, beginning with April 14th, he changed his tactics and thereafter counter-attacked with a fury almost unexampled. There was no more of that waiting to be attacked which had contributed so much to British confidence in the closing days of the Somme. From Bullecourt straight up to Lens the German thrust back again and again. Arleux, Oppy, Gavrelle, Greenland Hill, Roeux, Guémappe, and half a dozen other insignificant but henceforth memorable hamlets were taken and retaken innumerable times.

Left to himself there can be no question that Field Marshal Haig would have broken off the Battle of Arras on the 14th of April, as he himself stated in his official report, but in the week that followed, the French offensive had begun—and begun badly. Therefore, since he was under Nivelle's orders, Haig was compelled against his better judgment to renew the Battle of Arras on the 23rd of April by an attack on a nine-mile front from Croisilles to Gavrelle. In this renewed offensive local gains were registered but in every case strong enemy counter-attacks quickly beat down the assailants. Still the battle continued; on May 5th the front was further extended and there was terrific fighting about

Bullecourt where the Fifth Army attacked. Thereafter the battle slowly died out. Haig himself fixed May 5th as the final day, and British interest and effort were transferred from Artois to Flanders. In sum, in less than a month of fighting the British occupied rather more ground than they had captured in the Somme offensive which had extended from July to December. In Vimy Ridge they took a position vastly stronger than anything which had confronted them on July 1, 1916. They captured 257 guns, including 98 heavy pieces, 19,500 prisoners, 464 machine guns, and 227 trench mortars. They had engaged not less than forty divisions, twenty-three of which had been withdrawn exhausted from the line.

Viewed in its proper perspective—as no more than a holding operation designed to aid the French in their major offensive to the south—it is plain that the Battle of Arras was for the British not only a great success in itself, but also a far more considerable achievement than might have been expected, given the limited objectives.

Unfortunately, although the British performed their part in the Allied plan completely and accurately, the sacrifice was in the larger sense useless, since, in spite of it, Nivelle failed at the Craonne Plateau. Moreover, the later phases of the battle were exceedingly costly in men, and the prolongation made necessary by the French failure fatally delayed the main British thrust in Flanders.

The consequences were not long in unfolding. It had been a great concession on the part of the British to place their vast armies under the control of the French commander. Having made this sacrifice, and having loyally fulfilled the task assigned to them, the British saw the French fail, saw their own troops compelled to make desperate and hopeless assaults, saw their own campaign postponed until its failure was inevitable. As a result, they resolved against another experiment with a unity of command; and this resolution endured, with evil consequences, up to the moment when the great German victory of March 21st of the following year brought the whole Allied cause to the edge of ruin. Then, and only then, the British yielded; and Foch became generalissimo.

Viewed by itself, the Battle of Arras was a brilliant victory, which revealed the British army at its best. The taking of Vimy Ridge was one of the finest achievements of the whole war and, as the second act in the campaign of 1917 following closely upon the German retreat, it awakened hopes which were not warranted and led to disappointments which had far-reaching effects.

VI. BAGDAD

Four weeks before the British had opened the campaign in Europe with the victory at Vimy, another British army, far out in Mesopotamia, had achieved a success which retrieved the British position in the East and restored a prestige shaken at Gallipoli and well nigh destroyed at Kut-el-Amara. On March 11th General Maude's victorious troops entered Bagdad, henceforth to remain in British hands, after one of the most brilliant of the colonial campaigns of which the history of the British Empire is so full. Indeed only Kitchener's advance to Khartum along the Nile rivalled the new river campaign of Maude along the Tigris to Bagdad.

The failure of the army of relief to reach General Townshend's army, beleaguered in Kut-el-Amara, after the disastrous and reckless dash for Bagdad which had failed at Ctesiphon, had resulted in April, 1916, in the surrender of Townshend and the collapse of the Mesopotamian campaign. Thereafter, the British situation in the east remained difficult. The Turk had failed in his effort to cross the Sinai desert, pass the Suez Canal, and burst into Egypt. The Russian victory in Armenia and the capture of Erzerum had brought to an end all possibility of a successful invasion of Russian territory south of the Caucasus Mountains so long as Russia remained a fighting nation. On the other hand, the conquest of Serbia and the crushing of Roumania had eliminated the European front for the Turk, although several of his divisions were with Mackensen's army along the Danube.

Since he was able without any great effort to beat down an ill-conceived British counter-offensive seeking to enter Palestine by Gaza, the Turk was now able to concentrate a considerable army in Bagdad;

and his efforts, not wholly unsuccessful, were directed alike at holding the British forces on the Lower Tigris obtaining control of Persia, and raising the Moslem tribes along the frontiers of India.

It was the Indian phase of the situation that dictated British action in Mesopotamia. Indian troops had shared in the disastrous campaign which had terminated at Kut-el-Amara. All India knew of the breakdown of the British army and the British military system, which had resulted not alone in the disaster which included the surrender of the British army but also in the ghastly tragedy disclosed in subsequent Parliamentary investigation, which set forth the terrible sufferings due to inadequate medical supplies and insufficient communications. It was essential, therefore, as a matter of prestige and as a matter of safety for India, that the British should retrieve their position in the East and, having once set out for Bagdad, should arrive victoriously in that town.

The Commander-in-Chief of the Mesopotamian Army was one of the great figures of British colonial warfare. Had he long survived his victorious entry into Bagdad, General Maude might not impossibly have succeeded Haig himself when the failure of the British at Passchendaele gravely compromised the Commander-in-Chief of the European army. As it was, dying almost immediately after his triumph, Maude will divide with Plumer the honour of being the most successful British army commander in the whole of the war. In the second venture toward Bagdad, none of the mistakes of the first was repeated. River transport in abundance, boats specially adapted to the peculiar conditions of the Tigris, railway lines with all the material necessary for a campaign along the banks of a desert river—recalling the Khartum campaign vividly—were provided in abundance.

There was no longer any political motive leading the Government to press the military commander to take hopeless risks on the chance that he might provide some shining success which might offset failures in other fields. Two years before, the Asquith Ministry had hoped that the failure to get Constantinople, resulting from the defeat at Gallipoli, might be covered by the capture of Bagdad. Accordingly, Maude moved with utmost deliberation. At the outset of the campaign the

Turkish army occupied the locally famous lines at Sanna-i-Yat, a few miles below Kut-el-Amara on the Tigris River. The position was strong, the nature of the country advantageous to the Turks. The fighting began in January, but notwithstanding initial successes the first effort at Sanna-i-Yat did not succeed. It was not until February 17th, following a brilliantly successful crossing of the river, that the Sanna-i-Yat system was stormed. On the following day it was in British hands. Thus at last fell a position which for more than a year had balked all British efforts and had successfully held up the relieving army seeking to save Townshend at Kut. Kut itself fell immediately afterward and the river was opened to British gunboats. One week later the Turkish army was in full retreat and already Maude was able to report the capture of 4,000 prisoners, 39 guns, 22 trench mortars, and 11 machine guns, together with the re-capture of several British boats and much other war material.

In the first days of March the pursuit of the Turkish army, whose retreat was now degenerating into a rout, paused at Azizieh. After a week of reorganization and accumulation of supplies, the British advance was resumed on March 5th and continued until the Turks were standing in their last line along the Diala River, which enters the Tigris eight miles below Bagdad. On this line there was severe but relatively brief fighting and on March 10th the Turks again retired, permitting the British to enter Bagdad on the following morning.

The capture of Bagdad was an event of world importance. The news arrived in Europe at the very moment when the German retreat was in progress and when Allied publics were expecting swift and sweeping success. It therefore contributed to Allied confidence and optimism, the more as it represented final success in a field where there had been temporary disaster. But in the East the capture of Bagdad was bound to have a more far-reaching importance. Hitherto, although his empire had shrunk in Europe and in Africa, the Turk had clung to his Asiatic provinces. He had preserved his control over the Arab world, important alike on the religious and the political side; but with a British army established in Bagdad and pressing northward toward Mosul, it was clear that in no long time the Turk would lose control of the valleys of the Euphrates and the Tigris.   He would lose touch with Persia, and if Russian armies should continue their operations, he would have to face converging attacks coming from Armenia, Mesopotamia, and Egypt.   Nor was it less probable, as the events showed, that the Arabs themselves would go over to the enemy and the day of Turkish domination in Arab lands south of the Cilician Gate would be at an end.

For the British Empire the capture of Bagdad meant, not alone a restoration of prestige but an insurance for India.   The German had planned to make the Bagdad Railroad and the Turkish Empire weapons directed alike against India and Egypt.   He had hoped to follow the pathway of Alexander the Great and arrive both at Cairo and the plains of India.   The Turkish failure at the Suez Canal had ended the German's African dream.   The fall of Bagdad now alike terminated German imperial ambitions and dispelled the Turkish pan-Turanian mirage.

With the fall of Bagdad, British armies pressed northward rapidly toward Mosul, and on April 2nd for the moment joined hands with Russian cavalry coming down out of Persia; but the Russian coöperation was only brief since the Asiatic armies shared in the general collapse of the military power of the great Slav state.   Nor was the advance beyond Bagdad pushed far.   The campaigning season was over and, henceforth, with the prize for which it had striven safely in its hands, the Mesopotamian Army sat down in Bagdad.   The fighting in the valley of the great rivers was over.   The decisive defeat of the Turkish armies would be achieved by Allenby, who was just launching his Vimy battle when the Bagdad operation came to a glorious end, while with the death of Maude, only a little later, there disappeared one of the figures which in the British history of the war must continue to hold a commanding place.

It was Bagdad and not Vimy which really lifted the curtain in the campaign of 1917.   Coming so closely together their moral effect was tremendous; while alike on the military and the political sides, the capture of Bagdad from the Turks was an event of far greater importance— not impossibly the beginning of a new era in Western Asia.

CHAPTER SIX

THE FRENCH OFFENSIVE

I
NIVELLE

The Battle of Arras was a relatively subordinate detail in the spring offensive. The main blow was to be struck by the French army. In examining the plans of the French General Staff, it is necessary now to consider in detail the man who, for a few brief months, dominated the military situation, so far as the French army was concerned, as absolutely as had his great predecessor, and, in addition, exercised a complete control over the British army for that limited period of time necessary for the great battle which had opened at Vimy Ridge.

The circumstances of the selection of General Nivelle as Commander-in-Chief were unusual. When it became clear that Joffre must go, when the Briand Cabinet, after hesitating and vacillating, at last reached the decision which removed the victor of the Marne from the active control of the French army, it was a cause of surprise to the whole world that the victor of the Marne was not replaced by the saviour of Verdun. As Joffre's prestige began to diminish, that of Petain had grown apace.

Unhappily for the French and for the Allied cause, the rise of Petain to world prominence in the Verdun defence had had, as a concomitant circumstance, irritation and jealousy at Chantilly. French High Command, Joffre and those associated with him, had seen—with natural if censurable heart-burning—the unmistakable arrival of a new man. It had not been an easy thing to reach the decision which eliminated the chief who counted to his credit the greatest victory of modern military history and who, despite obvious limitations, had preserved an unbroken front to the great enemy, superior both in resources and numbers, for more than two years. Joffre and his friends were the more easily to be reconciled to this decision if it did not carry with it the selection, to replace the retiring chief, of the man whose success had made him unpopular at French headquarters.

In addition Petain himself was, despite his great qualities both as a soldier and a man, not unlike our own General Sherman, difficult to deal with, cold, with a gift of bitter speech, and, however considerate and careful with subordinates, overbearing with equals and contemptuous of politicians. He did not conceal his contempt for the latter and his biting phrases—applied equally to French politicians and Allied generals —contributed materially to produce a natural if unfortunate unpopularity, which led to the temporary substitution for a really great man and a supreme soldier, of a little man with strictly limited gifts who was as successful in the art of cultivating friends in public life as he was incapable of achieving victory on the battlefield.

Petain being thus out of the question, there remained Foch, the victor of the Yser, Joffre's most brilliant lieutenant in the Battle of the Marne and the commander of the group of French armies which, with the British, had fought the Battle of the Somme. But Foch at this time was regarded as exhausted. He had continuously held high rank and conducted great operations since August, 1914. The campaign of the Somme, regarded in Great Britain as a great victory, was held in France to be, on the whole, a check. Particularly in the closing days of 1916 —when the German retreat had not yet begun and Allied armies were still faced by formidable German defences with only minor gains of territory to show for tremendous casualties—the French considered the Somme more critically than did the British.

As a consequence, Foch was, in the French military argot, "*Limogés*"; his group of armies was broken up in the last days of 1916, and on December 20th there was assigned him a task which was in reality a disguised disgrace. The general who had on the whole displayed the greatest brilliance in action of any commander in the war, on either side—and was, one brief year later, first to halt and then to turn back the German flood, and as Commander-in-Chief of the Allied armies, to win the greatest military campaign in all human history—found himself

BELGIAN INFANTRY BREAKING THROUGH GERMAN WIRE ENTANGLEMENTS

From the picture by C. R. W. Nevinson

THE ROAD FROM ARRAS TO BAPAUME

A grisly highway through a land made ghastly by the hate of man.   The trees to right and left of the road have not
been wrecked by casual shells, but were systematically felled by German axes

From the picture by Major Sir William Orpen, A.R.A.

THE THINKER ON THE BUTTE DE WARLENCOURT

From the picture by Major Sir William Orpen, A.R.A.

THE GIRLS' COLLEGE, PERONNE

From the picture by Major Sir William Orpen, A.R.A.

ADAM AND EVE AT PERONNE

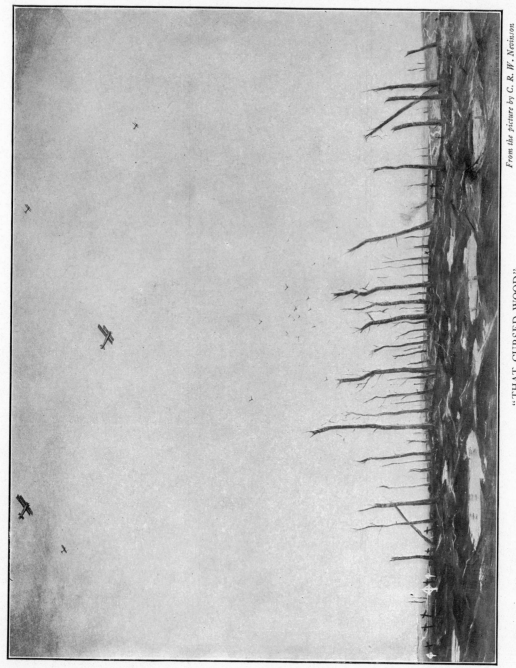

"THAT CURSED WOOD"

From the picture by C. R. W. Nevinson

Loathsome birds, startled by the drone of the aeroplanes, rise and fly screaming over a land of desolation and death

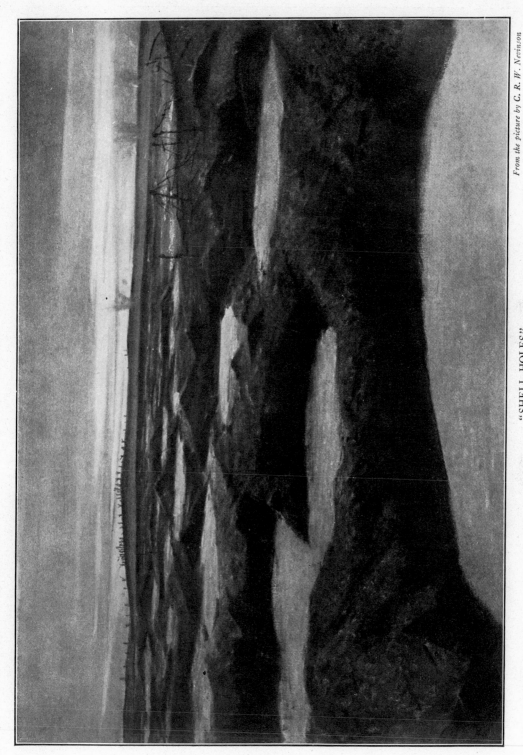

"SHELL–HOLES"

From the picture by C. R. W. Nevinson

This abomination of desolation makes one think of the third day of creation, before "God said 'Let the waters under the heaven be gathered together in one place'"

FRENCH ARTILLERYMEN GROUPED AROUND A FAVOURITE GUN

"A NASTY BIT OF GROUND"

British artillerists trying to work a big gun into satisfactory position in the opening months of 1917 exercising only a nominal command and actually engaged in making plans against a hypothetical German invasion of France through Switzerland. In that period both in France and England, men said, not without regret, that Foch was finished.

Aside from Petain and Foch, Nivelle was perhaps a logical selection. He had served with distinction under Petain at Verdun. When, as a consequence of his great achievements in defending the Lorraine fortress, Petain was promoted to command a group of armies, Nivelle, as his most conspicuous lieutenant, was named to succeed him in command of the Verdun Army. Under Nivelle's immediate command, although the supreme direction was Petain's, there had been organized that brilliant and amazing counter-offensive of October which had retaken Douaumont and Vaux and swept the Germans out of the area of the entrenched camp of Verdun. The last act of Nivelle before he departed to take over the supreme command was to direct the second Verdun counter-offensive, completing the liberation of the town from the German menace which for ten months had threatened it.

There was in addition the belief, wholly correct, that the coming of Nivelle to the supreme command would mean aggressive action. Joffre had on the whole advocated limited offensives; Petain was known to be hostile to great ventures which, if they failed, meant alike exhaustion of the man-power and the weakening of the morale of the French army; Nivelle was a champion of the attack. And a war-weary Allied world— and a France whose hopes for the liberation of her soil had been greatly deferred—longed for decisive action.

II. THE GREAT PLAN

Nivelle, as the subordinate of Petain and his successor in the command of the army at Verdun, shared in the closing phase of that campaign and shared disproportionately the reputation of his great chief. He was a man of charm and force, and must be considered one of the most amazing military figures of the entire war. To the statesmen of Britain as well as of France, he outlined stupendous conceptions with a coldness of manner and a calmness which captivated his auditors. He had executed Petain's conceptions in the retaking of Douaumont and Vaux, using Mangin as his instrument, and his orders to Mangin were so artfully written that if Mangin succeeded, the glory would be Nivelle's; if he failed, the responsibility would be Mangin's.

Nivelle thus came to the High Command with a great reputation. He came also with a colossal plan. Having seen Petain's success on a narrow front in the Verdun offensive—a success which was the result of carefully calculated estimates of the relations between the forces available and the possibilities of the situation—he conceived that if one multiplied the forces one could extend the front indefinitely. Joffre had planned in November a great offensive between the Somme and the Oise, and between Craonne and Rheims, to manœuvre the Germans off the Craonne Plateau. Nivelle proposed to attack from Arras to Rheims, to attack through and over the Craonne Plateau, and to break the German front. When he came to Paris to explain his plans, he told his amazed listeners that the problem was not one of short distances; that if his plans were put in operation, the question would be whether the German retreat would halt at the Meuse or at the Rhine. Accordingly when he came to Headquarters in December he totally transformed Joffre's plan.

Nivelle's statements fell upon willing ears. The Somme offensive had failed to break through because it had been an attack upon too narrow a front. The German submarine campaign, in the opening months of 1917, grew steadily to the point where it threatened to become a decisive factor and win the war for the Germans. Before the Allied spring offensive was launched, British naval authorities confronted the future with grave apprehension, if with unshaken courage. British policy therefore, quite as much as French, recognized the necessity of a decision, of a conclusive land victory before the end of 1917, of an absolute success in the spring offensive. All this Nivelle promised.

The Germans had made their attack upon Verdun in the latter part of February of the previous year and Nivelle promptly borrowed their time-table. In fact, he set the clock ahead and planned to attack in the early days of the month where the Germans had attacked at the beginning of the final week. Joffre's last plan, before his departure, had been to attack on New Year's Day.

Nivelle's plan contemplated confidently a gigantic Sedan. One group of French armies under Franchet d'Esperey—victor of Montmirail in the Marne campaign, and at a later time to be the conqueror of the Balkans—was to attack south of Amiens, advancing from west to east. Another group of armies, including the Fifth, Sixth, and Tenth—commanded by Mazel, Mangin, and Duchesne, respectively, and under the supreme direction of Micheler—was to advance from south to north on a front extending from Soissons to Rheims, but mainly straight over the great Craonne Plateau to Laon. Hundreds of thousands of Germans, innumerable cannon, and almost incalculable amounts of material, were to be captured as the two groups of armies closed behind the German rear, as on a far more modest scale Pershing's troops enveloped the St. Mihiel salient eighteen months later.

In Nivelle's conception the whole western front was thus to be ruptured; the war was to be won. In his opening conversations, Nivelle told the amazed and fascinated public men who were his audience not merely that his armies would arrive at Laon on the morning of the second day at dawn precisely but that he had prepared a time-table of the advance to the Meuse. Twenty-four hours after the first attack had been launched, the intensive exploitation of the initial success was to begin and, by the third day, war of movement—war in the open—was to commence.

As this great operation, which was to liberate northern France, could not succeed without full coöperation of the British army, Haig consented that Nivelle should exercise supreme command over the British and French armies with the single limitation that when the battle—Nivelle's gigantic battle—had terminated, full freedom in command was to return to Haig, while it was to be for Haig to decide when that battle had terminated. In the first hours of the exercise of this command, Nivelle was involved in difficulties with the British by the brusqueness of his orders, but the incident was politely forgotten. Upon the British, quite as much as the French, Nivelle made a great impression.   It is not true that British influence had contributed to his appointment. The selection was entirely a French matter.   Still his mother had been English and he spoke the language with a certain fluency, much exaggerated at the time.   His success with the British was due rather to his manner, to the distinction of his bearing, to the plausibility of his statements.   Thus he carried the British with him; and Haig, after preliminary objections, willingly and loyally enlisted as a subordinate in Nivelle's campaign.   Moreover, for Nivelle himself Haig acquired a real admiration, and to those who talked with him in this period, he spoke of Nivelle's fighting spirit in words of unqualified praise.

III.   THE FIRST MISTAKES

No sooner had Nivelle taken command than the very firmness of his faith in the success of his plan led him to amazing and fatal indiscretions.   By January his orders outlining his great strategic conception had been issued and transmitted down to the very commanders of companies.   By February every village in France, no matter how small, knew of the coming of the spring offensive and knew that it would be directed against the Craonne Plateau, and what the French knew the Germans were equally prompt to discover.   Preserving a certain element of common sense, Nivelle first invited Petain to command a group of armies whose mission it was to storm the Craonne Plateau.   Petain promptly pointed out the disproportion between the task and the resources.   He did not believe the great plan would succeed; he said so, and, as a result, one of his three armies was taken from his command and given to Micheler.   Petain was thenceforth ignored.

Meantime, conditions changed.   The Russian Revolution broke out. It became clear that Russia was out of the war for the time being.   This collapse brought paralysis to the Italian offensive which was planned to coincide with the attack on the western front, since it was plain that Italy would now have to bear the weight of Austrian troops which would be transferred from the Russian to the Venetian front.   Joffre's original conception—which fixed November 16, 1916, as the day for launching his offensive—included, as an essential condition, attacks by the Russians and by the Italians. Nivelle's plan had pre-supposed the same element, but now the Russians and the Italians were out of the reckoning.

More than this, in the first days of February the Germans suddenly began their great retreat. Slowly at first, rapidly later, they drew out of their positions on the Somme. They evacuated precisely those lines against which a great offensive might have been launched with some hope of success.

On March 4th, before the German retreat had become general or considerable, Franchet d'Esperey appealed to Nivelle for permission to attack at once as the enemy was about to retreat. Nivelle answered on March 7th—after a three-days' delay—that a German retreat was inconceivable since the Germans had so strongly fortified their positions surrounding Roye; but on the day after the Nivelle despatch reached Franchet d'Esperey, the Germans were out of Roye. Thereafter followed the retreat and pursuit until the Germans were well behind the Hindenburg Line.

Instead of an attack on lines Nivelle had foreseen, Franchet d'Esperey's armies now found themselves confronting beyond the glacis of desert twenty-five miles in width which was destitute of all means of communication, a position to attack which would involve months of preliminary preparation and the employment of formidable artillery which could not be brought up for many weeks owing to the destruction of the roads.

The great Nivelle plan had been comprehended in two formidable thrusts across the rear of the Germans in positions from the Somme near Péronne to Rheims, but the Germans, by retiring, had thus avoided one of the two converging thrusts. Nivelle had envisaged attacks from two sides of a square and on one side an attack was henceforth impossible.

This was not all. In addition, the Germans had reinforced their positions on the Craonne Plateau so that where there had been two lines in December there were four in February, as Micheler had reported.

They had concentrated their artillery, elaborated caverns and grottos on the Aisne heights, multiplied their concrete works, and created an almost impregnable position. At the same time they were working on their Hindenburg Line. Thus, by the middle of March, such chance of success as there had been for the Nivelle plan had vanished. The broad front had been narrowed by at least half; the remaining half had been sown with new defences, and German reserves released by the Russian Revolution were already beginning to pour westward. Meantime, while the chances of success were thus rapidly disappearing, circumstances had combined to create expectations out of all proportion to the remaining possibilities. The retreat of the Germans, actually one of the most skilful pieces of strategy in the whole war, was represented to the French army and the French public as a flight—as the beginning of the end—and the French soldiers were in a white heat of excitement. At the precise moment when the High Command, save for Nivelle and his immediate following, was unanimously assured of the impossibility of the great plan, the army was filled with an optimism as dangerous as it was tremendous. Nivelle and the common soldiers saw victory within easy grasp, but Nivelle's lieutenants, outside of a handful of subordinates at General Headquarters, saw the situation as it was. These generals recognized the impossibility of a supreme and crushing victory. They recognized the probability of a check after even greater losses than those at the Somme, with consequences to the army morale beyond calculation.

From all these officers protests now began to flow, and at this precise moment the Briand Cabinet fell. A new Ribot Cabinet arrived with Monsieur Painlevé as Minister of War, and no sooner had he come to office than Painlevé discovered the chaos that now existed. The relations between Nivelle and his subordinates were strained. The confidence of these subordinates in their chief was gone; yet, in the midst of all this anarchy, Nivelle's confidence had grown beyond belief. To those who questioned the possibility of success under changed conditions and asked him if he recognized the strength of the new German defences on the Craonne Plateau, he answered calmly that he already had the Craonne Plateau in his pocket, that the only question in his mind was whether he would have temporarily to halt his advance at the Serre or at the Oise, on account of the difficulty of moving up his supplies before he resumed the main thrust to the Dutch frontier.

For the new Ministry, there was then raised the acute question: Should there be an offensive? But here again was a new circumstance, for if the collapse of Russia had made a new offensive in the west difficult in the extreme; if it had removed a large fraction of the remaining chance of success; it had, on the other hand, certainly made such an offensive imperative alike to save Russia and to prevent the possible arrival of German troops on the Italian frontier—to prevent in the spring what actually happened in the autumn and produced the great disaster of Caporetto. Added to this were British anxiety and apprehension over the submarine peril, which was at this moment becoming terribly acute. The German submarine campaign was achieving inconceivable success. For the moment the British navy was frankly incapable of coping with the danger.

That Nivelle's grandiose plan could now succeed seemed impossible, both to his subordinates and to the French Ministry; but a lesser offensive, with limited objectives, carefully prepared and calling for small losses—an attack carrying with it the possibility of inflicting heavy casualties and achieving local and useful gains—still held out attractions. If the initial attack should result not in these modest gains but in that actual break which Nivelle foresaw, then the operations might be continued and expanded. This was the view of the Government and this was the extent of its consent to the Nivelle programme. As for Nivelle himself, he heard the words of warning of his subordinates and the words of advice of the civilian officials with a contempt born of supreme optimism. He still believed in a complete victory. At the moment of attack, he laid before the Government maps which showed an initial advance of twelve kilometres and this optimism did not desert him when 25,000 French dead and five hundred yards of gain were the total harvest of the first day of the offensive.

IV. THE CRAONNE PLATEAU

In Nivelle's original conception, his great offensive was to be on a front from Arras to Rheims, the British attacking in the sector above the Somme. The German retreat narrowed the British operative front to some twelve miles immediately east of Arras. Up to the very last moment, Nivelle hoped to employ Franchet d'Esperey's armies west of the Oise despite the German retreat, but a preliminary effort made by this group of armies on April 14th failed completely, and thereafter the fighting was restricted to the country between the southeast corner of the St. Gobain Forest and the heights to the north of Rheims. Across two thirds of this front stretched the famous Craonne Plateau which had seen desperate fighting in the days following the Marne, when Allied pursuit culminated in the First Battle of the Aisne, and one year later was to see the greatest French disaster of the war in the Battle of Chemin-des-Dames.

Resembling Vimy Ridge in certain respects, the Craonne Plateau is both higher and longer. It is actually the outermost rampart of Paris. Northward the ground slopes to the great northern plain, and invaders approaching Paris from the northeast encounter this great obstacle as the first barrier after passing the frontier of France. On the northern side, the Craonne Plateau drops down sharply for more than two hundred feet into the narrow, swampy valley of the tiny Ailette River. Seen from this northern side, it resembles a huge wall, its summit level against the horizon, with precipitous approaches—a military obstacle deemed impregnable until that subsequent May day when the German troops scaled it and pressed southward to the Marne again.

But on the southern side the Craonne Plateau descends more gently and slowly to the Aisne. Whereas the northern side is substantially a straight and solid wall, the southern side is cut by many deep ravines or glens through which brooks pass to the Aisne. On a relief map, the Craonne Plateau suggests a comb with the teeth pointed southward, the spaces between the teeth representing the little valleys. These valleys were of enormous importance in the battle of 1917 because they supplied admirable cover for machine-gun nests—cover which rendered machine-gun positions practically undiscoverable because the valleys were themselves filled with small woods and underbrush. Across the actual summit, following the crest from end to end—that is from the Laon-Soissons road to the village of Craonne—ran the famous Chemin-des-Dames, the scene of some of the most intense fighting of the whole World War.

In 1914 when Kluck retired, after the Battle of the Ourcq, he had halted his armies on the first slopes of the Craonne Plateau just across the river from Soissons. In the Battle of the Aisne the British had successfully passed the river, east of Soissons, and pushed part way toward the crest of the ridge. The French to the eastward had actually reached the crest at certain points and almost, but not quite, reached the outskirts of the village of Craonne. In January, 1915, during a period of high water on the Aisne, the Germans had vigorously attacked the French—who occupied the lines originally taken by the British—sharply defeated them, and forced them southward so that practically all the high ground remained in German hands. From this high ground the Germans were able to bombard Soissons at will, the city itself being less than a mile from their front at Crouy.

In the great retreat of March, the Germans again evacuated ground which they had taken in 1915, but continued to hold a bridge-head south of the Aisne near Vailly which constituted a sharp southerly salient dominated by the high ground on which stood the dismantled fort of Condé; then their line bent back sharply almost to the crest which it then followed to Craonne.

A more difficult military obstacle than the Craonne Plateau, as the Germans had organized it, would be impossible to imagine. The assailants were obliged to advance over open country in plain view of the Germans with an unfordable river behind them, and in places they had to cross the river itself under fire. For centuries this plateau had been worked for building-stone and was filled with immense caves and grottos which the Germans had organized for defensive warfare. The ravines were lined with machine guns which swept the flanks of the French waves as they advanced; the German trenches ran line on line backward up the gentle slopes to the summit, while the German heavy artillery was in position safely covered on the reverse slopes. Nor had the Germans relied simply upon natural defences. They had filled the whole zone with concrete machine-gun emplacements until it constituted a vast defensive zone from six to ten miles deep.

The traveller who hereafter passes over the Soissons-Laon road—reminiscent of the stretch of the Albert-Bapaume road, as it ascends to the summit of the Pozières Ridge, rising slowly to the plateau and following the highway as it marches between fields which for many years must retain traces of the terrible artillery destruction—will marvel at the courage or temerity which was responsible for an offensive against a position naturally as strong as that he sees about him.

Where it left the Craonne Plateau, at the point where the hill on the flank of which Craonne itself stands, towers above the plain in gaunt impressiveness—recalling Douaumont as seen from the plain of the Woëvre—the German line bent sharply southward crossing the Aisne at Berry-au-Bac, and extending to the dismantled forts above Rheims. Here the nature of the country was less favourable for the defence. For a stretch of ten miles on either side of the Aisne, the line ran across flat country covering a gap between the Craonne Plateau and the mountain of Rheims. Could the French penetrate this gap, they would cut the German armies in France in halves and take in the rear both the Craonne Plateau and the German positions eastward of Rheims. Through this gap Nivelle planned to throw Duchesne's armies once the Craonne Plateau and Fort Brimont had fallen.

But recognizing the natural weakness of this position the Germans had worked for nearly three years with characteristic energy and industry. Nowhere on the western front were so many concrete works to be found. The little hill near Ville-aux-Bois to the south of Craonne had been tunnelled, galleries had been constructed, every conceivable device had been employed to render impregnable a position which of itself was vulnerable. Southward from the Aisne at Berry-au-Bac to the heights about Rheims, the Germans had used the high ground east of the Aisne Canal and parallel to the Rheims-Laon highway; the keystone of their fortified system was the old fort of Brimont.

Against a surprise attack, neither the Craonne Plateau nor the position between Craonne and Rheims was perhaps invulnerable. Certainly the Germans were able to smash through on this entire front a year later—when the French occupied all the Craonne Plateau and many of the strongest positions to the south, which were in German hands in April, 1917; but the element of surprise restored by the Germans in the campaign of 1918 did not exist for the French. Nivelle himself had set the example of contemptuous publicity, and all the world, German and Allied alike, was aware of the front on which the French were to attack. Not only that, but the several postponements of the assault from January to April had permitted the Germans to construct four lines where they had had but two, and to multiply their concrete defences, their machine-gun nests, and their battery positions. To defend what was unmistakably the strongest single stretch of western front, the Germans had amassed forty divisions where the French sought —unsuccessfully, to be sure—to defend the same ground with six a year later.

The strength of the Craonne Plateau must be manifest to the merest civilian who looks up at the heights from the shallow valley through which flows the considerable Aisne, yet two successive struggles over these slopes have served largely to obliterate the innumerable trench lines which seamed the hillside. Strong as was the Vimy position itself it was incomparably less imposing and less considerable than that on which the armies of the German Crown Prince now awaited their French opponent, prepared to take full revenge for their own defeat at Verdun. So strong indeed was the Craonne position that Joffre himself, in planning an offensive over the same ground, had calculated to turn it from the north and from the south. Yet in Nivelle's great plan the essential circumstance was the advance of Mangin's Sixth French army straight over the Craonne Plateau. So complete was his confidence, he calculated that, by the dawn of the second day, his cavalry would be under the walls of Laon, whose cathedral, from a rocky eminence recalling the Acropolis at Athens, looks southward at the Craonne Plateau, and northward and eastward over the vast plain of northern France.

In the operation which we are now to examine, the main French attacks were made on the Craonne Plateau and Fort Brimont by the armies of Mangin and Mazel, respectively. In the latest phase of the offensive still a third attack was launched east of Rheims against the isolated Moronvillers Hills which dominate the whole of Champagne and constitute military obstacles hardly inferior to the Craonne Plateau itself. On this third field where the organization of the attack fell to Petain, the French were to win a considerable but useless success on the very ground which was to see the failure of the final German offensive —that of July 15, 1918. But despite the brilliance of this local operation, it had no effect upon the main battle. Actually, the decision was had in the sector between the Soissons-Laon road and the heights of Sapigneul around Fort Brimont. On this line the French attempted, by a brusque offensive extending over the widest front yet assailed in a single operation, to smash their way through the German lines as the Germans had endeavoured to hack their way first through Ypres to the Channel and, second, through Verdun to the heart of France.

V. THE BATTLE

Before the Battle of Craonne was joined, the chance of a wide-swinging success had utterly vanished. Almost without exception Nivelle's subordinates, aware of this fact, had advised him and the Government against the attack, and the Government itself had sought to limit the grandiose scheme to a modest local offensive—necessary both because of the Russian and the submarine situations.

But there were other conditions which made unlikely even a local success. Petain in his two Verdun counter-offensives—delivered on a three- and a five-mile front respectively—had calculated accurately and methodically the relation between the forces at his disposal and the artillery with which he could prepare the way. Before he launched Mangin in October he had spent weeks and months in the

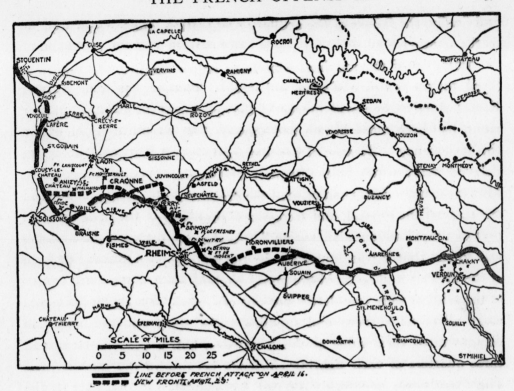

LINE BEFORE FRENCH ATTACK ON APRIL 16.
NEW FRONT, APRIL 25.

THE BATTLE OF CRAONNE

The solid line shows the French front at the opening of the attack of April 14th.   The broken
lines show approximately the extent of the French gains

preparation of communications and the organization of the rear.
Nivelle had dreamed of expanding the Petain method from a three- to
a sixty-mile front, but he was incapable of making the preparations
keep pace with the expansion.

Cannon, munitions, armament of all sorts, collected for the armies
which were to deliver the attack, were woefully insufficient; but had
they been adequate, the armies were insufficiently prepared both as to
ways of communication and as to the professional training of the combatants.   The medical service left much to be desired, as was subsequently established in official reports.   Three other circumstances
combined to abolish all possibility of the local success, which was now,
in the minds of all reasonable and informed observers, a maximum of
expectation.   These three circumstances were: the bad weather; the
stupidity, folly, and imprudence of the command in the Fifth Army;

and finally, the failure of the artillery preparation, due in some measure to the weather.

After one of the roughest winters in half a century, the month of April, 1917, was a time of snow and storm. The great British attack of Easter Monday, one week preceding the opening of the Craonne engagement, had been made in rain and snow and all April was marked with this inclemency. Because of weather conditions the offensive had to be delayed many times at the request of General Mangin himself. In March the newspapers had printed the precautionary warning: "Given the state of the ground, and recognizing that winter still lasts, all prospect of a rapid advance is Utopian." As the event showed the weather was so bad that it was impossible for the infantry to follow the barrage of the artillery. The rapid-fire guns, machine guns, and even the arms of the soldiers were completely put out of service. The infantry threw away all of its burdens and supplies. The black troops, which had demonstrated their value as shock units on half a score of fields, lost three quarters of their fighting efficiency because of the temperature. The assault was necessarily slowed down. All real observation and regulation of artillery fire was impossible. Transport failed. Testimony to these facts is found and re-found in the journals of operations of all the armies that took part in the attack. These show the mistake, now committed for a second time, of fixing a general offensive for the equinoctial period, as had already been done in the Battle of Champagne of September 25, 1915.

The second mistake grew out of an imprudence in the Fifth Army. Three days before the attack a sergeant—carrying the order of operations which indicated in detail the disposition of the attacks to be made by the 7th, 32nd, and 38th Corps and the Russians—was killed, and his despatch bag captured by the enemy. The order contained a synthesis of the attack on Fort Brimont. There the principal blow was to be delivered from the north to the south and it pre-supposed the capture of the heights of Sapigneul. Thus warned, the enemy reinforced the threatened sector promptly and the French advance here was nil, while the losses of the Seventh Corps alone in four days exceeded fifteen thousand men. For the officer responsible for the imprudence there was, however, this palliating circumstance. He had promptly and frankly confessed his fault in permitting a non-commissioned officer to carry a plan of operations, and the French High Command was aware that its offensive plan was known by the enemy down to its last detail, so far as three army corps were concerned. But, knowing this, what possible justification remained for risking the attack?

Finally, the artillery preparation was badly done. Ten days of bombardment were as unsuccessful in reducing the enemy works as had been the preliminary artillery preparation of the British at the Somme. Weather conditions, which prevented aërial observations, partially explained this failure, but beyond and above this was the fact that Nivelle lacked artillery in sufficient quantities and munitions in adequate volume to reduce the enemy works over so vast a front, particularly when for the larger portion of that front the enemy position rested upon magnificent natural obstacles reinforced by skilful military engineers.

In the face of all these circumstances; with doubts and hesitations amounting almost to insubordination among his lieutenants—interesting proof of which may be found in a letter of February 13th written by Nivelle to Micheler, commander of the group of armies which was to make the attack and containing unmistakable evidence of the lack of harmony and the almost unbelievable anarchy existing in the High Command—but with an army fired by the recent German retreats, knowing that their commander expected to break the German line, Nivelle, still unshaken, announced that he expected to succeed on the Craonne Plateau. This announcement was made to the Government after the first attack—that on St. Quentin—had been made on April 14th and had completely failed, thus dooming the whole enterprise. Nevertheless, fixing his attack for the morning of the 16th, Nivelle repeated his familiar forecast that he would arrive in Laon at dawn on the 17th, and that his cavalry would reach La Fère by sunset on the same day. Brimont was to be taken in five hours by that envelopment from the north of which the Germans had been so completely forewarned.

Therefore, just one week after the British had brilliantly delivered their offensive on Vimy Ridge, but at the precise moment when their advance had been pinned down, Nivelle launched his waiting armies. The armies of Mangin and Mazel left their trenches at six o'clock in the morning in the midst of a tempest of snow, rain, and wind. The aviation could not function; the artillery was dependent entirely upon ground observation. It was in vain that the trench mortars destroyed practically everywhere the enemy first line. An actual telescoping occurred on this first position with the mass of the German army which had received and executed the order to die on its first line rather than yield.

Warned long in advance, the Germans had no less than four lines, in a depth of eight miles. These lines were literally stuffed with light machine guns, hidden in the innumerable grottos and caverns of the porous cliffs. The French artillery did not completely dominate the situation as all the instructions of the High Command had expected. The tanks, in a gallant attack near Pontavert—which was designed to clear the gap between the Craonne Plateau and Brimont and open the way for the cavalry exploitation to Laon behind the Craonne Plateau—nowhere reached the third line, which had been their objective. The French armies were compelled to halt after the first hours, and the unforeseen pause jammed and blocked everything behind—organized for a great forward leap. This congestion and confusion of every sort still further aggravated the disappointment and disillusionment consequent upon a sharp check. All official records of the operations of the 16th and 17th of April, in both armies alike, reveal with truly tragic monotony the essential fact that the complete check of the French attack was everywhere due to the multiplied use of enemy machine guns which had survived inadequate artillery preparations.

The machine guns had not been completely destroyed anywhere by artillery preparation, and precisely this machine-gun fire, after the first hours, stopped the advance and broke the spirit of the best fighting forces of the French army. Some thousands of these guns, well placed and well served, were sufficient to stop in full cry the forward sweep of many thousands of veteran infantry soldiers confident of victory, and Americans will find food for reflection when they recall that a little more than a year later, in the great battle of the Meuse-Argonne, their own soldiers, with even less adequate artillery support, wrestled with these same machine-gun problems and suffered casualties well in excess of those which sufficed to destroy the French offensive of 1917.

On the morning of April 17th, when Nivelle's victorious troops should have arrived at dawn under the walls of Laon, they were actually only a few hundred yards from their starting place, holding with difficulty the second line of the Germans. All the plan for later intensive exploitation by Duchesne's Army pressing through the gap between Craonne and Brimont had crumbled into dust. Gains had been made, certainly not negligible; yet, given the glowing forecasts of the Commander-in-Chief, it is easy to understand the extent of the disillusionment alike of the Government and of the French people. And public opinion held responsible for this disillusionment that commander who had produced it, by the exaggerated grandeur of his conception.

VI. THE CONSEQUENCES

As to the offensive itself. Having failed to attain the expected rupture, Nivelle on the 17th, although he subsequently declared that he had stopped it absolutely at noon, directed Mangin and Mazel to shift their attack to the northeast and go on, and in accordance with the original plan Anthoine's Fourth Army was launched against Moronvillers. Severe fighting continued over the next four days, fighting which increased the casualties, already great, and resulted only in small rectifications of the line, the most considerable of which was the reduction of the Vailly salient and the elimination both of the German bridgehead south of the Aisne and the position about the dismantled Fort of Condé, from which the Germans had swept the valley of the Aisne east and west with enfilading fire. On April 21st Micheler informed Nivelle that it was now necessary to give up the fight. In this letter Micheler pointed out that there were only four divisions of infantry available, in the reserves of the three armies combined, to deliver the attack which would achieve that prospective rupture which Nivelle still expected. This letter is an interesting document in view of the later statement of Nivelle's champions that new French armies were ready to enter the fight. Micheler in his letter proposed also that local operations should be resumed on April 30th, which should include an attack upon Brimont still later on. In accordance with this suggestion of Micheler, on April 22nd there was considered, and decided in principle, the question of an energetic resumption of the general battle in the form of partial offensives—designed to gain both the Craonne Plateau, in order to uncover Laon, and the height of Moronvillers, to unblock Rheims. In point of fact, despite the later fighting, which included the taking of the Moronvillers Heights but was marked by a new failure at Brimont, the Battle of Craonne was over on April 25th. In ten days of terrible struggle the French army had been checked after a slight advance inconsiderable by comparison with the British progress before Arras; its fighting spirit had been broken; the soldiers recognized that they had been thrown against positions unshaken by artillery preparation; their confidence in their Commander-in-Chief was gone. They were defeated troops; no camouflage in reports of ground gained could disguise from these veterans the fact that, having set out for Laon and La Fère, they had actually arrived only at the second and third lines of their foe.

As to losses. On May 13th Nivelle made a remarkable statement to the Minister of War of his casualties between April 16th and 25th. Therein he cited the number of the dead—whose deaths had been witnessed by at least two people—as 15,500 and gave as missing 20,000, but only 5,000 of these 20,000 were afterward reported as prisoners; so in fact the killed in the ten days' fighting amounted to 30,000 while the other casualties approximated 70,000. The total loss was thus close to 100,000.

Against this terrible butcher's bill Nivelle could show only minor gains, which nowhere imperilled the main fighting position of his foe, and the capture of 23,000 prisoners, 175 cannon, 412 machine guns, and 119 trench mortars.

Nivelle's grand offensive, then, had failed and it was necessary for the

British to prolong their costly and useless battle for many days to relieve the strain upon the beaten French army, in which now, for the first time, certain signs of demoralization began to appear. Meantime, the Government in Paris had been more and more alarmed by the size of the casualty lists; by the ever-increasing protests from the officers; by the unmistakable demoralization in the fighting forces which was shown when veteran regiments, which had participated victoriously and gloriously in a score of struggles, declined to advance; and the Minister of War was called upon to sign death warrants of French soldiers who refused to be murdered in the hopeless gamble of Nivelle.

We have, then, in the first two weeks of May, a real crisis, in which Nivelle, having lost the confidence of the Government, his lieutenants, his soldiers, still continued on the hopeless enterprise of breaking the German line, until at last, on May 15th, he is summarily removed and Petain is called upon to undertake the task of restoring the French army, a task hardly more difficult or more doubtful of success than that which had fallen upon his shoulders a little more than a year before when he arrived at Verdun, after the mistakes of those who had preceded him had permitted Douaumont to fall undefended into German hands. At the same moment Foch succeeded Petain as Chief of the General Staff of the French army, a position which Petain had occupied only since April 30th, when the Government took its first step to limit Nivelle's authority.

About all this Nivelle episode there raged and continues to rage a great controversy. It is asserted that the politicians interfered to check a victorious offensive in the full cry of victory. Nivelle's champions, few but ardent, continue to declare that the Germans were on the point of retiring to the Meuse when Nivelle was removed and the French offensive stopped; but competent and universal testimony of French officers is directly in conflict with this. There is a common agreement, confirmed by the testimony of Micheler himself in the letter above cited, that on the 21st of April the offensive had so completely failed that it was necessary to abandon it. In the few months of his supreme control Nivelle had suffered a bloody defeat, shaken the confidence of the army and of the country. Thereafter he departed from active service, leaving to Petain and to Foch, whom he had displaced, the gigantic task of repairing his errors; and Petain's first warning to his British allies when he undertook his task was that many weeks must pass before the French army would be capable of another offensive. In point of fact, it was late October before they struck again at Craonne.

CHAPTER SEVEN

ITALY AND GREECE

I

THE MAY OFFENSIVE

It had been the original conception of Allied High Command that all the armies about the circle which encompassed Germany should attack the Central Powers at one time, exerting equal pressure on many sides, and, by virtue of superior numbers, exhaust German and Austrian reserves and either penetrate through some weak point or, by attrition, produce collapse.

We have seen that various circumstances combined to postpone Nivelle's Anglo-French offensive on the French front from February until April. By this time the Russian Revolution had so far paralyzed Russian military strength that even the last fatal Kerensky offensive was postponed until July. A similar delay had attended Italian preparations. Instead of being able to attack in April, combining their blow not merely with that of Nivelle but that of Brusiloff also, the Italians found themselves unable to depend upon Russian coöperation, compelled to postpone their attack from week to week, and finally to deliver it, not merely without Russian aid but against an enemy who was already reinforcing his imperilled front by divisions drawn from Russia.

The Italian campaign of 1917, between May and November, amounted to a gallantly sustained, terrifically costly endeavour—the third—to burst through that gap between the Julian Alps and the head of the Adriatic, and advance behind Trieste into Austrian territory.

By this time the world was as familiar with the Isonzo front as with the various sectors of British and French activity. When Italy entered the war the Austrians had stood between the Julian Alps and the sea on a front of a little less than forty miles, with the Isonzo as a deep and almost impassable moat from Tolmino straight down almost to Gorizia, where their lines crossed the river and held the height of Podgora covering the town. Thence their line recrossed the river and drew back from it across the Carso Plateau to the Adriatic.

This front had three contrasting geographical features. From Tolmino almost to Gorizia there was high ground, with crests passing 2,000 feet in elevation. This high ground was divided into two plateaux by the valley and depression of Chiaponavo, the northern half

THE ISONZO FRONT

Statute Miles

Railways   Roads
Frontier

ITALY'S BATTLEFIELD

bearing the name, henceforth memorable, of Bainsizza. The southern half was known to the Italians as the Selva di Ternova. Both these plateaux were tilted up on their western rims so that their highest ground rose straight from the Isonzo Valley and the peaks or hills which were now to acquire battle fame—Kuk, Vodice, Santo, San Gabriele, and San Daniele—confronting the Italians.

South of these two plateaux was the valley of the Vippacco stream, which comes down from the east and joins the Isonzo below Gorizia. Still farther to the south was the Carso Plateau, culminating not far from the Adriatic in the peak of Hermàda.

In 1916 the Italians had taken Gorizia and pushed a wedge eastward up the Vippacco Valley between the northern plateau and Hermada, but they were unable to advance this wedge further because it was a narrow salient in low ground commanded by Austrian artillery on the northern and southern elevations. It was plain that no further advance eastward could be made until both Hermada and the two northern plateaux, Bainsizza and Ternova, were reduced. Even if Hermada should fall, the distance between Ternova and the sea was too short to give Cadorna elbow room, while the Austrians remained on Ternova and Bainsizza.

The Italian plan, therefore, consisted in a series of movements which had for their objectives the reduction of Hermada and the occupation of Ternova and Bainsizza plateaux. On May 14th, just one month lacking two days after Nivelle had launched his unsuccessful attack in Champagne, Cadorna opened his battle by an attack directed against the southern edge of the Bainsizza Plateau and the western extremity of the Selva di Ternova. The peaks of Kuk, Vodice, Santo, and San Gabriele were the immediate objectives of this preliminary movement. Lodgments were effected on Kuk and Vodice; Monte Santo was taken and lost. There followed in the next few days furious Austrian counter-attacks, but the Italians hung on to their foothold on the Bainsizza Plateau.

A little more than a week later, on May 23rd, a second assault was directed at the Carso, the southern buttress of the Isonzo position. In a week of desperate fighting the Italians reached the western edge of Hermada, but by May 30th they were again held by a new series of Austrian counter-offensives, in which troops brought from the Russian front participated.

Cadorna had now tried to seize both the northern and the southern anchorages of the Austrian position by brusque attacks. Despite material progress two weeks of fighting had resulted in the failure to attain either end. Twenty-four thousand Austrian prisoners, thirty-eight cannon, and a number of positions of vast strength were the rewards of the effort, but Austrian official statements claimed nearly an equal number of prisoners and proclaimed a victory, since their lines still held. The whole month of June was consumed in beating off the Austrian counter-offensives, which made no considerable gain but precluded any renewal of Italian attack.

We now touch upon one of the contested questions of the war. Cadorna found himself unable to make further advance with such artillery and munitions as he possessed. Accordingly he and his government appealed to the Allies for guns and munitions, giving assurances that, were these provided, Italy could win a decisive victory which would put Austria out of the war. His request fell upon deaf ears. The British had launched their unfortunate Flanders venture; the French army was only just beginning to recover from the consequences of Nivelle's failure. Neither Petain nor Haig felt himself able to go beyond the despatch of a limited number of guns. In a word, while a certain restricted assistance was forthcoming, Cadorna and Italy met with a substantial rebuff from Britain and from France, and to this rebuff the Italians lay subsequent failure of their offensive and the supreme disaster which presently overtook their armies.

By the time he was ready to move again, Cadorna's situation had fearfully worsened. Russia had completely collapsed, Austrian divisions had streamed westward from Galicia to the frontiers of Venetia, while there was more than a hint that German divisions would also presently appear on the Isonzo front. Counsels of caution now would seem to have advised that the Italians, like the French, should renounce the offensive and gather up their resources for a storm which was bound to break. On the other hand, pressure, alike from the Allies and from the Italian Government and people, combined to drive Cadorna forward into precisely the sort of blunder which the British were making in Flanders, with equally disastrous results, though the British defeat at the Somme was not to come until March, 1918, while the Italian reverse at Caporetto was far closer at hand.

II. BAINSIZZA

Beginning on August 18th the Italians shifted their operations back to the Bainsizza Plateau. They sought to complete the clearance of the eastern bank of the Isonzo; to seize and hold all of the Bainsizza Plateau; to push southward, encircling first the plateau of Ternova with its dominating height of Monte San Gabriele and then all the Austrian positions east and south of Gorizia.

For a whole month thereafter the Italians slowly but successfully mounted the slopes of Bainsizza, cleared all the higher summits from Monte Santo to Kuk, and began to threaten the plateau of Ternova by an enveloping movement from the north.

It would be difficult to describe, and impossible to exaggerate, the greatness of Italian labour in this terrible month. They had to cross an unfordable river flowing in a valley almost comparable to a western canyon. They had to transport munitions and supplies over the eastern edge of the Bainsizza Plateau, here amounting to a precipice, and to maintain an army on the sterile plateau above.

The achievement of Italy on the Bainsizza Plateau was beyond praise. It must rank with the successful military operations of the war, but before it could result in decisive success Cadorna's munitions failed. His losses had been tremendous, amounting, even in the last phase of Bainsizza alone, to twice the cost to France of Nivelle's failure at Craonne. Moreover, he found himself daily confronted with new divisions drawn from the Russian front, and, at last, conducting an offensive with numbers only equal, if not actually inferior, to those with which the Austrians held positions beside which Craonne and Vimy were but insignificant ant-hills.

By the month of September the Bainsizza operation was over. It was a failure in all but local circumstances, a failure which had shaken the morale of the Italian army and the Italian people precisely as Nivelle's unsuccessful offensive had weakened his army and shaken the confidence of the French nation. The best of Italian shock troops had been sacrificed to gain a few miles of shell-torn slopes. A new offensive, designed to produce decisive results, had been beaten down without any penetration—without a break through of the enemy lines. Moreover, the ground which the Italians had now gained, if advantageous for a resumption of an offensive at a future time, was unmistakably dangerous to hold were the initiative suddenly to pass to the enemy. Having thrust forward on to the Bainsizza Plateau the Italians had materially lengthened their lines of communication by which the advancing troops were to be supplied and the Italian Second Army was

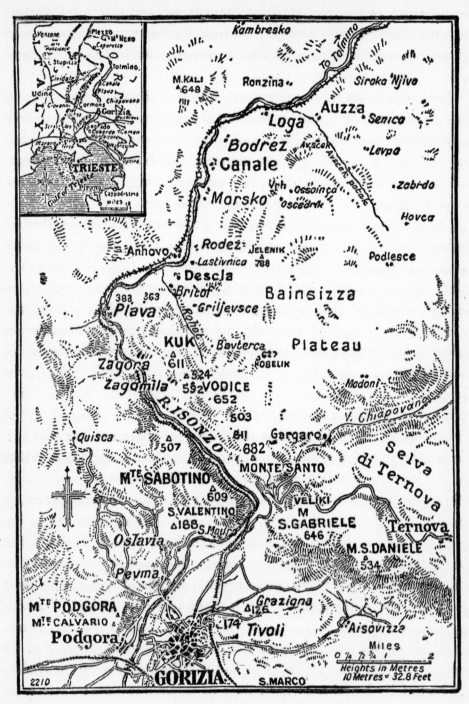

THE BAINSIZZA PLATEAU

now pushed forward in a dangerous salient exposed to a fatal disaster could the enemy to the northward break through the covering troops and, flowing southward, reach Udine in advance of the Italians on Bainsizza.

The Ypres salient—so costly to the British to hold, so perilous at all times during the war—had been born of an unsuccessful and uncompleted British offensive in October, 1914. More than once since that time the British troops in "the salient" had been in grave danger. Now the Italian offensive across the Isonzo had created a new salient far more dangerous. Having to choose between abandoning all his gains in a bloody campaign and running the obvious risks incident to holding them, Cadorna chose the latter course. The result was one of the greatest disasters of the war, but it is essential to see that, before the disaster came, Cadorna had fought his army beyond the limit of endurance—precisely as Nivelle had over-strained his troops at the Craonne Plateau and as Haig all but demoralized his armies in the bloody, useless Passchendaele offensive which had the disaster of the Somme for its consequence, as Cadorna's errors were paid for at Caporetto.

In many ways the Austrian defence of the Gorizia gateway, in not less than twelve battles of the Isonzo, was the most brilliant and successful of all Austrian campaigns during the war. The general who held this gap, Field Marshal Boroevic, must rank with the great commanders of the Central Powers. A still further circumstance, deserving of notice now because of its later bearing, was that while Austrian troops frequently proved themselves helpless in the presence of the Russians, and divisions from the Slav provinces displayed disloyalty even more than cowardice in the presence of Slav troops on the eastern front, Boroevic's armies, made up almost exclusively of Southern Slavs, fought the Italians with unflinching determination. The explanation is simple. However much the Slovenes, the Croatians, the Dalmatians hated the Hapsburg Monarchy and their Austrian and Hungarian masters, they preferred to remain under the rule of the rapidly decaying Dual Monarchy—until such time as they could realize their own aspirations of independence and association with the Serbs—to accepting a new partition which would give to a victorious Italy hundreds of thousands of Slovenes and Serbs and deprive the Southern Slavs of the Trieste and Fiume outlets upon the sea essential to the new state already existing in their dreams. This hostility between the Southern Slav and the Italian, always latent, was intensified by the years of struggle upon the Isonzo, in which Italy's great sacrifices and tremendous efforts were blocked by Southern Slav armies under a general of their own race.

Actually the spring and summer campaign of Italy had been fought for the possession of two hills, the northern and southern bastions of the Isonzo position—San Gabriele and Hermada. When the fighting, which began in May, terminated in September, half of San Gabriele was in Italian hands and the western slopes of Hermada were in no man's land, but Italian casualties in battle and as a result of disease had amounted to nearly three quarters of a million, and—precisely as French armies had set out for Laon and the frontier, to arrive only at the Craonne Plateau—Italian troops (who had confidently mounted to the assault with a vision of an arrival at Laibach and a successful reappearance along the pathway by which Napoleon in 1797 had led his army to the point where Vienna was in his grasp and Austrian surrender inevitable) were halted before the immediate objective had been attained.

III.   CONSTANTINE

At the moment when Italy was opening her spring offensive and Russia preparing the last despairing Kerensky offensive, there terminated in Athens the sordid and ridiculous drama which for two years had continued to humiliate Allied statesmen and soldiers and undermine Allied prestige in the Near East. On June 12th King Constantine abdicated in favour of his second son, Alexander, and, with the Crown Prince and his family, embarked for Switzerland, henceforth an exile.

When the whole story of the Greek episode can be told it will be a tragi-comedy unbelievable, so unreal and so preposterous were many of its circumstances. King Constantine himself was a field marshal of the German army and a brother-in-law of the Kaiser; a vain, stupid, obstinate man; dominated by his wife, and controlled by two passions: admiration for Germany, and hatred for Venizelos, the great Greek statesman.

We have seen how Constantine in 1916—having a year previous kept Greece neutral when Serbia was destroyed—continued by every conceivable act to aid the Central Powers. His agents warned the Germans of each projected operation of Sarrail's Salonica army. His officers had surrendered Greek troops and Greek fortresses to the hereditary enemy, Bulgaria, when Germany's allies had attempted a southward push in the spring and summer of 1916. In December, French and British sailors who had landed in Athens in one of those brief moments when Allied indecision gave way to ineffective Allied action, had been murdered and their murder had been accompanied by a pogrom of the political associates of Venizelos.

Constantine believed Germany would win the war. His confidence in the ultimate success of German arms was never shaken, and his comrades in the Greek army shared his admiration and worship for the German military machine. He was confident that the Kaiser would presently realize the grandiose scheme of Mittel-Europa; and, in that scheme, he saw Greece a secure and prosperous unit in a German system, and saw himself a great figure in this new Europe. He did not betray his country to an enemy. On the contrary, he was convinced that the salvation of Greece could be found only in alliance with Germany. However stupid and short-sighted the King was, he acted in the conviction that his own and his country's prosperity were equally menaced by the Allies and would be advanced by German victory.

Yet despite all Constantine's open and covert services to the Central Powers; despite the fact that the Allies knew that at a propitious moment the Greek army would be flung in the rear of Sarrail's forces at Salonica, and saw that Greek harbours offered ports of call for German submarines, Constantine remained master of Greece.

The reasons for this extraordinary persistence were manifold. In Britain, the Court and the Tory party set their faces stubbornly against the removal of the King.   In Italy the overthrow of Constantine and the return of Venizelos were correctly analyzed as certain alike to restore Greece and intensify Hellenic rivalry to Italy from Valona to Smyrna. In Russia, to the natural opposition of the Czar to the dethronement of a brother monarch there was added the selfish consideration that Greece claimed Constantinople, the prize of Russian wars for more than a century, and that if Greece regained Venizelos this claim might become annoying if not dangerous.   Only the French were neither concerned with respect for royalty nor by immediate selfish interests, but not until the Czar had fallen, the Revolution renounced Constantinople, and Italy's various claims satisfied in a degree by Allied pledges, were the French able to prevail upon their allies to take a step as logical as it was necessary.

As late as the last days of May and the first of June the new French premier, Ribot, and his most influential minister, Painlevé, soon to succeed him, found in London the familiar opposition to the removal of Constantine.   Long debates terminated in apparent deadlock, removed only by a private contract, between Painlevé and Lloyd George, in which it was agreed that France should undertake the responsibility for the ultimate disposition of Constantine with the understanding that Britain would disavow any failure.   What Lloyd George agreed to was that England would look the other way while France was removing a nuisance, but he warned that unless the thing were done swiftly, quietly, with respect for those decencies so dear to the British mind, Great Britain might be compelled to protest against the action which she consented, in advance, temporarily to ignore.

Happily the situation found the man.   To Athens the French Government sent Jonnart, Governor General of Algeria for many years, a man of firmness and decision.   Arrived in Athens, with the full authority of the French Cabinet behind him, in the decisive moment aided by the presence of warships and troops, he procured from Constantine the necessary abdication without using either.   At the very moment when Constantine set his signature to the document which ended his reign, the British Government was preparing to protest against the course of

Jonnart in Greece. The news of success silenced this protest. Great Britain acquiesced in an accomplished fact. Henceforth the situation in the Near East was to improve alike in Mesopotamia, Palestine, and Macedonia, while Constantine was to prove only the first of the kings and princes reigning in Central European states to lose his throne because he misinterpreted the course of events. Seventeen months later his illustrious brother-in-law was to flee his empire with far less grace and on infinitely worse terms than the man who had won for Greece greater victories than Hellenic history had known since the fall of the Byzantine Empire, and lost all by his fatal inability to perceive ultimate German defeat, or to make use of the services of a supremely great minister, who now returned to resume his task as the architect of a restored Hellenic state.

CHAPTER EIGHT

THE RUSSIAN REVOLUTION

I

CAUSES AND CHARACTER

We have seen that the French offensive had failed, that the British campaign for the year in Flanders had been delayed by the necessity of supporting the French by the Arras operation until all hope of decisive or even considerable success had vanished. The opening Italian attacks had been productive of no more than local or relatively inconsiderable successes. Meantime, the submarine campaign of the Germans, with its harvest of destruction, had assumed proportions which seemed to forecast complete triumph for this weapon and a consequent loss of the war by the Allies. While this situation was developing on the western front, Russia had entered upon that long, obscure, and bloody chapter of her history which led straight toward domestic anarchy and external impotence.

The Russian Revolution of 1917 is one of those great human convulsions whose causes are so mingled both with the history and with the psychology of a people that its origin, development, and meaning remain for long a sealed book to other peoples. Certainly the first three years of this tremendous convulsion were totally misunderstood and misinterpreted by the Western world, which knew little of Russia at the outset, and, so far from understanding the Russian causes, sought with ever-increasing folly to invest the Slavonic upheaval with the nobler and greater qualities of the French Revolution.

For the purpose of this history the Russian Revolution must be examined primarily to determine what its effect was upon the progress of the World War. It is not inconceivable, however unlikely, that out of this great convulsion new ideas and new forces may yet develop which will make it even more important than the world struggle itself in its

RUSSIA IN REVOLUTION

RUSSIAN SHOCK TROOPS CHARGING THE GERMANS

Russian soldiers were brave enough.   But they had much of the helplessness and ignorance of children and the simple-
hearted fellows were again and again betrayed by pretended friends

WHEN HOPE WAS THE ORDER OF THE DAY

Soldiers marching to the Duma with banner inscribed: "Down with Monarchy!   Long live the Democratic Republic!"

THE REDOUBTABLE COSSACKS

These splendid horsemen were Russia's stanchest defenders. When the Bolshevist blight fell upon the armies, most of the Cossacks stood fast. It is said that the Germans would have been troubled with no Russian Front at all in 1917 had it not been for the Cossacks and the famous Battalions of Death.

THE BATTALIONS OF DEATH

Above—Maria Botchkareva, organizer and commander of the Russian women's Battalions of Death, receives a dispatch from the hand of a respectful subordinate, while Mrs. Pankhurst, a sister militant but not military, is an interested spectator.

Below—The "march past" of the women recruits. Only those between the ages of eighteen and thirty-seven were permitted to enlist.

REVOLUTION'S HARVEST OF DEATH BEGINS

A deputation bearing wreaths of mourning to deck the graves of the first victims of the new struggle for liberty in Russia

FIGURES OF THE RUSSIAN REVOLUTION—I

For a time Kerensky, as here, held the centre of the stage. It is a sign of ill-omen that the crowd appears to have pushed him off the curbstone as he stands ready to salute a Cossack regiment which is marching by

FIGURES OF THE RUSSIAN REVOLUTION—II

Catherine Breshkovskaya, "Little Grandmother of the Revolution," returns in triumph from exile in Siberia

FIGURES OF THE RUSSIAN REVOLUTION—III

The sinister monk Rasputin was assassinated before the outbreak of the Revolution. Yet no figure was more prominent during the evil days which preceded it, among the pro-German traitors at the court of the Czar. He is here shown drinking tea with a characteristic group of women admirers.

AMERICANS IN RUSSIA

Above—Ambassador David R. Francis stands uncovered as the bodies of soldiers who have died for Russia are carried through a street of the capital.

Below—Chief Surgeon Egbert with the American Red Cross unit at Kief. He was troubled to find that two of the physicians on his staff were Russian pro-Germans, while one of the Russian nurses in the picture was an active spy.

THE END OF IT ALL

Many Russian soldiers dully, hopelessly surrendered to the enemy; while a faithful remnant, betrayed by their brethren, died a horrible death in a vain attempt to storm the German's defences

relation to human development. It is equally possible that it may continue, as it seems to Western civilization now, a supreme expression of anarchy, chaos—a mad, passionate boiling up from the depths of all the dark, incoherent, bestial passions and emotions of a race, or rather of many races, Asiatic rather than European.

The causes of the Russian Revolution are many, remote, and immediate. When Russia entered into the World War, that fabric of government which held together one hundred and eighty millions of human beings was already devoid both of vitality and of force. If a victory might conceivably have contributed to restore the machinery, to give it a new hold alike upon the respect and the obedience of the subjects of the Czar, it was inevitable that defeat, failure, disaster, easily traceable to the corrupt inefficiency of the ruling classes, would lead to the ultimate collapse of a system.

Moreover, as in the case of the House of Bourbon in the period preceding the outbreak of the French Revolution, scandal attached to the Court. The story of the influence exercised by that vile creature, Gregory Rasputin, upon the mind of the Czarina, upon the Russian Court, upon the Russian Church—constituted a chapter Byzantine in character, incomprehensible to the Western world, calculated to destroy —as it did destroy—the last vestige of reverence and respect among the Muscovite millions. Rasputin was finally murdered—"executed" perhaps is the better word—by a member of the Imperial Family jealous alike of the honour of the House of Romanoff and of that nobility daily smirched by the existence of this vile creature. But Rasputin did not die until his contribution to the general ruin of the fortunes of Nicholas had been made.

When the Russian Revolution broke, the Western world turned instantly to the parallels of the French Revolution, and particularly in Great Britain—that nation which had fought the French Revolution because of principles which Time has approved—sought to invest this new upheaval with virtues which Englishmen had rejected in that other earthquake a century and a quarter before. Moreover, the whole Western world recalled that the French Revolution, once it had been attacked by Europe, was roused to a sense of nationalism, of patriotism, to a military effort begun in self-defence which did not end until the French armies had occupied Moscow and Madrid and for more than twenty years victoriously traversed Europe and even penetrated into Asia and North Africa. Accordingly, Great Britain and France—recognizing that the Russian Monarchy in the closing months of 1916 and the opening weeks of 1917 had been disloyal to the Allied cause, that the creatures of the impotent Czar had betrayed both Roumania and Russia—hailed the coming of a liberal government and a new group of leaders as a sign that Russia would resume her place on the firing line of Europe, that Russian millions in arms would become imbued with the spirit which had moved the masses of the French Republic, still undisciplined, to march to the frontiers in 1792.

A more colossal misapprehension it would be difficult to imagine. France, at the moment of her revolution, was inhabited by a people whom centuries of association in battle and in common history had taught a sense of nationality and a spirit of patriotism. The orderly inheritance of Latin peoples, retaining the Roman conception of law and discipline, expressed itself promptly when the Ancient Régime fell. But Russia had never been fused into a national consciousness. It was a geographical expression, not a political nor even a racial fact. From Peter the Great to the last and microscopic Nicholas, Russian autocracy directing a huge army, had acquired province after province. The Pole, the Lett, the Lithuanian, the Armenian, the innumerable peoples of Asia, retained either a consciousness of a racial independence which had persisted under Russian rule or an allegiance to that state of semi-barbarism which had been interrupted by the arrival of Russian divisions.

Not only were the people of the fringes from the Arctic to the Caspian, from the Dniester to the Pacific, unassimilated, but the Russian family itself was divided, and the Ukranians of the South sought separation, not fusion. All this vast assemblage of peoples was held together by the double forces of bureaucracy and the army. It was held together by abnormal forces, by forces which had no roots in the separate races, and nothing was more certain than, when once this double pressure was removed, that Russia would resolve itself into its innumerable fractions and natural chaos succeed artificial unity.

There was a still further centrifugal force. The small but influential industrial element inhabiting the cities—which, as in the case of the French Revolution, rapidly laid hands upon the whole fabric of the Revolution—was not itself affected by the issues of the World War, but, so far as its leaders at least were concerned, was animated by the principles and dominated by the passions of that Marxian socialism whose essential doctrine is class war waged internationally. It was Capitalism, not Germanism, that the mass of the men and women who possessed even a shadow of intellectual illumination believed to be the enemy. The autocracy and the army, with a declining zeal and intensity to be sure, had accepted the challenge and made war upon Germany, but this very fact discredited the war itself in the eyes of Russian socialism. Moreover, other elements in the vast Russian population which had suffered from the iniquities, the oppression, the abuse of the bureaucracy which was the instrument of the Romanoff Dynasty, not only felt toward the Czar and his associates an inextinguishable hatred but were hostile to the war upon Germany itself because it had been made by the Czar and his government.

If in the first moment of the Revolution there was—or if there seemed to be—a re-birth of national spirit, and the men who took office and held power were alike moved by the influence of liberal ideas of the sort the West describes as democratic, and stirred by this patriotic emotion comprehensible equally to the American, the Frenchman, and the Briton, this was but a brief and transitory phase. It did not represent the fact in Russia and it totally deceived the western Alliance which welcomed the Revolution because it removed that reproach—ever present, ever felt—incident to an alliance between the three great democracies of the west and a reactionary Czaristic Russia. America, on the brink of entrance into the World War, was profoundly influenced toward her final action by the performance in Russia. For the moment critical voices were silenced in Britain and in France. Yet there never was a grosser deception, nor a more terrible awakening.

II.   WESTERN MISUNDERSTANDINGS

When the news of the Russian Revolution, with its relatively peaceful opening act, reached London and Paris and Washington, there was a
rejoicing difficult now to describe.   In every Allied capital the passing
of another tyranny was celebrated as a victory for human liberty by
those who were soon to recognize that, whatever else the effect of the
Russian Revolution might be, its immediate consequences threatened to
ensure the triumph of German arms.   There was an easy assumption
that revolution in Russia would be the preliminary step to the entrance
of Russia into that family of democratic nations whose institutions were
on the whole of a similar sort, founded upon a common conception of
social and economic principles.   There was not the smallest suspicion
that, when the smoke and dust of the first weeks and months of the
Russian upheaval had passed away, the terrible fact would be discovered
that those who dominated Russian affairs were animated by a spirit of
hostility to Western democracy far more intense than their opposition
to German autocracy.   There was not a suspicion that when the
Revolution found its man, as revolutions do, Lenin would preach a
doctrine of class warfare and direct all the great latent forces of Russia,
not against the German foe, but against that whole system of political
and economic life which prevailed in the Western nations.

The fact, as contrasted with the pleasant fiction long cherished in
the West, was this: The war had found Russia ripe, not only for the
overthrow of the autocracy and the elimination of the futile Czar, but
ready to burst into a thousand fragments as the unassimilated races and
tribes, relieved of the constraint of Russian imperial military power, undertook once more to take up their ancient pathways.   Russia had become
a geographical expression, a vast blot of colour upon the map, but it had
never been a nation in the western sense; and now, like so many empires
built by Asiatic conquerors whose swords enforced unity while they
lived, it was ready to return to the chaos from which it had been called
by a genius not long surviving to enforce his will.

In addition, the war itself had brought to the Russian masses indescribable agonies. Millions of Russian soldiers had perished because of the corruption and the treason of the civil government. The vast resources of the Russian Empire had been inadequate not alone to munition but to clothe and to feed the hosts collected at the call to the colours. The armies had been defeated; disasters in the field had followed one another with regular succession. The morale of the army had been weakened as the common soldier was called upon to face artillery and machine guns and offer himself as a consequence of the failure of his superiors and of his government to provide the necessary machinery of war. And great as was the suffering of the army, the misery behind the lines far surpassed it. All the machinery of national existence had broken down under the strain of the war; starvation reigned in provinces whose frontiers marched with the greatest wheat-producing regions of the world. In one section of the Russian Empire foodstuffs rotted, while, in another, women and children died of hunger.

In all the nations at war the progressive degeneration of national life and national industry was taking place. A sense of exhaustion, due to supreme suffering in consequence of the prolongation of the contest, was making itself manifest in every combatant nation, but in the western countries—however unmistakable the decline, the wearing-out alike of the human and the mechanical instruments of production, of transportation—there was still a functioning. The decay moved with slow if certain pace. Highly organized countries with disciplined populations submitted only slowly to the dislocation entailed by the conflict, but in Russia the organization was too elementary, the machinery in too woefully inefficient hands. Therefore that disease which was attacking the existence of the other peoples at war swept over the Russian Empire with the rapidity and the deadliness of some new scourge, while in the west it merely sapped the strength with the slow but steady march of a constitutional disease.

If the men who for the moment controlled the destinies of Russia, when the Czar and his régime had fallen, proclaimed their will, and the will of the nation to be, that Russia should continue the struggle against the German until her own territories were liberated and she and her allies had abolished the German threat, this was but the expression of now unrepresentative if noble patriots. The millions of Russia desired peace. There was no national consciousness which moved them to continue in the struggle while Austrian troops held Bessarabia or German divisions were in Poland. The people of France might continue, and did continue, to endure the agonies of the World War because even those agonies seemed less intolerable than the permanent surrender of Flanders, Artois, Picardy, and northern Champagne with the consequent enslavement of three millions of French men and women. But no corresponding sense of national pride or national sympathy induced a similar willingness to endure pain on the part of Russia.

The absence of a sense of nationality excluded the possibility of a real patriotic revival following the revolution, such as made the French Revolution one of the most splendid pages in the history of any people. What the Russian millions demanded was not national integrity but peace at any price, an ending of the now intolerable agonies incident to the struggle; and if the price of such a cessation of suffering was the surrender of provinces remote and won by military conquests of the now-fallen Czardom, it was a matter of no concern to them.

Nor were they more troubled by the fact that peace between Russia and Germany, a separate peace, meant the betrayal of the western Alliance, meant the possible victory of Germany, meant a supreme breach of national honour. France and Great Britain were not the allies of Russia, of the Russian people—in the eyes of those men who were rising to power. Rather they were the allies of that Czar and that autocracy to which the Russian people owed their centuries of suffering, owed their present misery. French gold had fortified the Romanoff power; British capital had supported the beginnings of an industrial system hateful to the men who were shortly to be the masters of the revolution. The obligations of Russia to the nations in the west were, in the eyes of these men, no national commitment but the pledges of a régime now banished. Moreover, since this was itself anathema, all its undertakings were suspect and the allies of the Czar were to be regarded as the enemies of the Revolution.

The first demand of the Revolution, when at last it found its voice, was peace. It was not concerned with the fate of France nor the fortunes of Britain. It was not influenced by appeals to the sense of national honour. It looked upon the western nations neither with sympathy nor friendliness. It regarded their appeals to Russia to stand firm in the fight against Germany as an invitation to Russians to pay a still further tax of blood and misery that the western Allies might realize imperialistic ambitions, and that capitalistic governments might fortify themselves at home by conquests abroad.

Become articulate, the Russian Revolution demanded that the west should lay aside every claim formulated in the progress of the war and now become an obstacle to peace. It renounced for Russia the possession of Constantinople and the acquisition of Turkish lands in Asia Minor. It demanded that France should surrender her aspirations to Alsace Lorraine. It proclaimed that Russia would accept a peace without annexation and without indemnity which would have left France and Belgium ruined by German devastation. Nor was it profoundly concerned if Germany achieved its ultimate objectives in the west. The millions of Russia desired peace at any cost. The men who rose to power in the Russian Revolution by promising the Russian millions peace were seeking a total overthrow of the economic and national systems which prevailed in Europe and in the world. The gospel preached by Lenin was a gospel destructive quite as much of British and of American governments and social orders as of German. American democracy was, in the eyes of Lenin, as evil a thing as Hohenzollern monarchy. Capitalism was the foe. Lenin was prepared to make peace with Germany, no matter how much it cost Russia in territory, that on such lands as remained he might organize Russia to become the agent of destruction directed against the governments and the systems of all civilized and industrialized nations.

In such a situation there could be but one consequence. When those men—moderates, who were collectively possessed of all the knowledge, understanding, and sympathy with the democracies of the west and with western civilization existing in Russia—had enjoyed their

brief hour of power and had fallen because they were not representative of a Russia which knew not patriotism, knew not nationality, and was dominated by a desire for peace; when they were
succeeded by Kerensky—a fugitive figure, representative in his
understanding of the masses but for ever chained by his comprehension of the western situation—and he had equally failed; then
at last power fell into the hands of a great man, prepared to give the
Russian people that peace which they demanded that he might obtain
the power that he sought to destroy the social order of the western world.
With the fall of the first provisional government all chance of a Russian
patriotic revival perished.   With the fall of Kerensky the last bond between Russia and her former western allies dissolved.   When Lenin
came there was no more a Russia.   All that remained was a certain machinery of government, hopelessly dislocated but still capable of a
degree of motion, and this machinery was thereafter operated, without regard to the war, to serve the purposes of a man who conceived
of overthrowing not alone German tyranny but also Allied democracy—
who looked upon the German system of government and rulers and the
Allied executives and parliaments as equally hateful, equally subversive
of the principles he had preached and practised during his lifetime.

Thenceforth Russia was in the hands of a man who saw the World
War not as a conflict between two principles, one right and one wrong,
but as a conflict between two sets of powers, each dominated by men
and representative of principles which it was his mission to destroy.
The more the war undermined and sapped the fabric of governments;
the more the several peoples engaged in the conflict murmured and com-
plained at the intolerable pangs of the struggle; the more confidently
Lenin looked forward to that day when these several peoples should
adopt his ideas, and Bolshevist anarchy and destruction which had
seized upon Russia and was transforming that country into a wilderness
and an economic ruin, should obtain equal sway in France, in Britain,
and in the United States.

All this was long hid from the Western world.   In the first hours the
west rejoiced that Russia had been converted to the religion of Western

democracy, just as it had clung, through all the revelations of the war, to the equally puerile notion that the German people were the victims of a government which by force, and by force alone, prevented them from adopting the beneficent systems of democracy of their western neighbours.   Mission after mission of eminent statesmen, ranging from Lord Milner to Arthur Henderson, from Elihu Root to Albert Thomas, visited Petrograd and returned with varying reports, were themselves bewildered by what they saw and heard, or even in a small but unmistakable degree impressed and influenced by the gospel which they heard preached.   But the masses and the governments of the peoples of the west remained impervious to the truth.   Not until Russia had made a separate peace and quit the firing line; not until they were aware not merely that Russia had deserted her old allies but that the men in control of Russian affairs were as hostile to the governments and statesmen of the west as they were to those of Germany and Austria—that in fact a new force or a new disease was abroad in the world; did the western powers at last in any measure comprehend Russian events.

In sum: between February and August the Russian Revolution ran the whole gamut from a protest of enlightened patriotism and moderate democracy to the anti-patriotic, anti-social Bolshevist fury of Lenin.   In that period Russian unity was destroyed; such machinery of government and production as remained was abolished.   The Russian army was first disorganized from within and then—after a brief, successful offensive—revealed, fleeing from a field of victory, no longer a force or a factor in the war.   Long before August arrived Russia had ceased to be an ally, had become a problem and even a peril.   Thereafter it was to continue an ever-growing menace, the doctrines of its leaders undermining and destroying national unity in Allied countries, while, freed from Russian danger, Germany was to bring her vast hosts to Picardy, and Austria and Germany to transfer still other divisions to the Venetian front, so that while Allied capacity for resistance behind the line diminished, actual defeat upon the battlefield and new onrushes of German and Austrian troops were still further to test the already war-tried temper of the French, the Italian, and the British peoples.

III. THE FALL OF THE HOUSE OF ROMANOFF

It remains now to trace rapidly the several steps in the Revolution. In January and February Russia was in the hands of the reactionary influences whose conspicuous representative was Protopopov. The assassination of Rasputin on December 30th, celebrated by the nation as a deliverance but viewed by the Czarina as a personal affliction, had been the signal for the loosing of the influences of reactionary tyranny. All through the first two months of the new year, while Petrograd had been filled with machine guns and with troops, one provocation after another had been resorted to in the hope of driving a hungry and exasperated populace to throw itself upon the prepared weapons of the agents of reaction. When at last the Duma assembled on the 27th of February, more than a month after the date set for its meeting, the atmosphere was tense, the signs of the coming storm were on all sides. Prior to the 8th of March there were bread riots. On this day there was a disturbance provoked by the Cossacks, which in the next day expanded to a real revolt. Almost spontaneously, with little sign of direction, the people of the Russian capital flowed into the streets; meetings of protest were held; and finally—sure concomitant of every revolution—the soldiers of tyranny fraternized with the people. Out of the fraternizing there developed a general and complete extermination of the police who had been the chosen tools of the bureaucracy and of tyranny for so many years. These wretched creatures were hunted down and slain wherever found. They were in fact almost the sole victims of the first phase of the Russian Revolution, which in every other aspect was orderly, and impressed the world with the absence of precisely those circumstances which one associates with revolutions even in their initial phases.

Between the 8th and 12th of March the Revolution had achieved complete success. The later date was marked by an assault upon the great prison fortress of St. Peter and St. Paul, comparable in many respects with that attack upon the Bastille which was the decisive act of the French Revolution. Ordered to fire upon the masses, even the chosen Guard troops fired upon their own officers, and before noon of March 12th the old Russian order had fallen.

Meantime, the Duma held aloof. Messages were sent to the Czar warning him of the crisis. One message was ignored; another, answered by the futile statement that the feeble Nicholas was coming to the capital. He never reached Petrograd. On this March 12th the Duma named a provisional government of twelve of its members, while at the same moment a Committee of Workmen, Soldiers, and Sailors was formed—an executive body destined to supplant the Duma in due course of time.

This First Provisional Government contained among others Rodzianko, Prince Lvov, Miliukov, and Kerensky. Two days later such government as was left in Russia consisted of the twelve named by the Duma and the Council of Workmen and Soldiers Delegates—that Council of the Soviets, destined in a few months to rival and even to surpass that Committee of Public Safety which, in the Terror of the French Revolution, established a record of violence till then unparalleled.

Meantime the armies and their commanders, Russky and Brusiloff, had accepted the Revolution, and on March 15th even the Grand Duke Nicholas advised the Czar that he must abdicate. To this decision Nicholas bowed and on that day abdicated in favour of the Grand Duke Michael. On this same day the Duma announced a new government. Already there was a clash between the Soviets, who sought a republic, and the Duma, which still advocated a constitutional monarchy. One day later the Grand Duke Michael, in his turn, was forced to renounce the throne. The House of Romanoff had fallen, in seven days. Still another week and Nicholas Alexandrovitch Romanoff was a prisoner at the Palace of Tsarkoe Selo, entering upon that long agony which was to end as tragically and even more sordidly than the similar experience of Louis XVI. This phase of the drama was complete.

IV.   THE DUMA

The second act was marked by the effort of the Duma, through its provisional government, to carry on orderly administration, to reform

Russia by degrees, to preserve Russia's association with the Western powers and to fulfil her obligations as a partner in the war against Germany. But while the Duma and the Provisional Government were seeking to ensure the peaceful evolution of Russia, the Soviets, assembling in congress, gave instant evidence of a totally different purpose. Renouncing for Russia all previous agreements by which Constantinople and other rewards were assured to the Czar, the Soviets demanded similar sacrifices from the western Allies as the sole condition on which Russia should continue in the war. Already in this initial assembly the voice of Lenin was heard preaching the gospel of class warfare, demanding not a continuation of the war against Germany but an expansion of the war to a crusade against all capitalistic governments, Allied and German alike, an appeal to the masses of the population of all the countries to rise against their own governments, and throwing off the bondage of nationalism and racial patriotism, to share in the common cause which had for its object the obliteration of national frontiers and the elimination of the bourgeoisie everywhere.

Lenin had long been the apostle of this gospel of class warfare and Marxian socialism. Exiled from Russia he had found asylum in Switzerland. When the Revolution came, German assistance had made possible his return to his own country, and, arrived at home, he served the German cause by assailing every influence in Russia which made for the continuation of Russia in the war against Germany. From the very outset of the later phase the Russian Revolution became a battle between Kerensky—himself a Socialist, too, but the champion of more moderate policies and of continued alliance with the western powers—and Lenin, a consistent and uncompromising advocate of the universal war against Capital, preceded by an immediate peace with Germany. Kerensky was compelled to urge the Russian people to new effort in a war which had become intolerable. Lenin promised immediate relief from this conflict. Kerensky appealed to the sense of duty; Lenin, to the selfishness and weakness of his fellow-countrymen.

In all this period Kerensky sought on the one hand to persuade the western powers to modify their war purposes and bring their policies into accord with the Russian formula of peace without annexation and without indemnity, while he endeavoured to hold the Russian people fixed to their alliance with the west. It was an impossible task for a man whose sole qualifications lay in a brilliant imagination and an unrivalled eloquence. Kerensky was able to sway every audience which he addressed, and when he was an exile in England he captured hearers who did not even understand the language which he spoke, but he had not the power of organization nor the iron will which the situation required. His task was probably beyond human strength at best but it was beyond all question hopeless when his ultimate resource was words.

Lenin's game was steadily played by the Central Powers. In April Austria made a proffer of peace and in the same month the calling of a Socialist conference at Stockholm was seized upon by Berlin to tempt the Russians and confuse the Allies. By the 16th of May the Provisional Government had broken down and the new government represented an attempted coalition between the Duma and the Soviets, although Prince Lvov, who had headed the first government, still retained his post, and Kerensky exchanged the Ministry of Justice for that of War and Marine. In this time a first effort of Lenin to seize control of the Government failed. For a single hour it seemed as if Kerensky had at least measured up to his task and would be able to control with an iron hand the elements of disorder within while he directed Russian armies into conflict with the foes without. In this period, yielding to the ever-growing insistence of the western Allies, already gravely compromised by Russian military quiescence, he agreed to an offensive, but the anarchy which had wrecked the domestic machinery had already permeated the army. The death penalty had been abolished; a discipline severer and more terrible than that which had prevailed in the German army now gave way to a method of control under which soldiers chose their own officers and debated obedience to or rejection of their orders.

V. THE FINAL OFFENSIVE

We have now to examine the final Russian offensive, which in its brief hour of success aroused hopes among western nations which would not stir again until American millions had replaced Russian and the final German western offensive, the "peace storm" of July, 1918, had ended in decisive defeat.

To understand the actual history of the Russian attack in Galicia it is necessary to recall certain facts familiar in 1916 but now forgotten. When in August Brusiloff's great offensive came to an end the Austrian armies in Galicia were standing in a wide semicircle about Lemberg and from forty to sixty miles east of that city. To the north, in Volhynia, the Russian advance had stopped along the line of the Stokhod River, some twenty miles east of the vital railroad centre of Kovel. Had the Russians reached Kovel a great Austro-German retreat from the Gulf of Riga to the Carpathians would have been inevitable.

In Galicia the Austrians were standing behind the upper stream of the Styr, which flows northward out of Galicia; their centre was along the Zlota Lipa, which rises near the Styr but flows southward into the Dniester, with their extreme right centre bent back north of the Dniester to the point where the Gnila Lipa enters it. South of the Dniester their line ran behind the Bystritza, just west of Stanislau, straight down to the Carpathians. They were actually in a temporary position, were on the point of drawing back their centre behind the Gnila Lipa, when the Russian offensive stopped. After the pause the Austrian and German troops held on.

The main mission of the Austro-German forces in Galicia was to cover Lemberg. Originally they had stood along the line of the Strypa, which parallels the Zlota Lipa to the eastward. They had fallen back to the Zlota Lipa, and the Russians had succeeded in passing the lower stretch of this river, thus turning the Zlota Lipa position. Actually, the Austrians had left to them the Gnila Lipa position; that is, the position behind this river which rises in the hills east of Lemberg and flows fairly straight down to the Dniester, which it enters opposite Halicz. This is the natural covering position of an army defending Lemberg, itself an open town; it is the position from which the Austrians had defended the town in August, 1914, and when they were defeated here they evacuated Lemberg.

The Bug River, rising in the hills that also see the birth of the Gnila Lipa and at one point coming within half a dozen miles of this stream, turns northward and flows across eastern Galicia into Russia and this makes a natural extension to the northward of the Gnila Lipa position, and together the lines of the Bug and the Gnila Lipa constitute the last and best defensive position before Lemberg. South of the Dniester the Bystritza, and behind it the Lomnica, serve as extensions of this Gnila Lipa-Bug Line.

In August, 1916, the world believed that the Austro-Germans would be compelled to draw back to the Gnila Lipa position. But they stood; their centre still advanced along the Zlota Lipa; and it was against this centre, and about the town of Brzezany, that the first Russian attack of 1917 was delivered on a wide front from north of the Lemberg-Brody railroad to the ground south of Brzezany.

This attack met with local successes. The town of Koniuchy, northeast of Brzezany, was taken; Brzezany itself was threatened; some 20,000 prisoners were captured, together with many guns. But these local successes were all that resulted. The Austrian line was reinforced and held on. Fresh Russian attacks were met by stiff resistance and brought heavy losses. The attack had begun on June 30th. By July 4th it was beginning to flicker out and there was no longer immediate promise of any renewal of the achievement of 1914 or of 1916.

The most that could be said for this first attack was that it had surprised the world by showing that Russia, apparently, was resolved to fight on; had revealed the Russian army as better prepared in artillery and other munitions than had been expected, and disclosed the soldiers as having a fighting spirit once more.

But had it ended with the Brzezany episode the Russian offensive would have had little real military value, measured by actual achievement. As it turned out this was only a beginning. After a few days' pause the Russians renewed the attack, this time south of the Dniester and along the Bystritza, west of Stanislau. Here their success was immediate and considerable. The Austrian lines were pierced and there began a drive momentarily quite like those of 1916. This victory was achieved by the army of Korniloff.

Recall again the relation of the various rivers to Lemberg. The Austrians still held a portion of the Zlota Lipa line. They could still retire to the line of the Gnila Lipa, as far as pressure north of the Dniester was concerned. But the Russians had passed both the Bystritza and the Lomnica, which are the natural extensions of the Gnila Lipa line south of the Dniester; they had crossed the Dniester from the south, opposite Halicz, which they had captured; and were thus west of the Gnila Lipa, north of the Dniester.

The situation south of the Dniester was perhaps more serious, for the Russians had passed both the Bystritza and the Lomnica, and having taken Kalusz were moving westward between the Dniester and the Carpathian foothills, driving a wedge between the Austrians north of the Dniester and those to the south, and threatening to open a wide gap through which their troops would pour in from north and west and threaten Lemberg. The real test of the Russian success was now their ability to reach the city of Stryj, thirty-odd miles northwest of Lemberg and an important railroad junction. If they got to Stryj, then the evacuation of Lemberg would be well-nigh inevitable.

It was possible that the passing of the river at Halicz might compel the abandonment of the Gnila Lipa River line by the Austrians and the eventual retirement west of Lemberg. It did in 1914, but it was less likely that this success would be decisive than that the fall of Lemberg would be determined by operations to the south of the Dniester, where there were more evidences of Austrian collapse.

Before there could be any determination of this battle, the whole Russian line north of the Dniester before Tarnopol and northward to the Lemberg-Brody railroad suddenly collapsed. There was no considerable German attack; there was no great engagement, but a panic—a rout—ensued. German spies, German agents, anarchists, and war-weary, deluded soldiers united in the destruction of discipline, and the army which had taken Koniuchy and threatened Brzezany two weeks earlier was suddenly transformed into a fleeing horde, comparable to that army which set out from the battlefield of First Bull Run for Washington.

And the effect of this collapse of the Russian centre in Galicia was to leave Korniloff's victorious army south of the Dniester in the air. It had no choice but to fall rapidly back for a hundred miles through Bukowina to the Russian boundary, surrendering all of Bukowina and all of Galicia held since the opening of the campaign of 1916. When the re-arrangement was complete the Austrians once more could boast a soil practically freed of the invader and this had not been the case since the very opening days of the war.

In men the Russians lost surprisingly few by this wretched per-formance. Official German figures placed the captures—up to mid-August, from Roumania to the Bug—at only 42,000 men and 257 guns. In their offensives in April the British and the French together had cap-tured over 55,000 German prisoners and more than 400 guns. The Russians in their first two weeks this year, while the armies still fought, had taken 36,000 prisoners, and captures in Roumania brought the balance even for the two forces on the southeastern front. Compare this with 150,000 Austrian prisoners taken by the Russians after Lem-berg in 1914 or 120,000 prisoners after the capture of Lutsk in 1916. The loss of guns was more serious, but the real disaster was the destruc-tion of the cohesion of the Russian armies.

At a critical moment the inevitable effect of the domestic agitations had been felt and Germany had been saved from deadly peril, the peril flowing from the opening of a joint attack in the east and in the west. Ludendorff himself subsequently declared in a military conference in Berlin that had this Russian offensive coincided with the Anglo-French attacks before Arras and at the Craonne Plateau the consequences might have been fatal to Germany. Now she could concentrate her attention upon Belgium and Artois, for even if Russian armies could be reorgan-ized and restored before the end of the campaigning season it was be-yond possibility that they could conduct a new offensive.

In point of fact Russia had collapsed. If Korniloff, who had planned the victorious offensive which ended so ignominiously, could in association with Kerensky make one more effort to restore discipline in the army, this association was destined to live but a brief time, and while Bolshevist uprising in Petrograd accompanied mutiny and desertion on the field of victory, Russia was slipping inescapably into the bog of anarchy. The break between Korniloff and Kerensky, a few weeks later, was to shatter the last power of resistance in the Provisional Government, in which Lvov had already given place to Kerensky.

Henceforth Russia is no more than a cauldron in which boil up all sorts of bubbles. It is no longer a nation or a state. It is no more capable of conducting war, of making peace, of manning the machinery of production and communication. Ukrainian, Polish, Lithuanian separatist movements destroy a physical unity already shaken by domestic anarchy.

The fall of Russia well-nigh lost the war for the western Allies. Had the Germans refrained from their submarine attack, which enlisted the United States, it is inconceivable that victory could finally have escaped the Kaiser. With the failure of the Russian offensive the whole Allied campaign of 1917 was doomed. The French had failed outright at the Craonne Plateau; the Italians, mounting with difficulty the Bainsizza Plateau, were condemned to find complete disaster after transient success; British armies were already floundering in the morass of Flanders in their tragically abortive campaign; while, with ever-increasing insistence, demands for peace—formulated by the honest but weak and the corrupt but influential—sounded in Allied capitals and countries.

In July, 1917, and in the succeeding months up to the Treaty of Brest-Litovsk we touch the dead low-water mark of Allied hopes, Allied prospects, Allied courage. Every calculation of victory had been predicated upon the participation of Russia. Again and again the western publics had been solaced for failure on their own front by promises of the arrival of the Russian steam roller in Berlin and Vienna. Such promises could be made no longer. The last illusion was disappearing; even the American hope lost appeal in the light of Russian deception.

There is another side to the Russian Revolution. The next two years were to show that the Russian collapse had not merely imperilled Allied prospects of military triumph immediately and greatly but that the disease which had seized upon Russia was destined to invade the west. Germany, which had procured the return of Russian anarchists following the Revolution—which had profited greatly by the disorganization in Russia—the work, if not primarily of its agents, at least the result in no small degree of its manœuvres; Germany herself was to suffer from the scourge, and no western power was to go unscathed. Henceforth, for the period of the war, for the period of the Armistice, when at last peace had been signed, Russia was to remain outside the circle of nations—outside the bonds of international association—suffering miseries unequalled in modern history, but, under the leadership of Lenin, despite indescribable weakness, to continue an immeasurable peril to the west—to Germany, as to France and Great Britain—a phenomenon as inexplicable to contemporary mankind as was the French Revolution a century and a quarter before.

CHAPTER NINE

THE SUBMARINE

I

THE GRAVER MENACE

Grave as were the military circumstances for the western Allies even before Russia had collapsed, the naval prospects were infinitely worse. In April and May Germany was winning the war with the submarine. In the former month upward of a million tons of shipping had been sunk, and Admiral Sims, going to London to establish relations between the American and Allied navies, was met by the appalling statement—made by Jellicoe and by civil officials alike—that, unless some new weapon or some new method could be discovered to deal with the submarine, and could be discovered promptly, then, not later than November, Great Britain would be starved into surrender, the war lost, the German victory on land and on sea inescapable. Mr. Balfour, when he came to the United States immediately after American entrance into the war, brought a similar message, and delivered it at the moment the American military authorities were learning from Marshal Joffre that the Nivelle offensive had failed and that the immediate presence of American soldiers in Europe, and in large numbers, was necessary.

We have now briefly to consider the submarine aspect of the war. It is plain that had the Germans, before the outbreak of the war, recognized the value of the weapon they possessed in the submarine; had they, instead of following the example of the British navy and embarking upon a pursuit race to overtake British sea power by the construction of capital ships, concentrated their energy and attention upon the construction of a really considerable submarine fleet; they might have won the war in the first three years, before the British navy had at last learned to cope with the new form of sea warfare. Nothing seems more clear than that the German submarine operations were the result of an appreciation, after the outbreak of hostilities, of the possibilities of this new arm directed against merchant shipping, rather than the consequence of marvellous prevision—just as the German mobile heavy artillery, which had been designed speedily to reduce French fortifications and open the way to swift victory, proved of incalculable value in unforeseen trench warfare, after having failed to procure the military decision which had been planned.

When the Germans abandoned their first campaign—which had nearly brought the United States into the war in 1915 and the first weeks of 1916—they then possessed an insufficient undersea fleet to accomplish their purpose; but thereafter, and particularly after Jutland, they concentrated their energies upon the construction of submarines, and were able to complete not less than three a week. When they resumed their ruthless sinkings in February they were able, thanks to new construction, to keep not less than eight or ten undersea boats at work at all times, and—contrary to all the reports of that period, official and otherwise—their loss was inconsiderable and far too insignificant to defeat the campaign itself.

Against a possible resumption of this campaign the British navy had neither fortified itself by the construction of destroyers—the sole type of craft capable of dealing with the submarine—nor had it formulated plans against such an emergency. Such destroyers as it had were almost all occupied in protecting the Grand Fleet. The few that were left for sea patrol were so ridiculously inadequate as to make hopeless the task assigned to them. Nor had the British Government foreseen the coming crisis and provisioned the British Isles in advance. In April, when the Germans put nearly a million tons of shipping under, Britain had six weeks of foodstuffs on hand, so that a continuation of the rate of sinkings for that month made surrender by November 1st inevitable.

It is essential to see the submarine element in the war accurately. The Germans did not risk involving the United States in the world conflict merely to make a hazardous gamble. They had calculated correctly, that as the British navy was fighting the submarine in February,

1917, and as it continued to fight it for months thereafter, the success of the new campaign was mathematically certain. They assumed that they would sink more than a million tons a month—perhaps two millions. They calculated that three months of this campaign would bring Britain to her knees; British calculations differed only as they doubled the period of grace. The German saw victory before America could be a real participant. He refrained from any attack upon American shores and from any considerable violence to American shipping in the belief that the war would be over before America could much affect its course, and with the thought that, in such circumstances, there would not be in America any such permanent hostility, dangerous to the after-war prosperity and commerce of Germany, as now existed all over Europe.

Conceivably, although the German hardly reckoned upon it, the submarine campaign might only prepare the way for one more western offensive. This was a possibility foreseen when Hindenburg devastated northern France and retired to his own front while German armies and German agents completed the demoralization of Russia. The mission of the western front was to hold fast until Russia had fallen and the submarine had either won the war, or so weakened British powers of resistance at home by the sure process of starvation, that an initial victory in the west, in 1918, would bring a collapse in Britain comparable with that in Russia.

It was the ever-mounting danger of the submarine that led the British to place their armies under the control of Nivelle, and welcome that alluring if disastrous strategy which envisaged a grandiose attack and the achievement of decisive military victory. It was the hope of the British and French governments alike, in the spring of 1917, that the Anglo-French armies might save the British navy. The Flanders offensive had, for its primary object, the sweeping of the Germans from the Belgian coast, and thus abolishing the main submarine base at Bruges, and laying hands on Zeebrügge and Ostend, the twin outlets of this hornet's nest.

II. IN APRIL

Admiral Sims has given the world a luminous description of the situation which he found when he reached London in the spring of 1917. For the moment Great Britain had lost, not the control of the seas by her navy, for the Grand Fleet still maintained a superiority vindicated at Jutland, but the use of the waters she dominated. Actually the British Isles were blockaded, and daily the harvest of submarine sinkings marched inexorably toward that point at which shipping would be so reduced that starvation would compel surrender. Such were the reports sent by Admiral Sims to the American Government. Such was the condition which confronted the Allies during all the period when their military efforts were failing and the collapse of Russia was resulting in the transfer to the western front of German and Austrian divisions sufficient to check Allied attacks in 1917 and compel British, French, and Italian armies to resign the initiative and await the attacks of victorious German armies, while German submarines cut their lines of communication, interrupted their supplies, destroyed the cargoes of foodstuffs and raw material essential alike for the maintenance of the armies and the civil population, and for the manufacture of munitions and guns.

It was only in June that the British Government at last, in a counsel of desperation, had recourse to the system of convoys, and even this ultimate expedient would have been impossible had it not been for the transfer to European waters of the Destroyer Fleet of the United States and a further contribution of a similar sort from the Japanese Navy. From February to September it was touch and go, and it was only in November that at last the convoy system, together with other methods, produced results which assured the Allies that—great and continuing as would be the injury of the submarine, difficult as would be the maintenance of sufficient shipping—the German could not win the war by this means alone. Slowly but surely the rate of sinkings fell; it was reduced by two thirds between April, 1917, and April, 1918. But once more the German victories in March and April of 1918 induced a

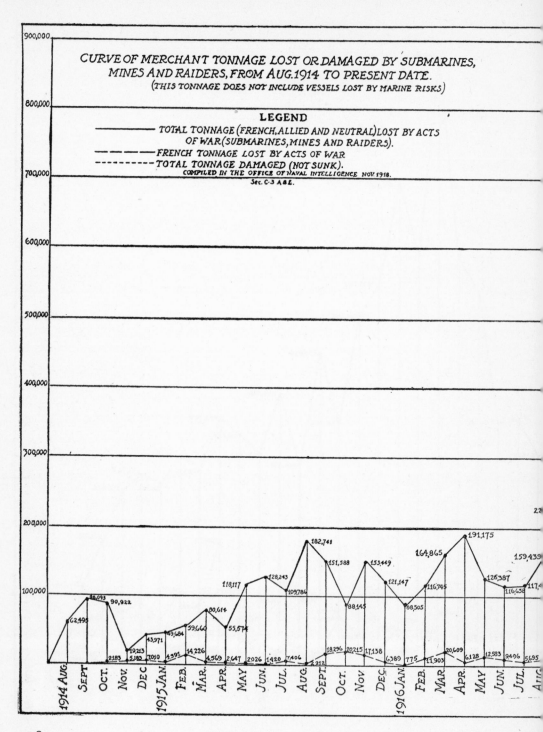

CURVE OF MERCHANT TONNAGE LOST OR DAMAGED BY SUBMARINES,
MINES AND RAIDERS, FROM AUG.1914 TO PRESENT DATE.
(THIS TONNAGE DOES NOT INCLUDE VESSELS LOST BY MARINE RISKS)

LEGEND
———————— TOTAL TONNAGE (FRENCH,ALLIED AND NEUTRAL)LOST BY ACTS
OF WAR(SUBMARINES,MINES AND RAIDERS).
— — — — — FRENCH TONNAGE LOST BY ACTS OF WAR
- - - - - - - TOTAL TONNAGE DAMAGED (NOT SUNK).
COMPILED IN THE OFFICE OF NAVAL INTELLIGENCE NOV. 1918.
Sec. C-3 A & L.

900,000
800,000
700,000
600,000
500,000
400,000
300,000
200,000
100,000

62,495   48,093   90,922   2,183   5,183   43,971   49,684   59,660   80,614   55,574   118,117   128,243   109,786   182,741   151,588   88,145   153,449   121,147   88,505   164,865   116,745   191,175   126,387   116,638   159,439   117,4

7,010   4,391   14,226   4,569   2,647   2026   1420   7,406   2,212   18,296   20,715   17,138   6,389   775   11,903   20,609   6,128   12,583   9,496   5,695

19,213

1914 Aug. | Sept. | Oct. | Nov. | Dec. | 1915 Jan. | Feb. | Mar. | Apr. | May | Jun. | Jul. | Aug. | Sept. | Oct. | Nov. | Dec. | 1916 Jan. | Feb. | Mar. | Apr. | May | Jun. | Jul. | Aug.

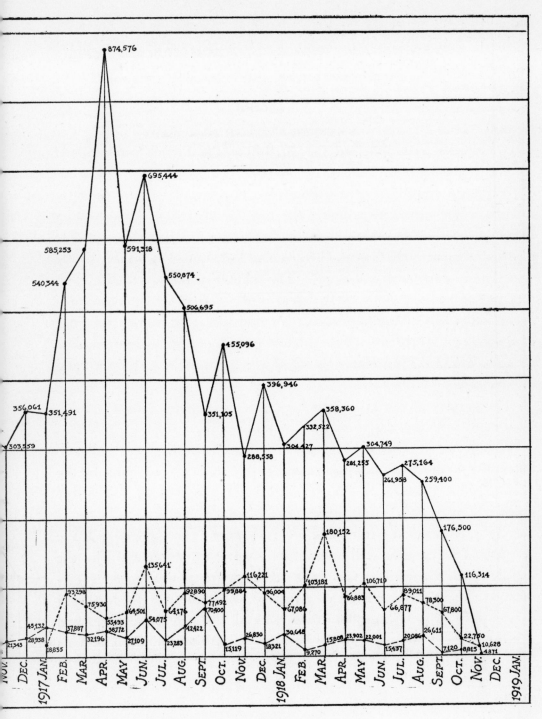

874,576

695,444

585,253
591,318
550,874
540,344
506,695

455,096

396,946

356,061 351,491
358,360
351,105
332,522
303,559
304,749
304,427
288,558
281,255
275,164
261,958 259,400

180,152

176,500

135,641
116,221
116,314
106,710
103,181
99,884
96,004
93,298
92,890
89,011
86,883
78,300
77,492
75,930
70,400
67,800
67,086
66,877
64,501
64,176
55,493
54,075
45,132
42,422
38,772
37,887
32,196
30,648
28,938
27,109
26,830
26,611
23,902
23,283
22,750
22,001
21,343
20,086
18,835
18,321
15,437
15,119
13,119
10,628
9,270
8,815
7,120
4,871

Nov. | Dec. | 1917 Jan. | Feb. | Mar. | Apr. | May | Jun. | Jul. | Aug. | Sept. | Oct. | Nov. | Dec. | 1918 Jan. | Feb. | Mar. | Apr. | May | Jun. | Jul. | Aug. | Sept. | Oct. | Nov. | Dec. | 1919 Jan.

WING THE COURSE OF SUBMARINE LOSSES DURING THE WAR

199

crisis when the necessity for the transfer of two millions of American troops to Europe suddenly removed an enormous tonnage from the service of supplies; in 1918, even more than in 1917, the British public suffered from a lack of food, and only the most rigorous system of rationing actually prevented famine. From the summer of 1917, onward, Great Britain was hungry, and even after the war had ended many months passed before the British or the French public could resume its former nourishment.

All things considered, the submarine campaign of 1917, in its early months, came nearer to winning the war for Germany than the first campaign to the Marne or the colossal March offensive of 1918. For a period of months the British Government lost control of the sea for the first time in more than a century. The submarine success, unlike a victory in the field, did not merely defeat or destroy an army; it attacked every individual in the nation. It brought Great Britain to the edge of starvation. It threatened British and French munition factories alike with the lack of the raw materials out of which armies were equipped and munitioned.

The gravity of the crisis was long hidden from the Allied publics. How near Germany was to victory by midsummer 1917, as a result of her submarine campaign, was not appreciated at the time, and can hardly be understood now, since no visible evidence to indicate the crisis of that time exists. Never in all her long history had Great Britain been so near to ultimate ruin, and until America could come, Britain was the last stronghold of resistance. To understand the progress of political as well as military events; to understand why the morale of the domestic as well as the military fronts weakened dangerously in 1917; to comprehend why the faint-hearted cried out for peace at any price, why treason flourished, why all through the summer and autumn back-stairs negotiations between the Allies and the Germans went forward in one fashion or another, it is necessary to grasp the actual achievements of the German submarine campaign, the success of which was carefully eliminated from the press and replaced by optimistic if mendacious appeals of statesmen designed to deceive the peoples of the Allied nations, and thus persuade them to continue in the struggle.

The German submarine campaign, in the end, failed. Its failure damns it, precisely as Napoleon's failure in his Moscow campaign made that venture a landmark in failure for successive generations. Moreover, the failure involved Germany in war with the United States and brought American troops to France in time to supply the western Allies with the necessary numbers to regain the initiative and win decisive victory. Exactly as the incursion into Belgium roused the world and gave a moral impetus to the Allied cause, in neutral as well as in combatant nations, without enabling the German armies to reach Paris or win the war, resumption of ruthless submarine warfare in February, 1917, without achieving its object, enlisted new enemies and ultimately ensured German defeat. Yet they were not mad, the Germans who risked contingencies that to human eyes seemed remote, in the pursuit of results which, if they seemed certain to German leaders in January—before the campaign was launched—appeared almost equally sure to British, French, and American statesmen, soldiers, and sailors in April and May—when the campaign was in full swing.

Like the devastation of northern France and the Hindenburg retreat, the use of the submarine for unrestricted sinking could only be the resort of a nation that was either desperate or certain of success. In 1917 the German was hardly desperate. He was by contrast still confident, not alone of victory but of swift triumph. By October, when conquest by the submarine arm alone had become impossible, his military prospects had so improved that he still had reason to believe that the submarine, plus the victorious armies now summoned from the Russian front, would gain the decision the forthcoming spring. But in using the submarine, as in transforming northern France into a desert, the Kaiser and his advisers invited terrible retribution if defeat should come. Nothing was more certain than that, if Germany lost the war, her shipping—one of the chief instruments by which the great development of German prosperity in world trade had been achieved—would be taken from her. Thus in 1917, on land and on sea, the German took irrevocable steps, whose consequences were to be written into the Treaty of Versailles two years later.   He sank hospital ships, laden with the wounded of the battlefield, to summon Allied destroyers from submarine patrol to the protection of these vessels of mercy, precisely as he bombed hospitals and peaceful cities far behind the battle-front, to recall Allied airplanes from active service.   He used all his weapons, and he exhausted the possibilities of all his machinery of destruction— not in savage rage, but in calculated ferocity.   The submarine campaign was the ultimate expression in the World War of the mean- ing of the German will for victory.   It came within an ace of winning the war.   It would have won the war if the British navy, aided by American destroyer fleets, had not turned to the convoy system, impossible till then because of the lack of destroyers.   This exposed the British navy as having failed, in the respite between 1916 and 1917, to devise adequate methods for meeting the submarine, and the British Government as having failed to provide in advance against a possible onset of famine.

To analyze the various elements that contribute to making victory or defeat in a nation is almost impossible either during or after the war. Yet it seems hardly an exaggeration to say that in 1917, disastrous as were Allied defeats upon the battlefield, they alone would not explain the decline of Allied morale among the peoples engaged.   It was the submarine campaign; it was the element of actual deprivation and proximate famine that gave secret strength to those successive peace offensives which so nearly gained the German his victory.   The armies had failed, but of themselves they could still fight on; but the govern- ments and the peoples behind the armies were assailed by an enemy whose advance long seemed irresistible and whose attack unnerved and weakened the whole population.

We shall see how at last, in 1918, the submarine campaign was de- feated—the peril well-nigh abolished.   In 1917 it was only halted.   It was not until autumn that there was at least a reasonable basis for belief that the submarine would not win the war, and in all the strain of military and political events during this long, grim period the influence of the submarine campaign must be recognized and appreciated.

III. THE STATISTICS

The following figures show the total tonnage lost during the war owing to the German submarine campaign, as compiled from American official reports:

SUBMARINE SINKINGS

1914			1917		
August . . .	62,495 tons		January . . .	351,491 tons	
September . .	98,093		February . .	540,344	
October . . .	90,922		March . . .	585,253	
November . .	19,213		April . . .	874,576	
December . .	43,971		May . . .	591,318	
		314,694	June . . .	695,444	
1915			July . . .	550,874	
			August . . .	506,695	
January . .	49,684		September .	351,105	
February . .	59,660		October . .	455,096	
March . . .	80,614		November . .	288,558	
April . . .	55,574		December . .	396,946	
May . . .	118,117				6,187,700
June . . .	128,243				
July . . .	109,786				
August . .	182,741				
September .	151,588				
October . .	88,145				
November . .	153,449				
December . .	121,147				
		1,298,748			
1916			**1918**		
January . .	88,505		January . . .	304,427	
February . .	116,745		February . .	332,522	
March . . .	164,865		March . . .	358,360	
April . . .	191,175		April . . .	281,255	
May . . .	126,387		May . . .	304,749	
June . . .	116,638		June . . .	261,958	
July . . .	117,473		July . . .	275,164	
August . . .	159,439		August . . .	259,400	
September .	229,616		September .	176,500	
October . .	320,974		October . . .	116,314	
November . .	303,559		November . .	4,871	
December . .	356,061				2,675,520
		2,291,437			

Total 12,768,099

IV. SIMS AND LUDENDORFF

At the moment in which I am completing this volume there are being published two documents which must for the future have great value in any analysis of the last phase of the submarine conflict.   One is the narrative of Admiral Sims of the American Navy, setting forth the story of the fight against the submarine, and the other is General Ludendorff's account of the last two years of the war, which includes an explanation of the reasons which led the Germans to embark upon their fatal venture.   These two documents are of unequal value because, while the truthfulness of Sims is not to be questioned, Ludendorff's book is plainly propaganda, designed to absolve the German military leaders from the responsibility of defeat.   Nevertheless, it has real value.

Moreover, setting the two narratives side by side one perceives first, what the German calculations were, from Ludendorff, and second, how nearly the calculations were correct, from Sims.

The explanation of Ludendorff is probably one of the most cold-blooded statements which the war has produced.   It shows no regard whatever for moral considerations.   It discloses the German Government and the German Staff concerned solely with the question as to whether the use of the submarine would be more profitable, despite its effect upon neutrals, or not.   Ludendorff explains that the campaign was not resolved upon until President Wilson's peace proposals of December, 1916, had failed and the success of German armies in Roumania had relieved the Central Powers of one source of anxiety and provided the necessary troops against the remote possibility that Holland and Denmark, and even more distant neutrals like Sweden and Norway, might enter the war as a consequence of a resumption of ruthless sinkings.

The most interesting single assertion of Ludendorff on the military side is that the German High Command saw the beginning of the year 1917 with grave anxiety, because they did not then suspect a Russian collapse such as took place, and he declares that since it was impossible to forecast the collapse of Russia, the Central Powers saw in the submarine the sole weapon which could avert defeat, and might produce victory.   The German calculation was that the submarine would bring Britain to her knees in six months.   Ludendorff himself doubled the period but accepted the statement of the naval authorities that the extent of the allied losses would preclude the passing of American troops to Europe in time or in numbers to affect the situation in 1918 even if the submarine campaign proved less immediately successful than was hoped for.

This amounts to a confession that if Germany had known of the forthcoming collapse of Russia in January, 1917, she would not have resorted to the submarine weapon, thus inviting American entrance into the war, and, as the event proved, insuring German defeat. In July, 1914, German High Command calculated that in six weeks, by violating the neutrality of Belgium, it could dispose of France whether Great Britain entered the war or not, and therefore the profit would be out of all proportion to the loss even if Britain should enter. In January, 1917, the Germans calculated that they could win the war in twelve months if they resorted to the submarine weapon, and that, for twelve months at least, America would be unable to intervene effectively. Both calculations very nearly proved correct, but failure by a narrow margin in each case led to fatal consequences. German military leaders were correct in calculating that not more than five or six American divisions need be reckoned with in Europe during the first year of American participation in the war, just as they were correct in assuming that the British Expeditionary Army would be small and play a relatively minor part in the first six weeks in the 1914 campaign. But in both cases there is disclosed that amazing German psychology which led to the taking of unheard-of risks without making any allowance for the intellectual and moral forces to be arrayed against them.

Ludendorff says that in January, 1917, expecting a renewal of attack on all fronts, not yet perceiving the approach of Russian collapse, having failed to procure peace by negotiation on terms which would have perpetuated the European condition created by Germany's opening victories, the Kaiser, the civil government, and the military leaders agreed upon a recourse to the submarine weapon without regard to the rights of neutrals, without concern for America, because it promised a decision within six months in the opinion of German naval officers, within a year according to the more conservative judgment of Ludendorff himself, and he concedes that the course would not have been adopted had German leaders perceived that Russia would soon collapse and the way would be clear to seek a military decision in the west in 1918.

As to Sims, he reports that when he reached London in April, after less than three months of unrestricted sinkings, he was bluntly told that Great Britain would have to give up the war by November if the submarine campaign were not checked and then he reported to Washington: "Briefly stated, I consider that at the present moment we are losing the war." He tells us that after spending his first four days in London and collecting all possible data, he wrote a four-page cable despatch setting forth the situation in its full gravity, and when he submitted it to the American Ambassador, Mr. Page declared that it was not strong enough, and wrote a much stronger despatch of his own. Thus are revealed the calculations of Berlin and the conviction of London in the first stages of the submarine campaign of 1917.

THE GERMAN SUBMARINE MENACE

THE LETTER "Z"

AND

HOW IT WAS MET BY

THE ALLIED NAVIES

THE WARNING

On Saturday, May 1, 1915, the day the *Lusitania* left New York on her last voyage, the above advertisement appeared among the steamship notices in the leading American newspapers

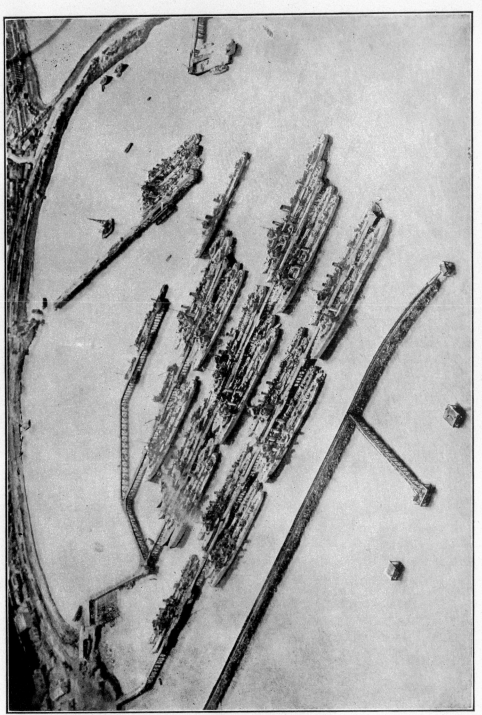

ONE OF THE BRITISH NAVY'S LAIRS

The *Lusitania* warning attracted wide attention, but few people took it seriously. Americans were unable to believe that the Germans would go so far in frightfulness, and Britons were proudly confident of the Royal Navy's ability to protect what was perhaps the finest ship in the British merchant marine

THE *LUSITANIA* SAILS FROM NEW YORK HARBOUR

The *Lusitania* sailed from New York Harbour on May 1, 1915. Despite the German warning her owners relied upon President Wilson's note of February 10th, which declared that the United States would hold the Imperial German Government "to a strict accountability" for such acts as were threatened

"SPURLOS VERSENKT"

From the painting by Paul Dougherty by, permission of Duncan Phillips

Many and revolting are the crimes for which the German officials must answer at the bar of civilization. But none is more dastardly than this which Mr. Dougherty has so strikingly portrayed—the sinking of an Allied hospital ship by a German submarine

From a drawing by Louis Raemakers

THE SURVIVORS

A *Lusitania* survivor stated that when the ship sank a submarine rose to the surface: "The crew stood stolidly on the deck and surveyed the scene. I could distinguish the German flag, but it was impossible to see the number of the submarine, which disappeared after a few minutes."

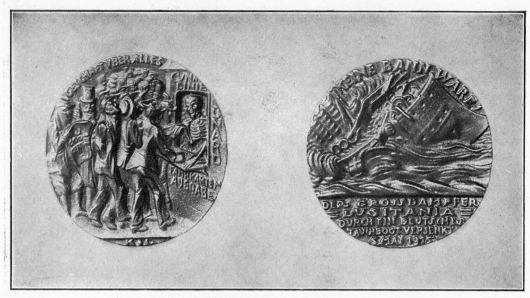

THE *LUSITANIA* MEDAL

This medal was struck by the Germans to commemorate their navy's "glorious" achievement. One side shows Death selling tickets at the Cunard Line's ticket-window, under the motto "Business before Everything"; the other shows the ship engulfed by the waves. It is noteworthy that the date stamped on the medal is two days earlier than that of the actual occurrence.

THE GERMAN SUBMARINE *U C* 5

In drydock after her capture by the British

A CONVOY IN THE DANGER ZONE

By steering a zig-zag course the food ships greatly increased the difficulty of the submarine's aim. This device helped
them to answer the heartfelt prayer of British children, "Give us this day our daily bread"

THE "RATS" IN THEIR HOLE

A group of German submarines lying in their base at Wilhelmshaven

ONE MORE ENEMY ACCOUNTED FOR

H. M. S. *Tempest* drops a depth charge as she dashes at full speed over the spot where a German submarine has just submerged

CHAPTER TEN

THE THIRD BATTLE OF YPRES—PASSCHENDAELE

I
HAIG AND GRANT

The operations in Artois—following the Battle of Arras, and designed to aid the French on the Craonne Plateau by occupying German divisions—died out toward the end of May, after having been prolonged for rather more than a month beyond the time Sir Douglas Haig had fixed for this subsidiary operation. By June 1st he was at last free to turn his attention toward that campaign which from the winter onward he had designed to be the principal British effort, in case Nivelle's offensive fell short of its far-reaching mission.

The campaign which we are now to examine was the bloodiest, on the Allied side, of the western front, comparable with the German attack at Verdun, and, like that stupendous German effort, destined to fall short of any larger objective and to be followed by a resignation of all the ground purchased at such an enormous price in human life and human effort. For American readers the Third Battle of Ypres, the new campaign in Flanders, has a striking parallel in Grant's operations in 1864 from the Rapidan to Cold Harbour and to Petersburg. The British army and the British public saw the opening of the campaign of 1917 with precisely the same confidence and hope with which the Northern public surveyed the beginning of Grant's first campaign with the Army of the Potomac.

The conditions were in many respects similar. Three years of war had in both cases seen the transformation of a civilian population into well-equipped and well-trained armies. The disappointments, the failures of three years of war had, on the whole, been without any disastrous consequences. The British army had suffered no considerable defeat. The Expeditionary Army, after it had at last found itself in the latter stages of the Battle of the Marne, had fought with distinction at the Aisne and won enduring glory at Ypres.

The gas attack of 1915, which was the striking circumstance in the Second Battle of Ypres, had resulted in loss of ground but had been without other serious consequences. If the British offensives at Neuve-Chapelle, Festubert, and Loos in 1915 and the far greater effort at the Somme in 1916 had resulted in no decisive victory; if they had indeed in the earlier cases ended in decisive checks and inexpressible disappointments, nevertheless, looking at the western front and marking the changes between November, 1914, and January, 1917, there had been a forward push almost everywhere along the British sector; the Somme had seen a considerable advance, and it had as one of its consequences a wide-swinging German retreat, a reoccupation of a thousand square miles of French territory, followed almost immediately by a brilliant success in the Battle of Arras.

The British public might well feel, as did the public of the North, fifty-three years earlier, that at last their army had reached the point where victory was in its hands, and their commanders had received the training essential to success, while the political generals, the incompetents, the failures, had been eliminated. "On to Richmond" was the confident watchword of the North in the next-to-the-last campaign of the Civil War, precisely as British soldiers and British civilians now expressed their confidence in forecasts that the autumn of 1917 would see Belgium liberated and the Germans behind the Meuse, if not behind the Rhine.

In the American case the high hopes of springtime faded in the terrible summer slaughter of the Wilderness, Spottsylvania, and the crowning tragedy of Cold Harbour. More than half of the army that Grant led across the Rapidan at the outset of the campaign were casualties by the time Cold Harbour had been fought. In that period the terrible costs, the sterile gains, shook the confidence of the public in its army, and of the army in its general. Grant, who had been hailed as the saviour of the Republic in May, was denounced as a butcher in September, and his achievements at Vicksburg and Chattanooga were tarnished by his failures in northern Virginia. The army which he finally took into trenches south of Petersburg was an army that was fought out and incapable of a new offensive for many months.

Fortunately for the Union cause, Grant's policy of attrition, his strategy of slaughter, was directed against an enemy whose last reserves were in the firing line. As a consequence, the very strategy which the North denounced in the autumn of 1864 demonstrated its efficacy in April of the following year. But had some change of circumstances wiped out the armies of Sherman and Thomas and permitted all the Southern armies of the West to flow to Lee's assistance, the closing act of Appomattox would not have occurred. Instead, Grant's opening attack in March, 1865, would have led to new repulses since it would have been directed against an enemy equal in numbers and resources.

Precisely this thing was what now happened in Flanders. The army of Sir Douglas Haig, with the proud consciousness of recent successes, with the confident hope of immediate victory, set its face once more toward those fields on which British soldiers had in 1914 won enduring fame. On those fields, after one brief flash of brilliant success, they were checked, halted with tremendous casualties, condemned to contest the shell-wrecked earth foot by foot. Time, so long proclaimed as the ally of the western powers, fought steadily against them; week by week and month by month, fresh divisions from the German front entered the conflict in the face of the ever-wearying British divisions.

To this circumstance were added two others. The weather, which had been unfriendly in the latter phases of the Somme, once more gave the Germans incalculable assistance. In the bogs and morasses, which extend over a large area about Ypres, the British armies floundered and suffered. German resistance was tenfold strengthened by the floods and the storms. One might speculate as to whether the British defeat of the Third Battle of Ypres was due more to weather or to German arms. Conceivably in the first days of August, had the weather held, there might have been a real success. Thereafter, weather conditions were almost sufficient to explain the failure, and the British soldier might well claim that his offensive had been drowned rather than defeated.

The second circumstance was the inefficiency disclosed in the general selected to conduct the army operations. The preliminary attack of June, under the direction of General Sir Herbert Plumer, was the high-water mark in technical efficiency on the British side throughout the war. In that opening battle Plumer displayed those qualities which presently earned for him, first the unchallenged title of the best battle commander in the British army and later, recognition as field marshal by his nation. When Plumer had struck the first blow with his Second Army it was Gough of the Fifth Army who was designated to direct the major attack, and this major attack failed. It failed so completely and at such a cost that Haig was presently compelled to call upon Plumer again. When Plumer came there was an immediate change. He mastered the "elastic" defence of Von Arnim, who had faced the British at the Somme and now confronted them along the Lys. But the hour when real success was possible had passed. As for Gough, his failure should have resulted in his recall. Instead, he was continued in command of his Fifth Army until the supreme disaster of the following March destroyed it and at last resulted in his elimination from the front.

Gough's failure, and the circumstances of that failure, shook the confidence of the soldiers in their High Command. They were sent against unbroken defences, as Nivelle had sent his troops against similar obstacles on the Craonne Plateau. They failed in the larger sense, as Nivelle's men had failed, and their spirit was broken to a degree as was the spirit of the finest fighting divisions of France a few months before. Men murmured for the first time against the useless sacrifice, as Grant's soldiers murmured even before Cold Harbour. This lack of confidence in commanders was also a factor in the disaster of March, 1918, while behind the army the British public daily became more impatient, more critical, more resentful, as each returning ship brought its terrible harvest from the battlefield and the official lists of casualties mounted higher and higher.

Here, too, begins a break between the Government, the Ministry, and the Army. There is political interference, marked difference of opinion, leading to an insistence in the close of the year on an extension of the British front at the moment when there is denied to Sir Douglas Haig those reinforcements necessary to re-build his shattered divisions. The spring campaign of 1918 will find the British holding a long front with thin lines, while hundreds of thousands of troops are held in England, others scattered from Salonica to Jerusalem, and the confidence of the army itself is shaken. These are the facts which one must consider in watching the development of the Third Battle of Ypres and the second British campaign in Flanders. They are more important than the local successes or failures of the day-by-day fighting.

II. THE STRATEGIC PURPOSE

The purpose of the campaign in Flanders in 1917 changed radically during the progress of the battle. It was the conception of Sir Douglas Haig at the outset that a brusque attack, a great offensive, breaking out of the Ypres salient and flowing down the Lys Valley, would shatter the western flank of the German armies between Lille and the sea; compel an evacuation of the Belgian coast, and particularly of the Bruges-Zeebrügge-Ostend triangle, whence came the greater portion of the submarine scourge; and force a general German retirement at least behind the Scheldt, with a consequent liberation of the great French industrial towns of Lille, Roubaix, and Tourcoing.

For the British the elimination of the submarine base of Bruges was of utmost importance. We have seen the extent to which the submarine attack had scored preliminary successes in March, in April, and in May. When Sir Douglas Haig began his offensive there was still more than a reasonable expectation that by winter the submarine would bring Britain to her knees. The liberation of French soil was bound to have a tremendous moral effect upon the people of France, but the expulsion of the Germans from the Belgian sea coast had become almost a matter of life and death for the British.

In a sense Sir Douglas Haig took up that offensive begun by Sir John French in October, 1914, and speedily transformed into a desperate defensive when Antwerp fell and the Kaiser set out for Calais. An ad-

vance of ten or fifteen miles down the Lys Valley westward toward
Roulers and Courtrai would cut the main line of communication between the coast and the German armies in France; a slight further
advance would bring the railroad from Ghent to Bruges under the fire
of the Allied long-range artillery, while the seizure of the crossings
of the Lys at Menin and Courtrai would ensure the German evacuation of Lille and of their whole front southward to St. Quentin.

Such, in substance, were the larger possibilities and purposes of British strategy in 1917. The British army, advancing out of the Ypres
salient, transforming it into a great sally port, was first to penetrate
between the German forces on the Belgian coast and in France, driving a wedge which would compel a retreat from the coast and the surrender of the submarine bases. So far it was an effort to do on land
what the Navy had failed to do on water, namely, to suppress the submarine weapon. In addition it was designed, by cutting the anchorage
of the western flank of the German armies from the sea to Switzerland,
to open a turning, an enveloping movement around the new Western
flank, compelling the Germans to retire until this flank again found
safe anchorage upon the forts of Antwerp. Conforming to this retirement all the German armies in France would be compelled to withdraw
until they stood at the French frontier. Nivelle had sought to break
the German centre. Haig now undertook to turn the German flank.

One year later exactly, this strategy was again put into operation,
this time under the direction of Plumer in association with King Albert
of Belgium, and in a few brief weeks supreme success was achieved.
Advancing over the Passchendaele Ridge, victorious British and Belgian troops, presently reinforced by French and even by Americans,
compelled, first the evacuation of Ostend, Bruges, and Zeebrügge;
then the abandonment of Lille; and, finally, a retreat to the line of the
Scheldt. At the moment when the Armistice came, this line had been
forced and British troops were in Mons.

It is plain, then, that the strategy was sound, that the calculations
were exact, and that, had British armies been able to accomplish in
1917 what they did a year later, the results would have been what the

THE THIRD BATTLE OF YPRES—PASSCHENDAELE 223

British public and the British High Command looked forward to in 1917. But the chance of success had practically disappeared before the battle opened. The Germans were not compelled to hold the Flanders front with a limited number of troops. On the contrary, they were able to bring division after division from the Russian front, with the result that not infrequently the troops that attacked were weary, while those that received the attack were fresh; nor was there any limit to German numbers which allowed the British any decisive advantage.

The supreme blunder of the Flanders campaign lay in undertaking it at all, after the events of June and July had demonstrated how completely the Russian Revolution had eliminated Russian armies and transformed the military situation. To persist—in the face of preliminary checks and in the face of the inescapable fact that each day German resources and numbers were mounting—was a blunder equally great. The British army was put to a task that no army could accomplish. It was kept at the task under conditions both military and climatic which could only result in the depression of morale and in the multiplication of losses due alike to the enemy's fire and to weather.

Haig and Sir William Robertson, following Grant's phrase, set out to "fight it out on this line if it took all summer"; but, unlike Grant, they were in the presence of an enemy who could replace men and material as rapidly as they themselves, so that to invoke attrition was as foolish as Mrs. Partington's celebrated attempt to dispose of the Atlantic with a mop. The ultimate failure led to the removal of Sir William Robertson and gravely compromised Haig. He survived both this decline in popularity and the subsequent further decline incident to his terrible defeats in the spring. His brilliant operation which began in August, 1918, regained for him no small share of his lost laurels, as Grant revived his shrunken fame between Five Forks and Appomattox; but in both cases, although with unequal justice, the campaign of attrition led to personal unpopularity and national depression.

As the struggle progressed, the objectives changed. The reduction of the Bruges submarine base, the approach to Ghent, the arrival at Roulers and Courtrai, became as remote possibilities as the taking of

Cambrai and Douai in the Somme time. By October a British army which had set out to turn the western flank of the German armies in the west was painfully struggling up the slopes of the Passchendaele Ridge. Its single purpose now was to finish the campaign in possession of that high ground to clear which had been its programme for the opening days of the offensive.

This much was achieved. When winter came, by the anniversary of the repulse of the final German effort in 1914, British troops looked down upon all the broad stretch of the plain of Flanders exactly as, the year before, they had passed the crest of the ridge south of Bapaume. They had won the ground for which they had striven. They had driven the Germans from positions that had seemed impregnable. The achievement of the British soldier was beyond praise, but it was a victory that yielded no fruits and opened up no horizons. Not only was it too late to push forward, but already the accession of German strength in the west had condemned the British, like the French, to the defensive, and only a few months after British, Canadian, and Australian troops had mounted gloriously to the crest of Passchendaele Ridge, they were compelled to evacuate it ignominiously and fall back into the old shell-cast area of the original salient exactly as the French a little later had to surrender in a single day the whole of the Craonne Plateau, won by months of effort and untold sacrifices.

III. MESSINES—"WHITESHEET"

Before Sir Douglas Haig could launch his major offensive at the Ypres salient, a preliminary operation was necessary. The salient itself had been born as a consequence of an incomplete British turning movement in October, 1914, followed by an unsuccessful German enveloping thrust later in October and in November. To understand the situation it is necessary to glance again at the topography of the Ypres salient. Two ranges of hills—one coming from the west eastward, and the other from the north, southward—make a right angle due south of the town of Ypres, which stands in the flats. Still a third and lower ridge, proceeding from west to east, north of Ypres, gives the

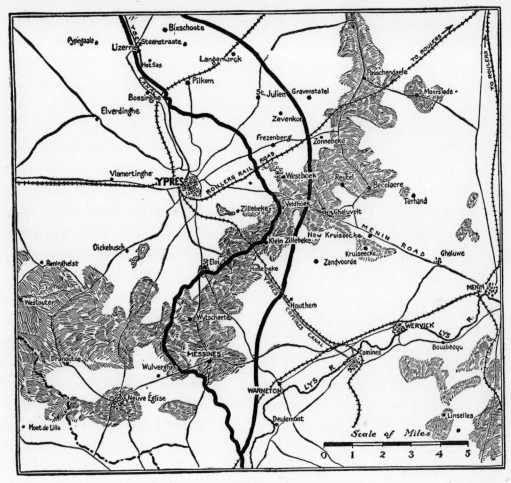

THE YPRES FRONT

The left-hand black line shows the front of the Ypres Salient at the beginning of the Third Battle of Ypres. The right-hand line shows the ground gained in June when Plumer captured the Messines-Wytschaete Ridge, and in August and September in Gough's two attacks. The shaded portions show the high ground, practically all of which, north of the Menin Road from Gheluvelt to Passchendaele, was captured in the last stage of the offensive.

impression, on the contour map, of three sides of a square enclosing Ypres itself. The southern ridge from west to east rises to the heights of Scherpenburg and Kemmel, memorable in the fighting of 1918, but until that time well behind the battle-line, and supplying the best British observation post in the whole salient. Where this Kemmel Ridge intersects the northern and the southern ridges there were situated the small towns of Messines and Wytschaete—the latter of which, in the argot of the "Tommy," was "Whitesheet." The northern side of the square takes its name from the town of Pilkem and appears in all the battle reports as the Pilkem Ridge. On November 1, 1914, the Germans had advanced over the Messines-"Whitesheet" Ridge and driven the British and Indian Cavalry into the flats south and east of Ypres. . In April and May, 1915, they had taken the Pilkem Ridge. They thus gripped the British in Ypres as one might hold an object between the thumb and the forefinger, the thumb representing the "Whitesheet" Ridge; the forefinger, the Pilkem Ridge; the object being Ypres. From the Pilkem Ridge the Germans looked down on Ypres itself, but from the "Whitesheet" Ridge they looked behind Ypres and had under their vision all the roads by which British troops and British supplies approached the ruined city. Entering Ypres by daylight was a hazardous feat and automobiles speeded over the road under shell fire, while even at night the highways were systematically "watered."

Actually this German position has been accurately described as resembling a stadium from the benches of which an audience looks out upon a football game. Like the players the British were far down, but, unlike the football players, their operations were greeted, not by cheers, but by shells. Nothing could move by day into or out of Ypres without inviting shell fire.

So bad was this position, the worst on the whole western front, that ever since November, 1914, a bitter controversy had gone forward in the British army as to whether Ypres should be held or evacuated. To evacuate it and fall back to the Kemmel-Scherpenburg Ridge and the still higher summits of the same range to the westward would have been to surrender ground of little value, costing many casualties each week to hold, and it would have brought the Germans down in to the plain under direct observation as they now held the British.

But as in the case of Verdun, the moral value outweighed the military. Because they had paid so much to hold Ypres, the British recognized the moral victory the Germans would win by laying hands upon the ashes of the old Belgian town of which there was nothing left intact save the lower walls of the old town jail. In addition, to surrender

Ypres meant to abandon the last remnant of Belgian soil and thus enable the Germans to complete their conquest of King Albert's nation.

So, week after week and month after month the British had held on to Ypres. The "Wipers" salient was held and the expense in life, which was great, was borne by the successors of that Regular Army, the flower of which slept on the forward slopes of those hills now just within the German lines. In April and May, 1918, when the German victory to the south brought the enemy even to the summit of Kemmel and the salient became ten times as bad, the British still held on.

But if there was to be an offensive out of the Ypres salient—if it were to be transformed into a sally-port—the first step must necessarily be the re-conquest of the "Whitesheet" Ridge, since no preparations within the salient could be made without German direct observation and except under direct German artillery fire as long as the Germans sat on the crest of the ridge marked by the ruined villages of Messines and Wytschaete. Therefore—precisely as Pershing, in the following year, before he advanced out of the Verdun salient in the great battle of the Meuse-Argonne, seized the St. Mihiel salient as a necessary preliminary—Sir Douglas Haig gave now his first attention to the Messines-"Whitesheet" Ridge.

Once more it is necessary to recall the fact that, in the level country of northern France and western Belgium, hills which elsewhere would hardly achieve a name are "mountains" and the merest swells decorated by the name of ridges. Messines Ridge at its highest point near Wytschaete was barely 200 feet high, while it was nowhere 150 feet above the walls of Ypres, some three miles due north. The British soldiers did not scale the heights nor even climb obstacles comparable with Vimy or with Craonne. They advanced over a gently rising slope, the upward pitch of which was hardly discernible to the eye from Kemmel or from Scherpenburg. By contrast they advanced over a country which for nearly three years had been in German hands and on which the Germans had lavished all their wealth of material and expended all their military ingenuity and skill in fortifications. If "Whitesheet"

Ridge was not a natural obstacle of forbidding strength it had been transformed into an extraordinarily difficult military obstacle.

The preparations for the attack had been under the immediate direction of General Plumer, whose Second Army had held the salient from the time of the Second Battle of Ypres onward. Plumer's Chief Intelligence Officer, Colonel (afterward General) Harrington to whom no small part of the credit for the achievement is due—had by skilful observation located all the German batteries, strong points, and "pill boxes." The position had been studied with every possible care; rail-roads had been built; roads had been pushed forward; material had been brought up; water had been piped with such great skill that eight days after the Messines-"Whitesheet" Ridge had fallen half a million gallons of water was daily reaching points which had been within the German lines at the opening of the attack.

A striking circumstance of the Messines-"Whitesheet" affair, unique not only in previous warfare but in the World War as well, was the explosion of nineteen mines which gave the signal for the departure of the troops. Twenty-four of these mines had been constructed; the work had begun as early as July, 1915, and greatly extended after January, 1916. A total of 8,000 yards of galleries were driven and over a million pounds of explosives were used in them. The Prime Minister of Great Britain, at his house in Downing Street, London, on the morning of June 7th, heard the boom of these mines when they were fired. Favoured for once with good weather in the days preceding the attack, and thanks to the skilful preparations and observations of Harrington, the British guns were able to take all the German works under their fire, precisely as, on the morning of attack, they were able to smother dugouts and trenches alike with their fire, which surpassed in intensity even the gigantic bombardment accompanying the attack at Vimy.

At 3.10 on the morning of June 7th the nineteen mines were ex-ploded simultaneously, the British artillery opened, and the infantry left their trenches. English, Irish, Australians, and New Zealanders were represented in the shock troops, while Ulster and South-of-Ireland troops competed for the honour of being the first to reach their objectives, and Major William Redmond, brother of the leader of the Irish party in Parliament, was one of the distinguished victims of German fire.

Two and a half hours after the British troops left their trenches, "Whitesheet" Ridge was in the hands of Ulster regiments; New Zealand troops reached Messines by seven o'clock, and before noon Plumer's victorious troops were moving down the eastern slopes of the Messines-"Whitesheet" Ridge. In the afternoon they penetrated battery positions and captured German field guns. Before sunset every single objective had been taken. The Ypres salient had been abolished, the eastern flank of Haig's forthcoming offensive had been established. On the previous day the enemy, as usual, stood on the "Whitesheet" Ridge looking downward upon all the roads leading into Ypres. The following morning the British stood on the same ridge looking downward over the plain toward Lille, toward Tourcoing, toward the whole valley of the Lys. From "Plug Street" to Hill 60 the high ground was British; 7,200 prisoners, 67 guns, 94 trench mortars, and 294 machine guns, were the harvest of material garnered in this battle, while the British losses were hardly more than double the total of prisoners, counting less than 16,000—an ultimate demonstration of the supreme skill with which the guns had been handled, while for once the Germans attempted no counter-attack.

Plumer's feat at the "Whitesheet" Ridge must be compared with Petain's two offensives at Verdun in 1916, and with his later operations at Verdun and Malmaison in the year we are now examining. In that comparison the British achievement loses nothing. On the technical side it would be difficult to imagine anything more perfect than this Messines-"Whitesheet" operation. It had no grandiose purpose. Its objectives were rigidly limited. There was no more thought of an effort to reach Lille than there was an idea to take Metz when Pershing abolished the St. Mihiel salient. The operation is not to be compared with the Somme or the later Flanders fighting to which it was the prelude. It was even less far-looking than the Vimy attack, but, within its limits, it was beyond praise; following the victory of the Third Army at Arras it thrilled the British public, gave new confidence to the army, and aroused hopes and expectations, the withering of which was bound to bring grievous disappointment and dangerous depression.

IV. THE ATTACK OF JULY 31ST

Having cleared his eastern flank, Haig planned to begin the main operation in Flanders early in July. But again unavoidable delays, in part at least due to conditions in the French army, compelled several postponements, and it was not until July 31st that he was able to begin. In this attack even the semblance of surprise was absent. The Germans knew long in advance where the blow was to fall and were able to make counter preparation. It was only after Cambrai and Riga that the element of surprise was restored. In this opening battle the British commander had under his direction and actually engaged three armies, whose positions from east to west were as follows: The French First Army, under Anthoine; the British Fifth Army, commanded by Gough; and the British Second Army, which, under Plumer's direction, had already captured the Messines Ridge while in later operations the Belgian army participated. The front on which he made his attack was some fifteen miles in extent, stretching from the Lys River east of Wytschaete to the Yser Canal at Steenstraat, some three or four miles north of Ypres.

It is necessary now to look once more at the topography of this country which had became familiar to British and French publics as the scene of two desperate battles in 1914 and 1915. From the ruined city of Ypres to the north and the east a number of highways radiate like the spokes of a wheel. Two of them, one leading due north and the other practically straight east, form a right angle. Between the two arms of this angle lies the battlefield of Third "Wipers," while the roads themselves —the Pilkem to the north and the Menin to the east—were the central circumstance in the Second and the First Battle of Ypres, respectively. It was the Pilkem road to Ypres which was opened for hours in April, 1915, after the first German "poison-gas" attack had broken the French Colonial troops. The Menin road shares with the Albert-Bapaume highway at the Somme, and the Bar-le-Duc national route to Verdun, the sombre distinction of being one of the three bloodiest highways in history.   Down this road toward the Lys Sir John French's first regiments had marched in October, 1914; and up this road, a few days later, from the valley had come German hosts, crowding on the way to Calais.   The Pilkem Ridge, north of the town which gives it its name, reaches the southern fringe of the forest of Houthulst, the most considerable woodland in western Belgium, while the Menin road four miles out of Ypres and just west of Gheluvelt reaches the crest of the high ground and begins its descent to the Lys Valley.   Houthulst Forest and the high ground near Gheluvelt were the two anchorages of the German position, which rested like an arch on these two abutments and between them curved inward following the high ground, with Passchendaele as the keystone of the arch.

Between the Pilkem and the Menin roads three other highways lead northward and eastward.   Just east of the Pilkem road is the Langemarck highway, on which Sir Douglas Haig had met the Germans in the 1914 battle.   East of the Langemarck road is that of Poelcappelle, also the scene of desperate fighting in October, 1914.   Eastward again is the Zonnebeke highway which intersects the Passchendaele-Gheluvelt road just east of Zonnebeke.   This last road extends from the Menin road at Gheluvelt to the Poelcappelle road at West-roosebeke along the crest of that Passchendaele Ridge which was now to become the chief objective of the new battle of Flanders.   It also marks fairly accurately the limit of British advance.   It was the purpose of British strategy, advancing on a front between the Pilkem and the Menin roads, to break the German arch between the Houthulst Forest and the high ground at Gheluvelt, and, driving northward through Roulers, reach Ghent.   The distance to be covered was less than that which the Allies had gained on the Somme front as a result of the Battle of the Somme and the subsequent German retreat, but the shorter advance would suffice to compel the Germans to abandon the Belgian coast.

The first blow, delivered on July 1st, was designed to penetrate the first, second, and—in places—the third series of German defences.   Its general front was marked, for the French army, by the town of Bix-schoote—rather more than a mile from their starting place at the Yser Canal at Steenstraat in the low ground touching the inundated districts surrounding Dixmude—and for the British, by the western bank of the little muddy brook flowing north across their front from the high ground on the Menin road just north of Westhoek and crossing the Langemarck road half a mile south of Langemarck, the St. Julien road at St. Julien, and the Zonnebeke road just east of Verlorenhoek. The objectives along the Menin road were Hooge and the tangle of woodlands and ruins to which the British soldier had given such picturesque names as Shrewsbury Forest, Stirling Castle, Clapham Junction, Inverness Copse, Glencorse Wood. The muddy brook, so important a detail in the battle despite its insignificance, is known along its course as the Hannebeek, Steenbeck, St. Jansbeek, and finally in the French sector as Martje Vaart.

At 3.50 on the morning of July 31st, after a long period of artillery preparation, the first phase in the major offensive developed. The chief work in this stage was to be performed by Gough's Fifth Army, which was in the centre. It was the mission of the French on the right and of Plumer on the left, to keep pace with the progress of Gough in the centre, and by their pressure upon the Germans, lessen the resisting power that Von Arnim could exert against Gough. The French share was the more interesting, minor as it was, because their objective was the ground lost by French Colonials in April, 1915, as a result of the gas attack.

The attack was, on the whole, a striking success. The French speedily reached all their objectives, and thereafter passed the little brook which comes down from Pilkem, and took Bixschoote. The British took and passed Pilkem; entered—but were unable to hold—St. Julien, although they captured it finally three days later; passed through Verlorenhoek and reached Frezenberg on the Zonnebeke road, while they took Hooge and reached "Clapham Junction" on the Menin road.

At the end of the first day, therefore, the Fifth Army had carried

HEAVY WEATHER IN THE NORTH SEA

The bow of this cruiser is drowned in a smother of foam, as she drives ahead through the big seas. The three round caps in the foreground are covers of the observation posts used by the turret captain and the gun captain of the bow-chasers

PIRACY PHOTOGRAPHED FROM THE AIR—II

The breaking up of a torpedoed merchantman. A few minutes after this photograph was taken she disappeared. But for the presence of the hovering airship this would have been another case of "*spurlos versenkt*."

From the painting by Wilhelm Ritschel

NO RESPECT FOR AGE OR SEX

On the *Lusitania* were women and little children by the score. Small wonder then that the sea viper had no pity for this hoary and majestic relic of the sea's more chivalrous days

THIS WAS FOUR HUNDRED POUNDS OF T. N. T.

This egg of a German mine-laying submarine was smashed by a rifle bullet, fired from the quarter-deck of an Allied destroyer

A COLD VIGIL IN THE NORTH SEA

A striking silhouette showing the forepart of an airship and two members of the crew. The U-boats feared aircraft no less than destroyers, for the airmen could spy out a submarine from afar and quietly let fall a bomb upon her, with little or no danger to themselves.

AFTER TWISTING THE DRAGON'S TAIL

H.M.S. *Vindictive*, back in port after the successful raid on Zeebrugge, was the proudest if not the nattiest ship in the British Navy. Her funnels were riddled with holes, part of her bridge was blown away and she was battered and scarred in dozens of places

MAKING ASSURANCE DOUBLY SURE

As she passed over a spot where a submarine had submerged, this destroyer evidently hurled depth charges to starboard and port from the "Y" howitzer on her stern

MANNING THE RAIL

This picture was taken from the fire-control station on the foremast of a battleship, as the King of England was reviewing the victorious Anglo-American fleet. After the review he inspected our *New York* and decorated our Rear-Admiral Rodman

all of the German first system between the Menin road and the Zonnebeke road.   North of the Zonnebeke road they had also taken the German second system as far as St. Julien.   North of St. Julien on the
Poelcappelle road they and the French had passed the German second
line, the British being close to Langemarck, the French in Bixschoote,
while the British Second Army south of the Menin road had fulfilled its
mission perfectly.   The British alone took 6,100 prisoners and 2,500 guns
while the French also took prisoners.

It had been the purpose of Haig to follow up the preliminary success
at once and push the Germans off the Pilkem Ridge, thus depriving them
of this second line of observation, as they had already been deprived of
the first on "Whitesheet" Ridge in June, by a prompt general attack.
Unhappily the weather now changed and there began that long period of
almost incessant rains which was as fatal to the hopes and prospects of
the British army in Flanders as the early onset of winter in Russia had
been to the Napoleonic army a little more than a century before.   Of
the consequences of this rain Sir Douglas Haig said in his official report:

The weather had been threatening throughout the day [of July 31], and had
rendered the work of our aeroplanes very difficult from the commencement of the
battle.   During the afternoon, while fighting was still in progress, rain began, and fell
steadily all night.   Thereafter, for four days, the rain continued without cessation,
and for several days afterward the weather remained stormy and unsettled.   The
low-lying, clayey soil, torn by shells and sodden with rain, turned to a succession of
vast muddy pools.   The valleys of the choked and overflowing streams were speedily
transformed into long stretches of bog, impassable except by a few well-defined tracks,
which became marks for the enemy's artillery.   To leave these tracks was to risk
death by drowning, and in the course of the subsequent fighting on several occasions
both men and pack animals were lost in this way.   In these conditions operations of
any magnitude became impossible, and the resumption of our offensive was necessarily
postponed until a period of fine weather should allow the ground to recover.

As had been the case in the Arras battle, this unavoidable delay in the development
of our offensive was of the greatest service to the enemy.   Valuable time was lost, the
troops opposed to us were able to recover from the disorganization produced by our
first attack, and the enemy was given the opportunity to bring up reinforcements.

Meantime two local offensives, one by the Germans and one by the
British, attracted attention without materially changing the general
situation.   From 1914 onward the Allies had maintained a bridge-

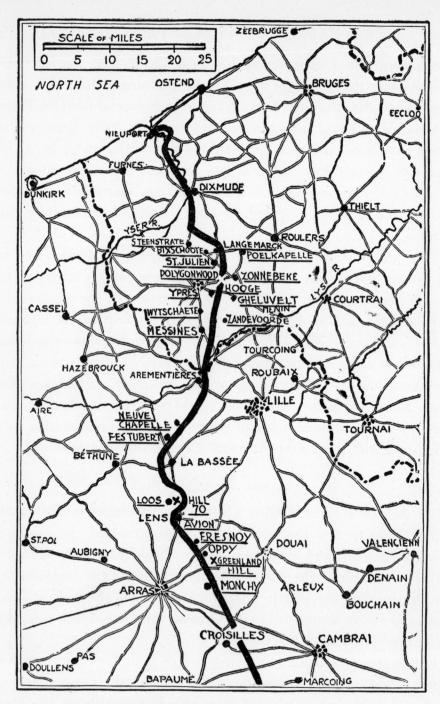

BRITISH BATTLEFIELDS IN MAY, JUNE, AUGUST, AND
SEPTEMBER, 1917

The solid black line indicates the front in September. The broken line in the
upper right-hand corner shows the Dutch frontier. One of the chief objectives of
this campaign was to drive a wedge between the German submarine bases at
Zeebrügge, Ostend, and Bruges and the German positions in France and thus
compel an evacuation of the Belgian coast and the submarine nests.

head beyond the Yser north of Nieuport and looking toward Ostend and the dunes that front the sea. On the morning of July 10th, almost immediately after the British had taken over this sector from the French, the German suddenly attacked on this two-mile front, destroyed two British battalions, and took the northern half of the bridge-head. His success in the southern half was less complete but to all intents and purposes this Lombartzyde affair abolished any menace at his extreme northern flank, while it scored for him a brilliant if relatively slight triumph.

To counterbalance this, on the 15th of August, the Canadians—who had already taken Vimy Ridge—moved up again over the barren plateau which had seen the costly failure of Loos; mounted the gradual slope to the summit of Hill 70, taken and lost by the Scottish on September 25, 1915; and consolidated their position looking down into the doomed coal town of Lens—already partially destroyed by the Germans at the Vimy time and now destined to become the most conspicuous of the many mournful ruined cities of northern France. One thousand prisoners and possession of one of the most valuable observation points along the British front were the gains of this brilliant little affair.

V. THE SECOND ATTACK

On the the 16th of August a slight improvement in the weather enabled Haig to deal his second blow. Meantime St. Julien, on the Poelcappelle road, and Westhoek, above the Menin road, had fallen. In this second phase the Allied objectives included the bridge-head of Drie Grachten on the Martje Vaart for the French, the town of Lange-marck and thence southward to the German third line, which crossed the Menin road just east of Gheluvelt.

In this attack Gough's Fifth Army, which again bore the brunt of the contest, failed almost completely. On the north, Langemarck was taken and held, but southward from the Poelcappelle to the Menin roads the gains were insignificant and the losses terrific. Von Arnim's system of "elastic" defence sufficed to break the force of British attack, while German reserves, pouring in at the critical moment, compelled the British to surrender practically all their gains south of St. Julien. Two thousand one hundred prisoners and thirty guns, with Langemarck on the British front and Drie Grachten on the French, were insignificant rewards for tremendous efforts and long casualty lists. The consequences of this failure were the revision of the method of British attack and the extension of the front of Plumer's Second Army so that thenceforth the major work fell on this army and its commander, whose new front now comprised practically all the major objectives, including the Passchendaele Ridge. Gough had failed and should have been recalled. Instead, he was permitted to continue—in a subordinate rôle.

Again it is essential to recognize the element of time. The Flanders offensive—which was to have begun in the first days of July and, before the middle of the month, to have ended in the clearing out of the Germans from all the high ground from the Houthulst Forest to the southern end of the "Whitesheet" Ridge—had by mid-August only reached the western slopes of the main Passchendaele Ridge and still fell short of the forest of Houthulst.

VI. THE END OF THE BATTLE

Following the attack of the 17th of August the weather turned bad again and it was not until September 20th that a new thrust was possible. On this day, under Plumer's direction, the British succeeded where in August they had failed. Before the skilful methods of the commander of the British Second Army the German's "elastic" defence crumbled. British artillery was trained, first, to deal with the "pill boxes," machine-gun nests and strong points, and second, to abolish the peril of German counter-attacks. Three thousand prisoners and the possession of that high ground along the Menin road west of Gheluvelt— which was one foundation of the German defensive arch—were taken, while desperate fighting on the following days in Polygon Woods at last yielded to the Australians the forward slopes of the final crest of Passchendaele Ridge itself.

On the 4th of October a new blow brought the British into Poelcappelle, through Zonnebeke, and to the outskirts of Gheluvelt, while the Australians, crossing the Gheluvelt-Passchendaele road at Broodseinde on the Zonnebeke road actually mounted the crest of the final ridge itself. Subsequent attacks stretching through the whole of this month brought the British and the French to the edge of Houthulst Forest, to the north of Pilkem and to the outskirts of Passchendaele itself. Finally, on November 6th, Passchendaele fell—a new achievement for Canada, whose sons had already planted their maple-leaf standard on Vimy Ridge and Hill 70. Four days later the capture of Goudberg Spur north of Passchendaele completed the mastery of the ridge and ended the Third Battle of Ypres.

Meantime, however, the Italian disaster at Caporetto had called British troops and General Plumer to the Venetian front. The Flanders success could therefore have no morrow. The British had won the ridge; they had taken Passchendaele, an "island in a sea of mud"; but an exploitation of their success—an advance down the valley of the Lys, the expulsion of the German troops from the Belgian coast—these things were no longer possible. Twenty-four thousand prisoners, 74 guns, 941 machine guns, and 138 trench mortars were captured by the British in three and a half months of fighting, and the smallness of these captures in men and even more so in guns is perhaps the best evidence alike of the stubbornness and skill of the German resistance and of the wholly limited character of British triumph.

Such, in its larger aspects, was the Third Battle of "Wipers." In it the British regained practically all of the ground lost in the two earlier battles. They took possession of positions which were in fact the keys to the Belgian coast and to the German front in Belgium. If, in the following spring, they could have attacked from the lines thus wrested from the foe, a German retreat would have been inevitable. When they were able in September of the following year to advance over Passchendaele Ridge, exactly the things that Haig had hoped to accomplish in the previous year were achieved, but unhappily with the opening of the campaign of 1918 the initiative passed to the Germans, and the successes of Ludendorff at the Somme and at the Lys in the following

March and April were to result in the entire negation of the hard-won British gain in the preceding campaign.

But for the Russian Revolution—perhaps in spite of the Russian Revolution—had the weather been the ally of the British rather than of the Germans, a far greater success might have resulted. As it was, the British had gained a position of great importance which they were subsequently unable to make use of, and the colossal losses which they had suffered had weakened the spirit of the army and shaken the confidence of the British public. Whatever one may say of the Somme there can be no real dispute of the fact that, despite the slight battle-field gain, the Third Battle of Ypres was, from all the larger strategic aspects of the war, a German victory which had consequences of utmost gravity in the following year. The German had held British and French armies off during the period necessary to realize the advantages gained by Russian collapse—henceforth for six months the superiority in numbers on the western front would be his—would remain his until America arrived.

CHAPTER ELEVEN

CAMBRAI—JERUSALEM

I
NEW METHODS

On November 20th, while the Flanders offensive was expiring in mud and misery, the joy bells of London were set in motion by a military success which opened one of the most extraordinary conflicts of the war. The Battle of Cambrai must, for Americans, not in its tactical circumstances but in its course, suggest that Civil War struggle known both as Shiloh and as Pittsburgh Landing. In that fight the army of Albert Sidney Johnston totally surprised Grant's force, and pushed forward until it became a matter of the closest calculation whether the Confederates would drive the Union forces into the river before night fell, or the Union forces would just hold out.

In the Battle of Cambrai, by the most successful single surprise attack up to that moment on the western front, the British broke through three of the four German defence systems, penetrated the fourth, and very nearly reached the open country beyond. A little more luck and the British cavalry would have been in Cambrai, but as the Union troops stood at Shiloh until night, when reinforcements arrived, and then turned and drove the Confederates from the field of victory, so the Germans held on and, receiving reinforcements, organized their counter-offensive with skill and deliberation, drove the British from every position of importance which they had captured, and in addition—within a week after they had themselves been the surprised—surprised and overran a long section of the British front.

Cambrai is important, however, not because of the outcome of the battle that was fought within sight of it, but because in that battle two methods of offensive were both effectively tried out and these two methods were both to be applied the following year and to revolutionize the character of the war: in the case of Germany to win stupendous successes which just fell short of a decision, and, in the case of the Allies, to turn the tide, after four years of strain and disaster. Different as were both methods of attack, each of them achieved the same result by restoring the element of surprise.

The three years which extended from the First Battle of Ypres to the fight before Cambrai are marked by many efforts to bring off a surprise attack, some of which, like the German gas attack at Ypres and their artillery avalanche at Verdun, scored partial successes. At Verdun the Germans actually got through all the permanent lines of French defence, but on a front too narrow to enable them to exploit their gains before French reserves arrived. At the Second Battle of Ypres the German progress distanced the expectations of the victors by so much that they were unprepared to take advantage of the opportunity during the hours when the Pilkem road to Ypres was open. At the Somme there was still an effort at a surprise, but the German was not taken unawares. In the Third Battle of Ypres no surprise was even contemplated. It had been accepted as axiomatic that the very vastness of the preparations necessary for commencing all but strictly local offensives precluded concealment, and German and British newspapers, with equal frankness, indicated that the British effort of 1917 would be in Flanders.

The elimination of the element of surprise had abolished any real hope of penetration to the extent of a "break through" on the western front, and the very belief that no surprise was possible was the foundation of the widespread conviction that the war would end with no great change in the position of the opposing lines. One set of staff officers after another had wrestled with the problem of restoring the element of surprise—of bringing off a surprise sufficiently great to enable large forces to break through all the lines in a given sector and begin that march to victory which would follow the shattering of the enemy's systems of defence. At the Somme the British had introduced the tank, but the tank had achieved only local and restricted success. By moving their field artillery forward the Germans were able to bring off many direct hits, disabling the new engines, while by mines they were similarly successful. Moreover, a tank was able to operate to advantage on relatively level ground only, and, once a battlefield had been torn up by the tremendous cannonades which were a detail in contemporary warfare, the tank became ineffective. The very size of the first tanks had been a further handicap, alike because of the target they offered the enemy guns, and the unwieldiness they displayed in operation.

At the Somme, despite local success in penetrating uncut wire and reducing machine-gun nests in ruined villages, in their first day, the tanks had fallen far short of the expectations their appearance had raised. In Flanders a year later they had proven a total failure, as a result of the character of the country, but in the Battle of Cambrai, in which tanks were tried again—with the foregone conclusion that a further failure would send them to the scrap heap—they demonstrated possibilities which had been unsuspected. In the first place, their field of operation was practically virgin territory, which had seen no considerable fighting and little artillery destruction. It was level country, but with sufficient elevation to escape the bogs and morasses of Flanders. In addition the tanks were used in huge numbers and handled with consummate skill. As a result, the Battle of Cambrai demonstrated that the tank would take the place of the long artillery preparation, which in itself could only be made after such an enormous concentration of guns and munitions as inevitably betrayed to the enemy the direction of the coming attack. The tanks themselves could be brought up secretly in the night; they could be launched without warning, and they could be counted upon to cut the enemy's wires and smash his strong points far mor esuccessfully than the old-fashioned artillery preparation, while the enemy would have no hint of what was coming.

Only the size of the tank proved a handicap. Already this had been perceived, and the French and the British—but particularly the French —were engaged in constructing in large numbers that "whippet" tank which was to play such an important rôle in the offensives of the following year. Thus while the tank attack at Cambrai, despite its initial success, just missed making possible complete victory, it disclosed possibilities which led to the reorganization of Allied offensive tactics, based upon a coördination of the infantry with the tanks, which in turn led straight to the completely successful surprise attacks of the French and Americans on July 18th, and of the British on August 8th in the 1918 battles of the Second Marne and the Third Somme—battles which together wrecked all German hopes of victory and at last prepared the way for the liberation of France and the defeat of Germany.

By contrast the German surprise tactics relied rather upon human than mechanical means. At Riga, in September, Von Hutier had completely overwhelmed the Russians by suddenly throwing against the rapidly disintegrating Slav forces large bodies of troops secretly assembled. The method of bringing these troops to the operative front was extremely ingenious. They were concentrated three or four days' march in rear of the front—so far back that, though their presence might be signalled by air observers, there was nothing to show where they would be put in. They were then moved up by night, concealed in villages and forests during the day, so that they arrived on the battlefield without having awakened the enemy's suspicions, and then they were put in, after a brief artillery preparation deriving its efficacy from the use of gas and smoke shells, which deluged the back areas, paralyzed the hostile artillery, and prevented the rapid approach of reserves.

Successful at Riga the Hutier tactics were then employed against the Italians at Caporetto, where they brought off one of the greatest successes of the war. They were then tried against the British in the final phase of Cambrai, where they transformed what had been a considerable British victory into a sterile venture, and finally, in the following year—in March in Picardy, in April in Flanders, and in May on the Chemin-des-Dames—they resulted in hitherto unparalleled successes, which almost won the war.

Thus, while its results were unimportant, the Battle of Cambrai is of utmost interest on the military side because in it were employed two offensive methods new in themselves, each of which restored the element of surprise without which victory was impossible, and the deadlock of trench warfare destined to be permanent. And yet, oddly enough, neither side sufficiently recognized the threat in the new enemy tactics to prepare against it. Since the Germans possessed the initiative at the opening of the next campaign they were able to employ their method first, and the circumstances of the British disaster of March 21st, on ground not far distant from the battlefield of Cambrai itself, exactly recalled their experience of November, 1917.

II. PURPOSE AND TOPOGRAPHY

British strategy at Cambrai was based upon the following calculations. The operation in Flanders had been drowned. It was no longer possible to move about Ypres, and the armies engaged in the conflict on the British side were exhausted by their efforts and shaken by their losses. Nevertheless, it was essential to do something before the campaign closed, if only to prevent the Germans from sending troops to that Italian front on which there had now occurred the disaster of Caporetto, which threatened to put Italy out of the war.

Sir Douglas Haig, and all Allied military authorities, had recognized that, as a result of the Russian collapse, the Germans would be able to pass to the offensive in the following year. But it seemed possible to strike one more blow, achieve a local success which might restore Allied morale, aid the Italians by diverting German divisions, and not impossibly improve the front on which the Allies would have to meet the storm that was soon to break.

Such an offensive could have no far-looking objectives. Sir Douglas Haig lacked the reserves to begin a new operation of the magnitude of either the Somme or of Flanders, while the season of the year precluded any long continuation of the battle. In point of fact, he lacked the troops necessary to venture upon any offensive. Such forces as he was able to muster were, as the events proved, incapable of exploiting a really great gain when it was made; were insufficient to continue the battle when the apparent approach of decisive victory again tempted the Commander-in-Chief to pursue the engagement; and were unable, in the last phase, to prevent the Germans in their turn from surprising British divisions, breaking the old British front, and coming within an acc of achieving as great a success as the British themselves missed by an equally small margin. The Battle of Cambrai, then, belongs to that considerable number of gambles of which Gallipoli and the first dash to Bagdad were even more unfortunate examples. Like them it had its brilliant opening phase, which aroused hopes incapable of realization, and in the end brought a depression dangerous in the extreme.

The country selected by Sir Douglas Haig for this offensive was a seven-mile front mainly included between two great national highways: the Amiens-Cambrai road coming up from Albert across the battlefield of the Somme and from Bapaume to Cambrai across the country devastated by the great German retreat, and the Péronne-Cambrai road coming up from the south and joining the St. Quentin road at the Scheldt Canal, a few miles south of Cambrai. This country is level with low swells, affording wide views. On the Bapaume road, where the British attack began, it is possible to see Cambrai, with its spires and chimneys, some eight miles away, with Bourlon Woods, one of the main circumstances of the battle, to the west of it. In the same way, standing on the Péronne road, one has an equally far-swinging view, although Cambrai itself is hidden behind the low hills north of the Scheldt Canal. The generally level nature of the country offered an admirable field of operations for the tanks. Nor were there any such elaborate systems of defences based upon natural obstacles as the British armies had met on Vimy Ridge and the French on the Craonne Plateau. The only considerable obstacle was the double barrier of the Scheldt River and the Scheldt Canal, which crossed the route of the British advance diagonally but behind three of the four German defensive systems. The Canal du Nord at the other end of the battlefield, while more considerable, was successfully turned.

It was the purpose of Haig, using the British Third Army—which Allenby had led to victory at Arras, and Sir Julian Byng, who had commanded the Canadians in the Vimy attack, now directed—to surprise the Germans in positions between the Bapaume and Péronne roads, break through their various systems of defence, push across the Scheldt

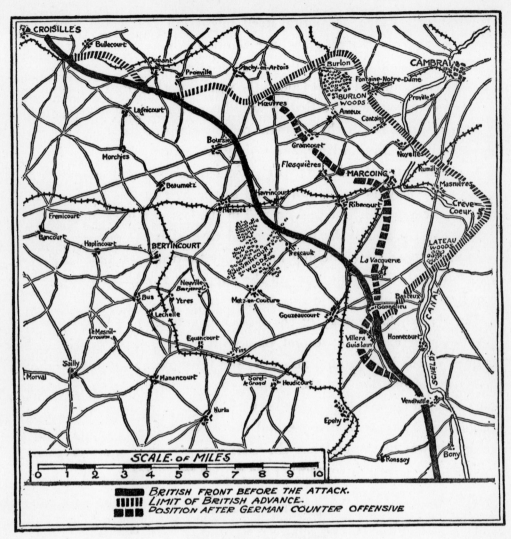

THE BATTLE OF CAMBRAI

Canal, take Bourlon Woods on the west and the high ground beyond the Scheldt Canal on the east.

The capture of this high ground behind the Scheldt Canal would so establish the British flank as to render it secure against German counter-attacks, while the possession of Bourlon would give Byng a position behind the Hindenburg Line, facing Arras, comparable with that the Germans occupied with respect of Ypres as long as they held the Messines-

"Whitesheet" Ridge. Cambrai itself might fall but would certainly be at the mercy of British guns once Bourlon Woods, which dominated it, were taken, and the Germans would lose effective possession of one of the most vital railroad centres along the whole western front. In Haig's plan he calculated that the British would have forty-eight hours, gained by their surprise, before the Germans could concentrate reserves in sufficient numbers. In that time, and mainly in the first twenty-four hours, he hoped to seize Bourlon, cross the Scheldt Canal, and establish his flank on the heights to the north and to the east of this barrier, and, through the gap which he had opened in the German lines, pour in his cavalry exactly as Nivelle had expected to exploit his victory on the Craonne Plateau by launching his cavalry toward Laon and La Fère. A retreat of the Germans from all the stretch of the Hindenburg Line from Lens to Cambrai would thus be inevitable.

But the whole strategy of the British commander depended, first, upon a complete surprise; second, on a swift passage of the Scheldt and conquest of the high ground above it; and third, on an equally prompt occupation of Bourlon Woods. Unless the close of the first forty-eight hours brought these things, together with the effective breaking of all of the German systems of defence and the successful penetration of the cavalry, it was inevitable that the Germans, who had more divisions available, would be able to smother the British resistance.

III. THE BATTLE

At 5 o'clock on the morning of November 20th the British guns opened on a 20-mile front from Bullecourt, which had been at the southwest extremity of the Battle of Arras, to Epehy in the St. Quentin sector. The artillery fire was of the briefest duration, of the sort subsequently described as a "crash" bombardment and a familiar circumstance in later offensives. A little more than an hour after the brief bombardment, British tanks, followed by British infantry, left their trenches on the front from just north of the Bapaume road south of the town of Moeuvres, which is on the Canal du Nord and was held by the Germans, to the village of Gonnelieu, just south of the Péronne road, which was held by the British. The distance between these points was rather more than six miles.

The surprise was complete. Favoured by mist and helped by smoke the tanks reached the advance line of the Germans before they were discovered, and overran it without difficulty. There then began an extraordinary forward sweep hardly paralleled before on the western front. The German troops bolted, the German defence collapsed, and all through the morning of November 20th the British had every reason to believe that the long-anticipated "break-through" had at last arrived. All through that morning the infantry continued to press forward. By noon Anneux, just south of the Bapaume road and almost half way between the British front and Cambrai, had been taken. In the centre the British had reached the town of Flesquières, while to the south Ribecourt had been taken and Marcoing approached. Still farther to the south the British had advanced along the Péronne road beyond the point where it is intersected by the St. Quentin highway. During the afternoon the gains were expanded, but along with much progress there came certain disappointments. Largely owing to the courage of a German artillery officer, who, single-handed, worked his guns in Flesquières, the British tank attack was long checked and many tanks put out of operation, while the Germans were able to destroy several of the important bridges across the Scheldt Canal from Masnières to Crèvecœur. The result of the resistance at Flesquières and the failure to get the bridges intact had fatal consequences. The British were unable on this first day to establish their right flank above the Scheldt Canal or overrun the fourth and final German positions. They were equally unable to reach Bourlon Woods. They had advanced four and a half miles in places; they had captured many thousands of prisoners and over a hundred guns, but the great cavalry operation had been impossible owing to the destruction of the bridges, and on the morning of the 21st the British found themselves in a salient quite as narrow as that which had persisted so long at Ypres. The enemy was still in Bourlon Woods and on the heights about Crèvecœur occupying vantage points entirely comparable with those held by the Germans about Ypres on the Pilkem and "Whitesheet" ridges before Plumer's June battle.   Moreover, twenty-four hours of the forty-eight in which the surprise ensured superiority in numbers to the assailants had now passed and already German reserves were beginning to arrive.   On November 21st the battle was resumed.   This time a brief success carried the British into Bourlon Woods through the village of Fontaine-Notre-Dame, three miles from the centre of Cambrai itself, but it did not enable them to establish their right flank by the occupation of Rumilly and Crèvecœur which from the beginning had been recognized as essential.

By night of the 21st the forty-eight hours of grace had expired.   No further profit could be derived as a consequence of the surprise.   The German reserves were arriving from all directions and would at no distant date outnumber the British.   Only the now weary troops of the Third Army were available, since proffered French reserves were to have been used only in case of the maximum gain which had been foreseen but not realized.   As the situation now stood, the British must either go forward or back.   They had thrust their neck into a vise, the jaws of which were represented by Bourlon Woods and the high ground about Crèvecœur, and they must either break at least one of the jaws or retire before the vise closed.

Sir Douglas Haig chose to risk a further attempt to advance, defending himself subsequently by the following summary of the situation:

. . . It was not possible, however, to let matters stand as they were. The positions captured by us north of Flesquières were completely commanded by the Bourlon Ridge, and unless this ridge were gained it would be impossible to hold them, except at excessive cost. If I decided not to go on, a withdrawal to the Flesquières Ridge would be necessary, and would have to be carried out at once.

On the other hand, the enemy showed certain signs of an intention to withdraw. Craters had been formed at road junctions, and troops could be seen ready to move eastward. The possession of Bourlon Ridge would enable our troops to obtain observation over the ground to the north, which sloped gently down to the Sensée River. The enemy's defensive lines south of the Scarpe and Sensée rivers would thereby be turned, his communications exposed to the observed fire of our artillery, and his positions in this sector jeopardized. In short, so great was the importance of the ridge to the enemy that its loss would

BRITISH CAMPAIGNS
IN THE EAST

IN MESOPOTAMIA

"A close one which held us up a bit"

THE BRITISH IN THE HOLY LAND—I

The Camel Corps near Beersheba, the city where Abraham dwelt and "planted a grove." General Allenby began his active campaign for Jerusalem by the capture of Beersheba, October 31, 1917

THE BRITISH IN THE HOLY LAND—II

Troops resting before their attack on Gaza. Its capture on November 7 was the second step on their road to Jerusalem. It will be remembered that Samson once carried off the gates of Gaza, and afterward met his death there by pulling down the pillars of the house wherein he was held captive. "So the dead which he slew at his death were more than they which he slew in his life."

THE BRITISH IN THE HOLY LAND—III

General Allenby's entry into Jerusalem, December 11, 1917. "Then the city was broken up and all the men of war fled, and went forth out of the city by night." Seven times in its long history has Jerusalem fallen, before the besieger. Assyrians, Babylonians, Greeks, Romans, Arabs, Christians, and Turks have held it. Before its latest capitulation it had been out of Christian hands for nearly seven centuries.

A TALKATIVE PRISONER

This Arab sheik volubly protests his innocence with oriental plenitude of word and gesture, but his British captor pays no heed at all and stands so stolidly that only proof of the authenticity of the photograph convinced us that he was not a stuffed lay figure.

THE ARRIVAL OF RATIONS AT A BRITISH OUTPOST IN THE SINAI PENINSULA

This ship of the desert had journeyed 130 miles

THE WAR IN WEST AFRICA

Germans in a border fortress firing on a reconnoitring British cavalry patrol

THE WAR IN EAST AFRICA

These men of the King's African Rifles have encountered a hostile patrol in the jungle and are having a brush with them

probably cause the abandonment by the Germans of their carefully prepared defence systems for a considerable distance to the north of it.

The successive days of constant marching and fighting had placed a very severe strain upon the endurance of the troops, and, before a further advance could be undertaken, some time would have to be spent in resting and relieving them. This need for delay was regrettable, as the enemy's forces were increasing, and fresh German divisions were known to be arriving, but, with the limited number of troops at my command, it was unavoidable.

It was to be remembered, however, that the hostile reinforcements coming up at this stage could at first be no more than enough to replace the enemy's losses: and although the right of our advance had definitely been stayed, the enemy had not yet developed such strength about Bourlon as it seemed might not be overcome by the numbers at my disposal. As has already been pointed out, on the Cambrai side of the battlefield I had only aimed at securing a defensive flank to enable the advance to be pushed northward and northwestward, and this part of my task had been to a great extent achieved.

An additional and very important argument in favour of proceeding with my attack was supplied by the situation in Italy, upon which a continuance of pressure on the Cambrai front might reasonably be expected to exercise an important effect, no matter what measure of success attended my efforts. Moreover, two divisions previously under orders for Italy had on this day been placed at my disposal, and with this accession of strength, the prospect of securing Bourlon seemed good.

After weighing these various considerations, therefore, I decided to continue the operations to gain the Bourlon position.

The 22nd November was spent in organizing the captured ground, in carrying out certain reliefs, and in giving other troops the rest they greatly needed. Soon after midday the enemy regained Fontaine-Notre-Dame; but, with our troops already on the outskirts of Bourlon Wood, and Cantaing held by us, it was thought that the re-capture of Fontaine should not prove very difficult. The necessary arrangements for renewing the attack were therefore pushed on, and our plans were extended to include the recapture of Fontaine-Notre-Dame.

Meantime, early in the night of the 22nd November, a battalion of the Queen's Westminsters stormed a commanding tactical point in the Hindenburg Line west of Moeuvres known as Tadpole Copse, the possession of which would be of value in connection with the left flank of the Bourlon position when the latter had been secured.

That this decision to go on was unwise, every subsequent circumstance seems to indicate. Haig had now taken 10,500 prisoners, nearly 150 guns, and his losses were still inconsiderable by comparison with those of the Germans. He grossly underestimated German resources and reserves and he unmistakably exaggerated the further fighting strength of certain units in the Third Army, at least one division of which had been practically annihilated in Flanders, and now, with green troops, was in position in a vital sector.

Having made the decision Haig put the Third Army at work again and in the following days acquired and despite certain fluctuations, maintained, a firm hold on Bourlon Woods, but he was not able to make any considerable change or improvement along his right flank nor did this brief tenure in Bourlon Woods lead to any German retirement on the Arras front. Continuing their counter-attacks on Bourlon the Germans hung on elsewhere.

Meantime, the news of the success at Cambrai, reaching Britain not long after the crushing tidings of Italian disaster and the not-less-manifest evidence of failure in Flanders, roused widespread enthusiasm and for the first time in the war the bells of St. Paul's were rung. English and Allied publics continued to look hopefully ahead to the arrival of British troops in Cambrai long after Cambrai had become as far removed from British reach as Berlin itself.

Meantime, once the temporary disarray incident to the surprise was over, the enemy—under the command of that General Marwitz, who, as a cavalry leader, had already checked the British at the decisive moment at the Marne and a year later was unsuccessfully to strive to check the Americans in the great battle of the Meuse-Argonne—took his measures. His strategy was simple, the strategy invariably employed in dealing with an enemy salient. He sought to pinch it out by attacks from the sides similar to those successfully made by Pershing at St. Mihiel, and he hoped, by breaking in the sides behind the nose of the salient, to capture large numbers of British troops and guns, as Pershing captured German soldiers and guns at St. Mihiel in September, 1918.

To accomplish this task he assembled an overwhelming force secretly, the actual arrival of which in battle was the first clear evidence to the Allies of the extent to which the Russian collapse had released German divisions for western service. These troops were brought in by the Hutier method so successfully that while the British knew a counter-attack was coming, and knew, as every soldier would know, where the blow must fall, they were in the end totally surprised along a vital section of the front. On November 30th, ten days after the British attack, sixteen fresh German divisions were thrown against the British, the main masses being used on the north and south sides of the salient the British advance had created, that is against Bourlon Woods, and against that portion of the British lines where the new front of the salient rejoined the old front.

It is the attack on this latter sector which is more interesting, as it was more successful. Preceded by a bombardment of gas and smoke shells, aided by the fogs of morning, and carried out by overwhelming masses of shock troops, several details of this attack recall with unfortunate exactitude the circumstances of that far vaster and more disastrous assault on a forty-mile front on March 21st of the next year.

Before the British were aware of the peril, German infantry had overrun their lines. The division immediately assailed—which had been cut to pieces in Flanders and was now occupying a supposedly quiet sector training its replacements—gave way, opening a wide gap in the British front through which the victorious German troops pressed rapidly forward, occupying the villages of Gonnelieu, Villers-Guislain and Gouzeaucourt on the Péronne road itself. In these first morning hours it seemed inevitable that the Germans would be able to advance behind the whole Cambrai salient and make a vast capture in men and material.

While the Germans on the southern side of the salient were thus making their successful advance, following their astonishing surprise, other German divisions were pounding with terrific energy on the northern side of the salient about Bourlon Woods, and thence eastward and southward along the whole salient. Fortunately for the British no such collapse took place on their left and centre as had resulted through the German advance on their right. By afternoon the Guards Division, which was in reserve, together with certain cavalry units, had been pushed into action and had re-captured Gouzeaucourt and reëstablished the imperilled flank.   The Germans had no longer any real chance of bringing off a huge success.

Nevertheless, there was no further possibility of holding the Cambrai salient or maintaining a grip on the all-important position of Bourlon Woods.   The effort to transform the local and considerable momentary success into a permanent advantage had not only failed but had invited a German counter-thrust which had resulted in gains by the Germans both in prisoners and guns totally counterbalancing the original British profit.   Moreover, such elation as had been excited by the initial success inevitably gave way now to a depression the more intense because this failure coincided with equally depressing situations elsewhere.

Such, in its brief form, was the Battle of Cambrai.   "The Cambrai Fright" as Ludendorff later described the tank surprise.   The British, when they had with skill and success re-organized their line, were still able to point to a certain number of square miles of territory permanently gained and to the possession of the ruins of a few villages which had been inside of the German lines when the attack of November 20th opened. They had released some hundreds of French inhabitants of these villages. They had for a moment threatened to achieve a complete rupture of the German front, but actually in casualties and prisoners the gains of the two armies were at least even, while to the man in the street it seemed that the British had completely missed a great opportunity—while the Germans had extricated themselves from a dangerous position with consummate skill and turned temporary defeat into incontestable success.

Cambrai, then, was no counterweight for the Flanders failure. It contributed nothing to restore the confidence of Allied publics, shaken alike by the Italian disaster and the Russian collapse; and, what was of even greater importance, the successful employment by the Germans of their new Hutier tactics did not open the eyes of the British to the perils this new method had for their own troops, untrained to defensive warfare. Finally there was discoverable, in the collapse of a British division, symptoms of a decline in morale and in fighting capacity not hitherto disclosed in all the terrible tests of more than three years.   Cambrai should have been a warning. However much Sir Douglas Haig and his associate commanders may have blundered in risking the offensive with inadequate resources, in persisting in it when all real chance of further gain had vanished, the real indictment must be found in the fact that from this failure, from the German success, they were unable to derive lessons which, if learned, might have prevented, four months later, what was to prove the greatest military disaster in all British history, for what happened to a division on November 30th happened to a whole army on March 21st.

IV. JERUSALEM

As the year closed British success in a far distant field served in some small degree to relieve the depression arising from the unbroken list of losses and failures elsewhere. On Tuesday, December 11th, Sir Edmund Allenby, who at the opening of the year had commanded the British Third Army at Arras, entered Jerusalem after a brief but brilliant campaign which was to prove but the prelude to that far greater success in the following year. This later triumph would in its turn drive the Turk out of Syria as well as Palestine, destroy three of his armies, and after long centuries avenge the failures of the Crusaders, while for the victor it would earn the reward of promotion to the rank of field marshal.

When Allenby came to the Holy Land the British forces, under General Murray, had suffered a severe check at Gaza on the edge of the Egyptian frontier and all further advance seemed forbidden, but under Allenby's direction a railroad had been pushed across the desert from the Suez Canal, the waters of the Nile had been piped into the wastes of Palestine, not only quenching the thirst of thousands of British soldiers, but, in the minds of the superstitious Turk, now presaging defeat— since there was a legend that the Turks would stay in Jerusalem until the waters of the Nile arrived in Palestine. By the last of October Allenby was ready. His first operations cleared Beersheba and his advance thereafter followed the sea coast and the Hebron road. By November 16th he had occupied Jaffa, the port of Jerusalem, and by November 21st his troops looked down on the Holy City from the west. On December 9th other British troops, following the Hebron road, were north and east of the city and across the Jericho road. All German efforts to prevent the disaster arrived at nothing. Falkenhayn, the engineer of the Verdun offensive, visited the front and returned convinced that nothing could be done. Finally, on December 9th, on the day of the festival celebrating the recapture of the Temple by Judas Maccabeus in 165 B. C., the Turkish garrison of Jerusalem capitulated. Two days later, on foot, through the Jaffa Gate. Allenby entered the town.

In the subsequent weeks, the British advance pushed forward until the new front was well beyond the range of the city and there the campaign paused, while the British began those preparations which, in the following autumn, were to lead to one of the most amazing victories in military history won on the Plain of Armageddon. Thus two British successes, both against the Turk, one of which carried Bagdad and the other resulted in the capture of Jerusalem, supplied bright spots in the darkness of this year of unmistakable depression, and disclosed two British generals whose achievements in the eastern theatre won enduring glory and were rivalled in British armies on the western front only by those of Sir Herbert Plumer. Maude, Allenby, and Plumer were thenceforth recognized as the great British army commanders of the war, and but for Maude's untimely death it is hardly doubtful that he would have been called to higher command on the western front.

In his report of military operations for the year 1917 Sir Douglas Haig announced that British armies had captured 114,544 prisoners, of which 73,131 were taken on the French front, and 761 guns, 530 of which were taken in France, while the losses in prisoners were 28,279 and in guns 166, practically all on the French front. This was a better showing in men captured than in the previous year but worse in guns, most of which were lost at Cambrai. These figures were, however, to seem insignificant as compared with the German and Allied captures in the coming campaign.

CHAPTER TWELVE

CAPORETTO—AND PETAIN'S ACHIEVEMENT

I
THE DISASTER

On October 24th Italy was overtaken by the first of that series of military disasters which destroyed, successively, an Italian, a British, and a French army; in each case resulted in far-swinging advance on the part of the enemy, and placed the whole military establishment of the nation assailed in gravest jeopardy.

Two years after the great disaster of Caporetto an Italian military commission reported that there had been three causes for the collapse of the Italian Second Army. These causes were: first, the failure of Cadorna and his subordinate generals to provide necessary reserves and adequate second and third positions; second, the successful progress of enemy and socialistic propaganda in the Italian army, and third, the new German tactics.

The destruction of the British Fifth Army in March of the following year was to recall in many details the Caporetto disaster, while the British and French collapse on the Chemin-des-Dames in May was to reproduce still others. In the case of the British there was no propaganda but there was an army wearied by its exertions and strained by its losses in Flanders, without adequate reserves and with insufficient support lines. In the case of the French and the British on the Chemin-des-Dames there was again no propaganda, while there were an infinite number of support and secondary defence systems and two considerable rivers behind to serve as defence lines.

As a consequence of these later experiences of the armies of Italy's allies, there has been a revision of the judgment passed upon Cadorna and the Italian troops at the time. The fact seems to be that the Germans had now devised a system of offensive—used at Riga and subsequently employed at Cambrai—which was destined to bring them victories and to prove irresistible until a successful answer was discovered and developed by General Gouraud and by him employed to break the last German offensive of the war on July 15, 1918, in Champagne. Perhaps the best analysis of this German method was supplied by Gouraud himself in an interview which he gave to the press after his great victory. In this—having pointed out that, with slight modifications, the tactics which had failed against him were precisely those that succeeded at Caporetto against the Italians, in Picardy against the British, and on the Chemin-des-Dames against the British and French—he said:

The Von Hutier system broke the trench warfare deadlock in the German favour by two factors: First, the element of surprise—that is, development of unexpected strength both of men and guns at a given point—and secondly, by neutralizing the land—or trench—defences by a brief bombardment of tremendous volume, followed by a smoke screen against which the defenders that escaped destruction were virtually powerless.

Beginning usually four hours before the zero hour, fixed around dawn, the enemy would open fire with four or five times as many guns as the defender thought he possessed in that sector. During the preceding weeks they had been "registering" on every worth-while objective, but taking care to space the registering shots so as to conceal their great strength. The bombardment would contain a fixed proportion of gas and high explosive calculated to render the defence positions untenable for a considerable depth. During the final hour smoke shells, at the rate of about two to one, would be added. Then at the zero hour the infantry, masked and lightly equipped, would charge forward at full speed through the gas and smoke, literally swamping the defenders and often penetrating right to the artillery positions before the isolated groups in the front-line defences realized that they were surrounded.

General Gouraud also pointed out at this time that the infantry divisions employed in these operations had been carefully trained in readiness, and brought up at the last moment by forced marches at night, during which every precaution was taken, and taken successfully in all cases, to avoid detection by airplanes. Not until the Battle of Champagne was the element of surprise eliminated but on this occasion Gouraud not only knew where the attack was coming, but the precise hour of the very morning on which it would be launched. For the attack upon the Italians, in late October, preparations had been made over a long period.   Not only were German troops sent to the Italian front for the first time during the war but the whole Austrian military forces were placed directly under the German General Staff, and Ludendorff himself assumed charge of operations.

As a consequence of the Italian local successes through the spring and summer, the Italians occupied in October a situation satisfying if they were going to continue an offensive but perilous in the extreme if, as was now the case, they were to be attacked.   Their Third Army continued to hold the positions between the Adriatic and the foot of the hills above Gorizia—positions which had in the main been held for a long period of time and were properly organized alike for defence and for further offensive operations.   Far different was the situation of the Second Army.   In the operations against the Bainsizza Plateau it had

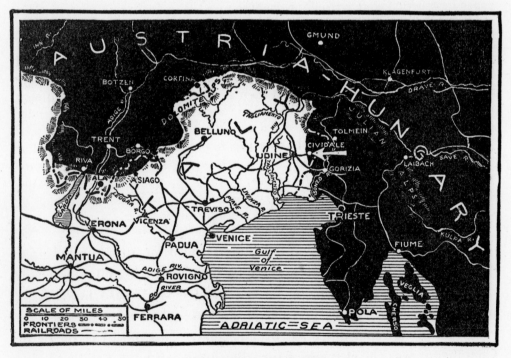

THE ITALIAN DISASTER

Solid black shows territory occupied by the Austrians on the day following Caporetto. The white arrow indicates the point at which the Germans broke through and their line of advance through Cividale to Udine cutting off the retreat of the Italians.

pushed across the deep canyon of the Isonzo, climbed up to the mountain rim of the Bainsizza Plateau itself, and then attempted to envelop Monte San Gabriele which was the final barrier to a forward advance to Trieste. This fighting for Monte San Gabriele had as completely exhausted the Second Army as the Flanders operations had used up the offensive qualities of the British troops.   Along with this exhaustion, due to too greatly prolonged strain, was a decline in morale resulting from the use made of the Pope's recent Peace Note by German, socialist, and clerical propagandists, the generally bad economic condition of Italy; and the growing unrest in the civil population.

Thus the Second Army, on the morning of October 24th, was an army already shaken in spirit, weakened by losses, fought-out in a campaign in which too much had been asked of it, and it occupied a perilous position with its centre and one flank thrown across an unfordable river, having at its rear only such communications as it had been possible to construct during battle, while the northern flank, parts of which were on opposite sides of the river, was composed of second- and third-line troops without adequate reserves or sufficient second-line defences.

A glance at the map discloses the full extent of the peril.   Could the Germans break the northern flank of the Second Army and seize the crossings of the Isonzo at Caporetto, they would have a straight road to Udine and it might be possible for them, pressing southward to and through this town, to cut off all of the Italian Second Army as well as the Third and achieve that colossal Sedan which they had sought in France in the opening days of the war.

Moreover, in choosing their time for this attack, the Germans followed a system which by this time had become familiar.   In 1915 they had closed a year of alternating success and failure by crushing Serbia and opening the road to the Golden Horn.   They had terminated the campaign of the following year by entering Bukharest and crushing Roumania.   It was of utmost importance to them to end the campaign of 1917 by a shining success which would serve alike to depress the morale of their enemies, raise the spirits of their own civil population, and supply the basis for further propaganda and pacifist operations.

The position occupied by the Italian Second Army, on the Bainsizza Plateau, was a pronounced and perilous salient. Now, as at Cambrai, the Germans undertook to "pinch out" this Bainsizza salient by a surprise attack. In the case of Cambrai they attacked from both sides of the British salient and were successful on only one. In the case of Bainsizza they attacked on only one side, but with extraordinary success. The operation which followed is perhaps most closely reminiscent of that at the Dunajec. In April, 1915, the main Russian armies were across the Carpathians about the Dukla Pass and were pushing onward into Hungary, while their flanks were covered by the armies of Dimitrieff along the Dunajec River and of Lechitsky on the crest of the Carpathians south and west of the Dukla. When Mackensen attacked Dimitrieff and destroyed his army the position of the main Russian masses under Ivanoff was critical; there were some days before it was clear whether the Russians would escape or suffer a Sedan. They got away, but they left prisoners, guns, and flags in German possession, and so great was the dislocation of their front that they were unable to make a successful stand until early autumn; and in point of fact neither the army nor the Government ever recovered from the effects of the disaster.

Now the German blow of October, 1917, was similar to the thrust at the Dunajec in May, 1915. It was levelled at that portion of the Italian forces guarding the flank of the Second Army on both sides of the Isonzo from Tolmino to Flitsch, and particularly at those troops occupying the bridge-head of Caporetto on the road to Udine. Once this force had been crushed the Germans would be able to advance southwestward upon Udine by the Cividale Valley, and a few hours after the Italian lines collapsed they were actually nearer to Cadorna's headquarters in this town than much of the Italian Second and all of the Third Army, and were approaching the line of communications by which the Second and Third armies must retire. Favoured again by mist, by driving rain, and even by snow in the upper mountains, six German divisions under Otto von Below fell upon the flank of the Italian Second Army, after a brief bombardment on the whole extent of their front from Zaga on the north to the edge of the Bainsizza Plateau. The attack was immediately successful, the surprise was complete. Certain units made no resistance whatever, some even laid down their arms in advance of the arrival of the assailants, and in the briefest possible time the left or north flank of the Second Army had ceased to exist. In a subsequent official statement Cadorna himself charged those responsible, officers and men alike, with treason. This declaration was softened by the substitution of the term "insufficient resistance" for the allegation of treason, but otherwise the statement was permitted to issue and was as follows:

The violence of the attack and an insufficient resistance on the part of certain units of the Second Army have permitted the Austro-German forces to break through our defence on the left wing of the Julian sector. The valiant behaviour of the other troops did not suffice to prevent the enemy from penetrating to the sacred soil of our fatherland. Our line retires according to plan. The depots and munition stores of the territory evacuated have all been destroyed. The splendid courage of our soldiers in so many famous battles fought and won during the two and a half years of war encourages the High Command to hope that on this occasion the Army, to which is entrusted the honour and the safety of Italy, will know how to do its duty.

II. TO THE PIAVE

The consequences of the collapse of the left flank of the Second Army were of utmost gravity. Below's German troops were now behind the Second Army, sweeping over the Julian Alps across its rear to Udine. In the following days this army broke up, ceased to exist. Its artillery, its vast stores of munitions, by far the greater part of its troops—officers and men alike—were captured. The fate of the Second Army was sealed once Below had passed the Isonzo at Caporetto and the Italian troops had failed to react on their own side of the river. The destruction of the Second Army was more complete than that of Gough's British Fifth Army in the offensive of March 21st of the following year. Its resistance was incomparably less determined, yet in both cases, although with different preliminary resistance, an army collapsed and left a great gap on a whole front through which the enemy poured in.

The single problem that remained after the first few hours following the Caporetto disaster was whether the Italian Third Army, commanded by the Duke of Aosta and occupying the Isonzo front from Gorizia to the sea, would be able to get back before it was enveloped by the German armies coming from the north and cutting its roads and railroads. Could it make such a retreat and escape envelopment there was a chance that the Italians might be able to rally at the Tagliamento, on the east side of which the Austrians had temporarily held up Napoleon in his great campaign of 1797.

By the narrowest possible margin the Italian Third Army succeeded in passing the Tagliamento in advance of the German and Austrian troops which were seeking to envelop it, but it only escaped by sacrificing all of its material and most of its artillery. But precisely as in the Dunajec time the Russians were able to halt but not to hold at the line of the San, the Italians rallied but were unable to remain at the Tagliamento. On October 29th the enemy was in Udine; on October 31st he had reached the Tagliamento, and three days later he passed the river north of the Treviso-Udine railroad.

The next position on which an Italian stand was possible was behind the Livenza, a smaller river which parallels the Tagliamento, but the fighting at this stream was less considerable than at the Tagliamento. By November 6th the enemy was across this river, still following the Treviso-Udine railroad, and by November 9th he was on the east bank of the Piave, the last position from which the Italians could cover Venice. By this time they had evacuated not merely all of the Venetian plain east of the Piave but all of the upper valley of this stream from Feltre to Cadore including the eastern slopes of the Dolomites, familiar to all alpinists. The Fourth Army had been brought back from the Carnic and Cadore fronts which it had held with such great distinction from the outset of the war, and the Italian front now stood from Lago di Garda along the mountains, followed by the old frontier as far as the Piave, at the point where it leaves the mountains, and thence behind that stream to the sea hardly twenty miles east of Venice. If the Italians were turned or forced out of the Piave position they would have to go behind the Adige, abandoning Venice, Vicenza, and Padua to the enemy, bringing the Austrians and Germans close to the forts of Verona and surrendering to the Austrians practically all of the province of Venetia.

Moreover, the Italian situation behind the Piave, while strong in the plain where the river offered a considerable barrier to direct advance, was weak on the hills, as had been disclosed in the Austrian offensive of 1916 when the Italians had been driven off the Asiago Plateau and the Austrians had almost reached the plain. On their north flank the Italians were now open to an attack down the Astico and Brenta valleys which, if successful, would have precisely the same peril for them as the recent German advance down the Cividale Valley. In other words, it was impossible for the Italians to stand at the Piave if their troops to the north failed to hold the foothills of the Alps between the Adige and the Piave, and if they were unable to hold the Piave line they would have to give up Venice and go back of the Adige and the Po, while any disaster in the hills would infallibly ruin all the remaining Italian armies, carry the victors to Milan, and force the Italians to make a separate peace. Already French troops, commanded by Fayolle—Petain's ablest lieutenant, who had fought with the British at the Somme—were on their way to the Italian front, and the British, after momentary hesitation, were sending Plumer with other troops; but considerable time must elapse before this aid could arrive and in this time Italy must still rely upon herself. Unless she could save herself, no aid from her allies could be of any value. In the immediate presence of Foch, however, she found assistance, and the great French soldier now appeared upon an Italian field of disaster and played something of that rôle which four months later he was to play in the presence of a British disaster even more perilous to the whole Allied cause.

Fortunately Italy measured up to the supreme test. The country rose behind the army; the whole national spirit of the people was touched; "defeatism" gave way to patriotism; political intrigues collapsed; the nation from the king to the peasant echoed Petain's immortal words at Verdun—"They shall not pass"—which proved the watchword of vic-

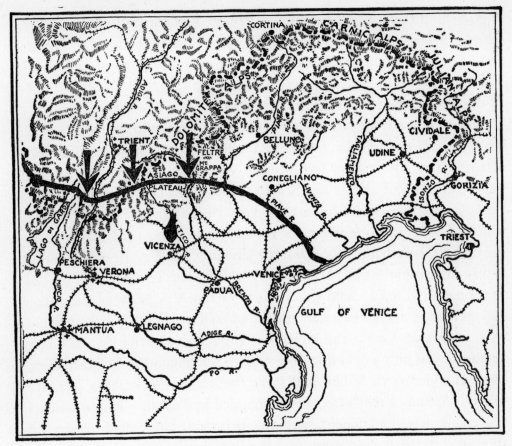

ITALY'S STAND AT THE PIAVE

The three arrows indicate the valleys by which the Austro-Germans attempted to descend to the plain behind the Italian front. The severest fighting was at Mt. Grappa and on the Asiago Plateau.

tory at the Piave as it had at the Meuse.   Through December the Austrians, with gradually declining German aid, strove to transform a victory into one more decisive battle of the world.   The main attacks were delivered not on the Piave front but in the mountains, although the Austrians succeeded in crossing at several places notably in the lagoons nearest to Venice.   They gained ground but they fell short of their objectives, and snow and winter came together with French and British troops, while the Italian lines still stood fast at the Piave. The greatest victory on the western front during the whole war—with the possible exception of Ludendorff's supreme success in March of the next year—had no morrow. In the following year the Italians were to endure and defeat one more offensive at the Piave, and then at last, passing to the offensive, see the Austrian armies dissolve before them between the Piave and the Isonzo in that same country which had beheld the heroic and successful retreat of the Italian Third Army.

But if the German victory at Caporetto missed decisive results by a narrow margin its moral effect was tremendous. While the Italian armies were still struggling to escape destruction, the British offensive in Flanders came to its mournful end. Cambrai was won, and lost, and the French armies, despite successful local offensives, were still under the shadow of the Aisne defeat.

Moreover, Russia in this same time finally vanished as a factor in the war and the realization was brought home to the Allied publics of Britain, France, and Italy, not only that their campaign of 1917 had been a failure, but, provided with a new system of attack and enabled to bring all their best troops from the east to the west, the Germans now possessed the initiative, and the sole chance of winning the war rested henceforth upon the size of American armies to be sent to Europe and the rapidity with which they would arrive.

Almost on the same day that the Italian Second Army had collapsed, the first American contingent had appeared on the French front facing Alsace-Lorraine, but American forces in Europe were still insignificant, and if the submarine menace had been countered to a degree it did not yet seem possible that ships could be found to move to Europe those millions of American troops without which victory was impossible and defeat might yet become inevitable. As a consequence of Caporetto, Cadorna joined the considerable number of generals—Allied, German, and Austrian alike—whose failures had led to their disappearance from active command. He was succeeded by General Diaz, one of his ablest lieutenants, whose victory in the Second Battle of the Piave the following summer marked the turn of the tide in Allied fortunes.

Even more important was the first step taken toward unification of command on the Allied side as a direct consequence of the successive

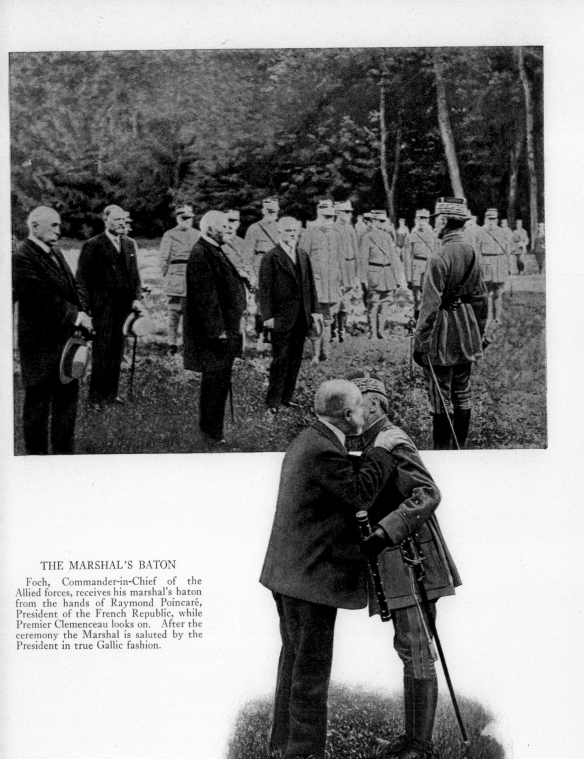

THE MARSHAL'S BATON

Foch, Commander-in-Chief of the Allied forces, receives his marshal's baton from the hands of Raymond Poincaré, President of the French Republic, while Premier Clemenceau looks on. After the ceremony the Marshal is saluted by the President in true Gallic fashion.

failures of the several armies under divided leadership.   It was a halting step.   It produced only that Versailles Conference which in fact was little more than an abstraction, since it had no actual authority.   Out of the Versailles Conference four months later Foch emerged as generalissimo of all the Allied armies, and in the final campaign Italian troops fought in France as British troops shared Italian success in Venetia.   But if this first step toward unified command carried with it the promise of victory in the future, at the moment when it was made it was an insignificant circumstance in the minds of the Allied publics, which saw in Caporetto an unparalleled disaster, which had cost the Italians 250,000 prisoners, more than 2,000 guns, most of their military material—the whole accumulation of two and a half years—and enriched the Austrians not merely by these military prizes, but by considerable foodstuffs as well, and enabled them to occupy more than 2,000 square miles of Italian soil, while depriving the Italians of almost every foot of Italia Irredenta which had been gained in three campaigns and at appalling sacrifice.

III.   PETAIN'S ACHIEVEMENT

While the British army was failing in Flanders, the Italian army going to disaster at Caporetto, the Russian army dissolving, what was the position of the French?   When Petain had succeeded Nivelle in May he took over an army shaken in morale, no longer responsive to that discipline which for more than three years had been a circumstance alike in heroic defence and in splendid offence.

Following his accession to the High Command, Petain promptly informed his British allies that they could expect from the French nothing in the way of offensive operation for at least two months to come. In fact, it was not until August, when the Flanders offensive had already touched approximate failure, that the first French blow could be delivered.

Meantime, the immediate task of Petain was hardly less considerable than that which confronted him when he was called to save the compromised situation at Verdun.   He had to restore the confidence of the soldiers in their commanders.   He had to satisfy certain of their legitimate demands. He had in many cases to find new generals and await the construction of new staffs. All of these things he did with consummate success. The French army which entered the campaign of 1918 was incomparably superior to the British. If it was no longer capable of such efforts as had marked the French forces in 1914 and 1915 it was to demonstrate in the crucial hours of March and April the old Verdun capacity for holding and in the counter-offensive of July to disclose at least a flash of that *élan* which had made the French infantry famous for centuries.

The first military problem faced by Petain was left over from the abortive Nivelle operation on the Chemin-des-Dames. When the French abandoned the offensive here the Germans seized it and eagerly sought to take advantage of the temporary disorganization within the French ranks. All through June and July the German showered terrific attacks along the whole of the Chemin-des-Dames position and particularly on the eastern half from Heurtebrise Farm to Craonne. Just above the little ruined village of Craonne, the eastern end of the Craonne Plateau culminates in two relatively narrow level plateaux, while the ridge itself, seen either from the north, the east, or the south, assumes a dominating character reminiscent of Douaumont, and one of the most impressive landmarks of the whole front.

The French had cleared this eastern end with its two little plateaux of Californie and Casemates in the May attacks. Now the Germans sought, by repeated assaults, coming up the steep slopes out of the marshy valley of the Ailette, to regain those crests which in all the German military reports are known as the "Winterberg"—the same crests from which the Kaiser on May 27th, of the following year, surveyed a field of victory. Time and again they mounted to the attack, effected a lodgment, lingered for a few hours, and were driven off. Eight weeks of almost continuous fighting gained them no permanent hold anywhere along the lines the French had established in the April offensive. Any hope that deflection in French morale would open the way to a victory such as was subsequently achieved at Caporetto proved illusory. If the French veterans would no longer attack impregnable positions,

would no longer consent to be led against unbroken wire and unde-
stroyed machine-gun nests, they still retained the spirit and the
strength necessary to convince their German opponents of the folly of
similar ventures.   The fighting of this June and July, largely filling the
press of the time, had no permanent value.

While the French lines thus held at Craonne, Petain reorganized his
armies.   Late July saw a French army despatched to the Flanders
front to share with the British in the Third Battle of Ypres and perform
there a useful if subsidiary service wholly comparable with that performed by the French armies in the Battle of the Somme.   But it was
not until August 20th that Petain was at last ready, and his first blow
coincided almost exactly with that second phase of the British opera-

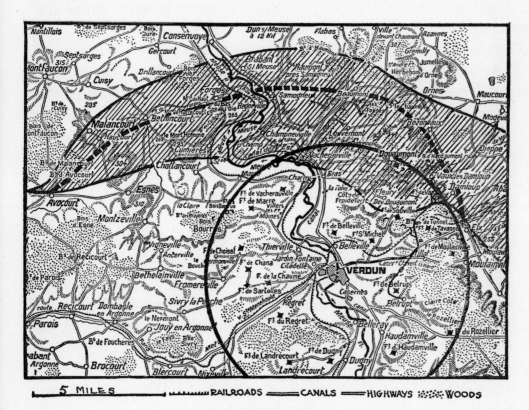

THE VERDUN SECTOR

The shaded portion shows the ground captured by the Germans between February and
July, 1916.   The circle indicates the area of the entrenched camp of Verdun.   The broken line
marked the front attained by the French after Petain's successful offensive in August, 1917.

tions at Ypres which resulted in the capture of Langemarck but was nevertheless, over most of the front, a failure which doomed the whole enterprise.

For his first operation Petain chose the Verdun front, where he had achieved enduring fame in defence and subsequently demonstrated his supreme ability in the organization of a local offensive by those two attacks, one of which wrested Douaumont and Vaux from the Germans and the other released Verdun from the fatal German embrace which for many months had threatened it with strangulation. At the close of these two offensives Verdun was unblocked. Practically all the vital positions on the heights of the Meuse were retaken, but the Germans still clung to Hill 304 and Dead Man's Hill on the western bank, the fruits of their second attack in 1916. Possession of these western hills would give the Allies ground from which they might in the future operate out of the Verdun salient, as the British were now attacking out of the Ypres salient. Actually the Petain offensive of August, 1917, made possible the American attack of September and October a year later, which carried the victorious American troops to Sedan and cut the vital German railroad lines connecting Metz with Lille and the Alsace-Lorraine front with that of Belgium. From the ground that Petain took from the Germans in the third and fourth weeks of August Pershing's armies advanced to their successful opening attack on September 26, 1918.

At 4 o'clock on the morning of August 20th the French troops on both banks of the Meuse left their trenches, supported by a tremendous artillery fire, and almost without resistance seized the Côte de Talou in the bend of the Meuse on the east bank, from which the Germans had direct observation up the Meuse Valley to Verdun, Hills 344 and 240 north of the line established in December of the previous year, and on this front occupied all the ground from which they had retired on the second day of the First Battle of Verdun, including the town of Samogneux on the Meuse itself. On the west bank the progress was less considerable. Dead Man's Hill was taken, but 304 held out. Two days later it fell and the French line was restored all the way westward from the river south of the little Forges Brook, across which Pershing's troops moved to battle thirteen months later.   In the first action 8,000 prisoners were captured, while the number was increased to 10,000 in the next few days.   Subsequent German counter-offensives led to nothing.   The French position at Verdun was now completely reëstablished within sight of the line on which the German flood of February, 1916, had broken, and Verdun, having been for three years a bulwark against German attack, was now to be the sally port from which America emerged in the final campaign of the war.

While the victory at Verdun was primarily due to Petain it reflected credit upon the new commander of the Verdun army, Guillaumat, who had succeeded Nivelle and was presently to replace Sarrail at Salonica and plan that victorious operation executed by Franchet d'Esperey after Guillaumat had returned to Paris to participate brilliantly in the last phase of the war.   Guillaumat at Verdun, Gouraud in Champagne, De Maistre at the Chemin-des-Dames, were three of the new names which were to be heard with increasing frequency in the next few months, together with those of Fayolle and of Mangin, who, despite disgrace due to his share of the Nivelle failure, was to return as an army commander to the same field in 1918 and achieve a still greater reputation.

Two months after the Verdun operation, at the precise moment when the Italians were collapsing at Caporetto, Petain launched his second blow.   This time he selected the front on which Nivelle had failed in the spring.   He sought no grandiose objective.   His purpose was limited to clearing that western end of the Craonne Plateau on either side of the Soissons-Laon road which, in German hands, imperilled the whole French position on the Craonne Plateau and was in fact a wedge driven into the centre of the entire Allied front.   The key to this position was the high ground just off the Laon road, the ground occupied by the dismantled fort of Malmaison, which looked across the Ailette Valley squarely at the spires and walls of Laon.   On this position Nivelle's great offensive had broken with tremendous casualties.   It was one of the strongest sectors on the whole German front, recalling in its immediate circumstances the crest of that Pozières Ridge held for so long by the Germans in the Battle of the Somme. On the west the German lines touched the Ailette and ran along the Vauxillon Plateau to the ridge where once the mill of Laffaux had stood. This point was "the Laffaux Corner" of Ludendorff and other German commentators. Thence they followed the high ground south of the Chemin-des-Dames eastward for several miles. The position had been fortified with utmost skill and care before the attack of April 16th. In the succeeding months its fortifications had been still more largely increased. Nevertheless, on the 23rd of October—after a six-day bombardment, which succeeded

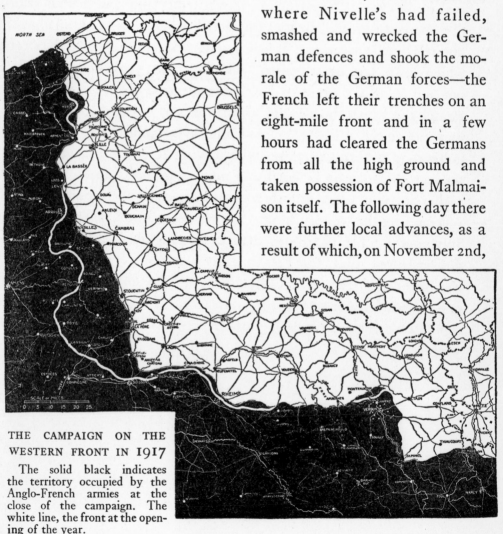

where Nivelle's had failed, smashed and wrecked the German defences and shook the morale of the German forces—the French left their trenches on an eight-mile front and in a few hours had cleared the Germans from all the high ground and taken possession of Fort Malmaison itself. The following day there were further local advances, as a result of which, on November 2nd,

THE CAMPAIGN ON THE WESTERN FRONT IN 1917

The solid black indicates the territory occupied by the Anglo-French armies at the close of the campaign. The white line, the front at the opening of the year.

the Germans evacuated all the ground still held by them on the south bank of the Ailette and for the first time since August, 1914, all of the Craonne Plateau was in French hands. More than 11,000 prisoners and 200 guns were captured, and the effect was a real if small counter-weight to the Italian disaster which gave the French armies and the French people still further confidence in Petain and won for De Maistre, who commanded the army actually engaged, a place among the success-ful generals of the war.

The German victory on this ground in May of the following year robbed the 1917 victory of all its permanent value and much of its real importance. Nevertheless, it was a brilliant and a final example of a successful employment of the tactics which aimed at local objectives and restricted successes. It was in a sense the perfection of the strategy which Joffre had described as "nibbling" two years before, but it did not and could not produce decisive results and it gave way to the new strategy in which the element of surprise was restored both on the Ger-man and on the Allied side. As Cambrai is significant as disclosing the methods of restoring surprise and achieving at least a measure of a break through, Malmaison is worthy of note as the final appearance of that earlier method which for three years achieved the most considerable successes on the western front. By his defence at Craonne in June and July and by his victorious attacks in August and October, Petain demonstrated that the French army was not yet conquered and by the opening of the next campaign would be able to make new and great contributions to the common cause. This, after all, was the real significance of the French operations between May and the end of the year.

CHAPTER THIRTEEN

POLITICAL EVENTS

I
1864 AND 1917

In the political even more than in the military events of 1917 students of American history will find a parallel in the year 1864. In the earlier year the prolongation of the Civil War, the long postponement of victory, the never-ending cycle of bright hopes in the spring and disappointments in the summer and autumn, had produced an atmosphere out of which there came many direct and indirect demands for peace, and more than one effort to compromise the difficulties which war had so far failed to settle.

The year 1864 was a year in which the courage of the weaker failed; faint-hearts, feeble spirits, counselled and even clamoured for an end to the struggle which had now resulted in the slaughter of a large fraction of the best manhood of America. Horace Greeley could demand peace at any price; President Lincoln himself, clearly as he saw the impossibility of compromise, was forced by public agitation to consent to that abortive Fortress Monroe conference which half a century later finds its counterpart in the mission of Smuts to Switzerland, in the activities of the British Minister at the Vatican, while in 1917, as all through this period of the Civil War, there were back-stairs negotiations, intrigues, manœuvres, important at the time, forgotten afterward, and buried now in the vast accumulation of official and unofficial papers defying the patience of later generations to examine.

In 1917, as in 1864, there arrived one of those hours in which the spirit of nations and of men began to falter—in which the clear vision, the gallant challenge to death and privation which marked the opening period of the war, had begun to give way. The very best of the manhood of France and of Britain, the spirits which knew no thought of surrender or of compromise, were buried in all the mournful graves which stretched from the North Sea to Switzerland. There was a decline in morale everywhere. Human nature itself began to revolt against the protraction of an agony daily becoming more intolerable and daily seeming more utterly beyond remedy.

The similar period in the Civil War commands little attention and less comment now. Those Americans who know the military history of the great struggle are infinitely less well acquainted with the grimmer and less attractive phase which reveals human nature on its weaker side precisely as the battlefield discloses it in its most splendid phase. By common consent, when war has ended, men of all nations combine to dismiss from memory and from history those circumstances which detract from the glory of the unselfish sacrifice. Thus it is that, although only two years have passed since 1917, the record of the intrigues, the falterings, the weakness, is already blurred and will in no long time disappear almost completely, and later generations will think of the men and women who lived and dared and suffered in the period of the World War rather as demigods than as human beings. We shall have one more legend which, by doing utmost violence to the facts, vindicates anew the claim of fallible human nature to possession of those qualities with which the ancient Greeks decorated their gods in Homeric legend.

But if one is to understand 1917 on the military side it is essential to know it from the political angle. The intrigue, the treachery, the treason of this year, these circumstances are inextricably linked with the deeds on the battlefield. Treason behind the lines, domestic disorder, suffering of the civil population, selfishness on the part of the politicians, these things went far to explain the collapse of the Italian army at Caporetto, while, before the French tried and failed at Craonne, Caillaux had forecast a surrender peace for his country in which he should play the rôle of the supreme dastard. And as the year closed, Lord Lansdowne, former Secretary for Foreign Affairs—under whose direction Anglo-French association had hardened into military understanding, under whose immediate direction France had been encouraged in the Tangier time to challenge Germany—uttered a document, which, however moderate in tone and reasonable in character, could have and did have no other meaning than to urge that Great Britain should make a negotiated peace with her great enemy, while that enemy was still victorious on the battlefield and confident in the possession of a continental empire greater than that of Napoleon. In the very opening weeks of the year President Wilson had spoken of "peace without victory," and when the President of the United States had so modified his views as to lead his nation into the World War these earlier sentiments remained to give courage to those weaker if not less honest spirits for whom the supreme tragedy of the war had become so intolerable that peace at any price—the "white peace" of contemporary euphemism— seemed preferable to war under any circumstances. The voices of selfishness, in class and in mass, alike, were joined with those of cowardice and treachery. All over the world there was beginning a dim perception that the destruction incident to the struggle had gone so far that there was now little chance of restoring much that had seemed an essential part of orderly government and methodical existence. As revolution in Russia more and more fiercely flamed up and the forces of anarchy attacked institutions and obliterated systems, there spread a growing consciousness, a mounting apprehension, that while armies still faced each other in the trench deadlock, Bolshevism might conquer Western civilization as it had mastered Russia, and civilization itself would disappear.

Day by day it became clear that the war had strained human institutions, governmental systems, the endurance of men and women themselves, so much that even peace when it came could not bring that immediate or possibly that eventual restoration of the world of 1914 to which the peoples of the nations at war had hitherto looked forward confidently.

There was an ever-increasing appreciation of the fact that, whatever the issues of the war, there was now little reason to question the old German assertion that civilization itself was committing suicide and, that, without the settlement of those questions which had provoked the war, the nations in arms were becoming bankrupt—were more and more sacrificing not merely the flower, but the larger fraction of their male population. Hunger, misery, forebodings of actual starvation, these were in the minds of millions. The submarine at sea, the bombing airplane in the clouds, the ceaseless roar of the artillery, all combined to break the morale of the civil populations quite as much as it attacked the military resources of the nation.

All of this the German turned to his own advantage, while Bolshevism, which he encouraged and fostered, destroyed Russia as a military force; and as a nation, at the precise moment when Bolshevist leaders were uttering words which were interpreted by western dreamers and idealists as a new gospel, as a further revelation comparable with the doctrines of the French Revolution, German politicians and leaders gave lying echoes to those principles and those utterances. "Peace without annexation and without indemnity," demanded by Russia, which had renounced every Romanoff claim, was now championed in the German Reichstag by politicians who never for a single moment contemplated the evacuation of Belgium, the surrender of Poland, or even the restoration of the invaded districts of France. And in this period there was faltering in the statesmanship of all the Allied countries. In Britain those Liberal elements which had opposed British entrance into the war at all, now acting in the name of humanity, urged a settlement which could not come except by the surrender of Britain's allies to Germany. Lloyd George himself publicly suggested that Germany might find compensation in Russia with Allied consent, while Smuts and other British representatives journeyed to Switzerland and Spain and elsewhere in vain efforts to find in secret conference with the enemy some basis for negotiated peace which would leave to the Allies a degree of security, if only a small fraction of honour.

In France there was even more faltering. There was even more treachery. Between the spring and the winter the Republic had four cabinets. In that time treason flourished openly, peace was preached almost publicly. German agents passed through Paris, French newspapers were purchased by German gold, and the trail of intrigue led from the banks of the Seine to those of the Hudson and La Plata.

Defeatism flourished; cowardice, disguising itself as liberalism and as humanity, now appeared from the dark corners in which it had hidden. France was at the point of moral collapse when in despair she turned to Clemenceau, finding once more—as so frequently in her long history—a supremely great spirit who was to lead her out of despair, through fortitude, to victory.

But of the three European allies the plight of Italy was worst. On the economic side her condition was incomparably inferior to that of her two associates. The German submarine campaign in the Mediterranean deprived her of the coal, the raw materials, and the food essential alike to her industry, her war making, and the existence of her population. The old breach between the Clerical party and the Monarchy reasserted itself and the appeal of the Pope to the belligerents to make peace was seized upon by at least a section of the Clerical element to undermine the morale of the army. Moreover, socialism and anarchy responded in Italy even more than in France to the pronouncements of Bolshevism in Russia. In losing Russia the Allies were not merely deprived of millions of soldiers, whose departure permitted Germany to move innumerable divisions to the western front; almost more deadly was the effect of Bolshevist propaganda. It was a madness which could not have assailed the minds of men and women had the way not been prepared by the endless torture of the war. But to those in despair it held out a promise of relief as unreal as the mirage that thirsty travellers see in the desert, but to be pursued with the same frantic zeal.

In this period the appeal of President Wilson for peace at the opening of the year; the bid of Socialism, advocated in Russia, propagated by Germany, expressed in the Stockholm Conference; the appeal of the Pope; and, finally, the counsel of Conservative selfishness voiced by Lord Lansdowne, combined to unite the most diverse elements and the most inimical classes. Mankind was attacked at once on the side of humanity and of selfishness, of reason and of passion. The peace offensive broke lines hitherto unshaken. It is almost impossible to exaggerate the degree to which the whole Allied cause was imperilled in this time and by these various factors. Not even the military defeats of the next year—which once more put Paris in jeopardy and again seemed destined to open a road to the Channel—were actually as deadly menaces as those other dangers which filled 1917.

And yet, since in the main these perils attacked the spirit—since they were in their very nature imponderable, not to be disclosed by battle maps, not to be explained by the citation of debates in the Reichstag, or Parliament, of speeches in the market place—since the whole phenomenon was, after all, a product of the emotions, the passions, the agonies of the hour—it is almost impossible even now to describe or to preserve the facts which made up the inner history of 1917.

Yet, out of the turmoil and welter there does emerge the one clear and unmistakable truth. The belligerent world was rapidly approaching the moment of complete exhaustion. The bonds of discipline, of government, of civilization itself, were loosening. Conditions hardly paralleled since the days of the Thirty Years' War were appearing in western Europe, and men and women everywhere, aghast at the abyss which was opening at their feet, turned to the thought of peace without victory, without decision, even without honour, as holding out the single promise that the world could be saved from that chaos into which Russia had already disappeared and toward which the rest of the world was drifting headlong.

The circumstances of the political history in this period are of relatively minor importance. All the scheming and the treachery of the selfish, the seduced, the corrupt, led to nothing. All the back-stairs negotiations, the secret exchanges, the international conclaves, arrived nowhere. The appeal of the Pope, like the proposal of the President, did not shorten the war by a single hour. In the end the struggle went forward because the German—perceiving his public as yet less shaken behind the firing line and his army not only more successful than the opposing armies but now in a position which held out the promise of speedy and supreme victory—declined to abate by one degree those claims, or moderate in one particular those ambitions which he had held when he set out to achieve world power. Had Germany been wise, clear-sighted, possessed of a statesman like Bismarck, she could have made a peace in 1917 which would have left her far forward on that imperial road which she had deliberately entered three years before. But her mood was the mood of Napoleon in 1813. The blindness, the overweening self-confidence, which made that great soldier refuse the advice of friends, disregard the warnings of statesmen, invite the ruin which overtook him, now afflicted the German war lords. By contrast, despite all the weakness, there was still left in Allied manhood the strength for one final struggle. Western civilization was in its last ditch, but when the Treaty of Brest-Litovsk revealed that all the smooth and appealing words so recently and frequently in German mouths had meant nothing, and that still, as always, the choice was slavery or resistance, western Europe rallied; and there was left to it just sufficient strength to hold the line until American millions should transform the whole situation and demonstrate that German victory was henceforth and forever impossible.

II.   IN GERMANY

The summer of 1917 was marked by the first direct break in the political solidarity of Germany. Before the British failure in Flanders, in advance of the Italian disaster, and while Russia was still maintaining armies in the field, there was in the Reichstag a sudden outburst which for a moment seemed to promise that the German people and a controlling faction of German statesmen would be able to throw off the control of the military and the Junker elements. All through the summer debates in the Reichstag, changes in the Chancellorship, a multiplicity of circumstances combined to create the impression that Germany was at last ready to abandon the old ideas and the old ideals which had provoked the war—prepared to renounce those ambitions which made a peace of understanding impossible—and there was a widespread belief among the Allied publics that the war might be terminated by negotiation rather than by battle, since Germany was at last yielding to more liberal ideas and the control of German affairs was passing from the hands of the soldiers to those of reasonable statesmen.

In July, Erzberger, one of the leaders of the Roman Catholic party, precipitated a political crisis by a sudden attack upon the Government for its failure alike in the diplomatic field and in the department of domestic affairs. Bethmann-Hollweg's halting efforts to answer the charge were of no avail. The Emperor himself, after a conversation with the military chiefs, issued a decree granting immediate and equal suffrage to Prussia, a step recalling concessions of a similar sort made by one of his predecessors in the face of similar conditions and thereafter repudiated when the conditions changed. The Emperor's concessions roused violent protest from the Prussian Junkers, but, so far from satisfying the Reichstag element, now in revolt, it merely provoked a demand on the part of Erzberger and his associates for a statement of the war aims of Germany.

As a consequence of his failure to check the political uprising Bethmann-Hollweg resigned and disappeared. He was not a great men. The distance between him and Bismarck was incalculable Yet the circumstances of his position had made him one of the most conspicuous figures throughout the conflict. His declaration that the invasion of Belgium was wrong created a profound sensation in the world. That, left to himself, he would have followed a wiser course seems at least possible, but in fact the critical decisions were made by the military element and he was compelled to defend policies which he did not originate and of which he frequently did not approve. It is not impossible, therefore, that time will deal more gently with the first German War Chancellor than did contemporary criticism.

The departure of Bethmann-Hollweg did not silence the political tumult. On the contrary, it encouraged still further uproar, which culminated on July 19th in a declaration adopted by a decisive majority in the Reichstag advocating peace, endorsing a peace of conciliation, and adopting the Russian phrase of "No annexation and no indemnity." This action made a great stir over the world. It made a profound impression upon Liberal and Radical elements in Great Britain, France, and the United States. Germany seemed to be yielding to democratic ideas. The influence of Russian revolution upon Hohenzollern policies seemed only less great than upon those of the Romanoffs. Influenced by military failures, affected by the growing conviction that military decision was impossible, many elements in the Allied publics welcomed the events in the Reichstag as a sign and a promise.

Unfortunately, whatever may have been the sincerity and the reality of this movement in Germany at the outset, any chance of success was speedily destroyed by the complete transformation of the military situation. Had German armies continued unsuccessful, threatened alike on the east and the west; had Russia endured a potential enemy, it is conceivable that the beginning made in the Reichstag might have been followed by still further progress toward a liberation of the German people from the control of the soldiers—a deliverance accomplished by Germans alone. But while this protest was still in its initial stage Russia collapsed and ceased to be a factor in the war, and the military party was able again to point to the possibility that, with Russia out, decisive victory, with all its unlimited rewards, might be achieved.

With this change in the circumstances the military party resumed its control, but resuming its control it undertook to use what had happened as propaganda. In other words, it made the ideas and the principles which had been voiced in the Reichstag the cover for its own campaign. It did not repudiate what had been said; rather it sought at one time to delude Allied publics with the impression that Germany had become liberal, and prepared the way for the old-fashioned military decision with all its attendant circumstances of forcible annexations and enormous indemnities.

The Pope's appeal for peace came at a fortunate moment to supply the German leaders with new material. The Kaiser had selected as his new Chancellor an old bureaucrat, Dr. George Michaelis—an unknown man of no particular ability, responsive only to the old autocracy—and the new Foreign Secretary, Kuhlmann, an adroit and skilful intriguer, undertook to deceive the world by new protestations of German fidelity to ideas acceptable to the western Allies, momentarily advocated by the Reichstag and now abandoned when the promise of victory had reappeared. Kuhlmann endeavoured, not without success, to foment unrest and division in Allied countries by using publicly that formula

BURSTING SHELL

This remarkable painting of a bursting shell is the work of Christopher Richard Wynne Nevinson, who received his honourable discharge from the British army, with the Mons star, in 1916. The following year he was appointed Official Artist with the British Armies.

"TANKS"

From a painting by Major Sir William Orpen, A.R.A., representing two of the clumsy monsters about to wallow across a ditch

FRENCH INFANTRY CREEPING FORWARD TO MAKE A SURPRISE ATTACK

SERBIAN BOMBS

Above—A bomb-throwing attachment for the rifle, used by Serbian troops.
Below—A rifle-thrown bomb barrage on the Serbian front.

ONE OF THE MOST REMARKABLE PHOTOGRAPHS OF THE WAR

Allied aviators have managed to set fire to this German's observation balloon. So he has hooked on his parachute harness and jumped clear. The parachute is just breaking away from the balloon. The aviator who took this photograph does not know whether the balloonist reached the ground in safety or not.

ON THE BRITISH FRONT

German shell breaking near a British battery. One of the "Nissen huts," invented by Lt. Col. Peter Norman Nissen, may be seen at the left

BRITISH FIELD DRESSING STATION NEAR MONCHY

These stretcher-bearing Tommies seem rather heedless of Fritz's shooting, though his shells are bursting not far away

RIGHT THROUGH THE ROOF OF THE BAKERY

Lawrence Scanlon, an American aviator, lost control of his machine 500 feet above the French aviation school at Avord. It crashed down through the roof of this building and when Scanlon scrambled unaided out from among the débris, he was astonished to find that he was without a scratch.

MACHINE GUNNERS ADVANCING

These French troops are going forward as their artillery prepares the way

IN THE WAKE OF THE HUNS

The retreating Germans concealed a quantity of explosives in a corner of this building and then built a fire in the opposite corner. The explosion occurred some
time after their departure, as was intended

which he and his associates had privately rejected and were, at Brest-Litovsk a few months later, to repudiate altogether.

German diplomatic, German political leadership, having been forced to submit momentarily to a revolt in the Reichstag, predicated upon liberal ideas, now endeavoured to make the fact of this revolt produce disarray in Allied countries and cover that period in which Germany was making the necessary preparations for the great Ludendorff offensive of the next year. How successful she was the Italian disaster at Caporetto presently disclosed. Thus the German conducted a new peace offensive pending the time when he should be ready to make one more stupendous bid for military conquest, and used as ammunition the precise words urging peace and conciliation which his own fellow-countrymen had uttered in the Reichstag in July. The Devil was no longer sick, but well he still retained the monk's garb.

All through the late summer and autumn these manœuvres went on. Kuhlmann's deliberate effort to create a "peace atmosphere" was echoed and seconded by peace speeches of Count Czernin, the Austrian Prime Minister. In October a naval mutiny was seized upon in the Reichstag as a pretext to refuse to vote a war credit. But before October had ended Caporetto had been won; the last semblance of sincerity in the protestations of German liberals had vanished. The Kaiser now called Count Hertling to replace Michaelis, and Hertling was frankly and unmistakably the tool of the military party. Moreover, the military situation was such that he was now able to resume where Bethmann-Hollweg had left off. The movement for peace in Germany had collapsed in the presence of a promise of victory. The words spoken in the Reichstag in July of 1917 and the terms written into the Peace of Brest-Litovsk in February, 1918, measure the distance between the two states of mind.

Had the German movement of July continued, had the spirit which it had expressed prevailed, nothing seems more certain now than that a negotiated peace would have followed. The mass of facts which are to-day becoming public property indicate how willing Allied statesmen were to listen to any reasonable overtures coming from Berlin. General

Smuts journeyed to Switzerland; the British Minister to the Vatican received, if he did not make, preliminary proposals. No Allied government could have continued had its people been convinced that it had rejected a sincere or moderate German proposal of peace. That Bismarck would have seized the opportunity to assure for Germany reasonable profit for her great sacrifices cannot be doubted, but such Allied interrogations as were made, directed inevitably at ascertaining Germany's position on the all-important question of the liberation of Belgium, were met by evasive or defiant answers. Germany was not willing to give any assurances that she would evacuate Belgium and her refusal destroyed all chance of a negotiated peace.

Napoleon after Dresden and before Leipzig made a similar blunder, with consequences which were less disastrous on the whole to his country but equally fatal to himself. He chose to fight—and lost his throne. The Kaiser and his advisers now decided to risk all on a similar venture and their decision took the Kaiser to Amerongen as Napoleon's decision carried him to St. Helena. Germany, all through this fateful summer, remained faithful to the Bernhardi gospel of "World power, or downfall."

The explanation for the success of the military party in Germany in repulsing a peace movement in their own country before they skilfully turned it to their own use abroad must be found in the circumstances of the Russian Revolution. Had Kerensky been able to prevail upon revolutionary Russia to continue in the trenches Germany might have consented to a negotiated peace by the end of 1917, but the collapse of Russia served to reanimate all the old appetites and all the early ambitions of the German people. The postponement of victory for three years led to the incipient German revolt of July just as similar and even greater disappointments had led to larger protests in Allied nations. But the new promise that plunder and power could be had silenced all protests. Even though sinking into anarchy herself Russia did a final and incalculable injury to Germany. Her helplessness invited Germans to a new revelation of their purpose, and this revelation led straight to that Armistice of November 11, 1918, which deprived Germany not merely of the fruits of her earlier victories in the World War but of her conquests in all the wars of aggression since Frederick the Great started Prussia on her predatory pathway.

III. AUSTRIA

Following the declaration that war existed between the Imperial German Government and the United States, the Austrian representative in the United States—who was acting in place of Dr. Dumba until Count Tarnowski, Dr. Dumba's successor, arrived—demanded his passports. Diplomatic relations with Austria were thus severed although actual war was not recognized to exist until December 7th. So far as the United States was concerned then, Austria continued in a relation which was neither war nor peace and supplied an opportunity for various peace manœuvres. In point of fact, the Austrian Government not merely "played up" to the German peace campaign, but various gestures were made, the most famous of which—a letter of the new Emperor to his brother-in-law Prince Sixtus, under the date of March 31, 1917—contained the startling statement: "I beg you to convey secretly and unofficially to Poincaré, President of the French Republic, that I shall support by every means, and using of my personal influence with my Allies, the French just claim regarding Alsace-Lorraine." The publication of this letter a year later by Clemenceau, following a debate carried on between the statesmen of the warring countries, produced a real sensation and was followed by the resignation of Count Czernin.

It may be assumed that this letter was an unmistakable evidence that the Austrian Emperor and the Austrian Court were eager for peace. This fact was common knowledge all through the summer and autumn of 1917. It was the explanation of several conferences in Switzerland, conferences in which both British and French representatives sought a common ground on which to base real peace negotiations. Unquestionably Austria was sinking. The complete collapse of the Dual Monarchy in the autumn of 1918 was the result of too long and too great a strain, which shattered the relatively slender bonds uniting the several races and populations of the Hapsburg Empire. Badly organized, lacking alike the German genius for organization and the German solidarity, Austria-Hungary suffered infinitely more during the war, and in 1917 the approach of a collapse was revealed by many circumstances. That the young emperor, eager to save his throne, had earnestly and honestly struggled to free himself from German control, seemed unmistakable. It was this situation which led to the transfer of German troops to the Italian front, and the victory of Caporetto, following the collapse of Russia, gave Austria a respite and for the moment served to save the Empire from impending ruin. It is worthy of note that all through this period the Allies, who in the early days of the war had formulated a programme which amounted to nothing less than dissolution of the Hapsburg Empire, more or less publicly renounced this ambitious prospectus. Like Germany, Austria could have saved herself by making peace any time in 1917.

Like Germany, moreover, Austria made many preliminary movements in that direction. She was prepared to, and she did renounce for herself any war gains. The destruction of Russia had eliminated the great menace which for a generation had hung over the Monarchy. Russia had disappeared, Serbia had been crushed, Italy had been checked and was presently defeated. Peace on the basis of the *status quo ante* would have given that security which Austria had long sought. The defeats of Serbia, Roumania, Russia, and finally of Italy, combined to achieve the real war ends of the Hapsburg Empire. Unhappily for her, despite many efforts—some of which were revealed in public statements which made a stir all over the world—Austria-Hungary could not regain her freedom of action. Compelled to share German successes, which were now without profit for herself, she was equally compelled in the end to share in a ruin which for herself was complete.

IV. THE POPE'S APPEAL

The most significant of the various Austrian efforts in the direction of peace was disclosed in that series of political operations in which the Austrian Parliament, the Roman Catholic party of the Centre in Germany, and various Roman Catholic elements all over the world, rallied to the support of that peace proposal made by the Pope himself on the 15th of August.

The appeal of the Holy Father to the several warring nations suggested in many respects that document which President Wilson had uttered a little more than six months before. Like the President, the Pope in the nature of things was compelled to address both sets of contestants in words which were equally courteous and similarly devoid of content which might indicate sympathy with one set of contestants as contrasted with the other. He was obliged, like the President, to deal only in generalities, and since the President's note to the belligerents had been frankly only a preliminary, Mr. Wilson had been able to escape the necessity faced by the Pope of suggesting some basis for settlement. The basis suggested by the Holy Father—the only basis which could be suggested, given the circumstances of the conflict—included the waiving of all claims for indemnity and "entire and reciprocal condonation." Belgium was to be evacuated; her independence restored. German colonies were to be returned to her and she was to restore the occupied districts of France. The vexed questions of which Alsace-Lorraine and Italia Irredenta were the most conspicuous examples, were to be referred to peaceful negotiators, while similar disposition of the problems of the Balkans, of Poland, and of Turkey was suggested.

The rejection of this Papal appeal by Great Britain, by France, by Italy, was a foregone conclusion. "Reciprocal condonation" was in itself nothing more than a confession of equal guilt and responsibility for the war by the Allies, who had been attacked. For three years Germany had conducted a war of aggression in the manner of a barbarian. She had attacked her neighbours without justification. She had taken their territory, enslaved their peoples. She had assailed neutrals as well as belligerents. She had defied every convention, she had outraged every doctrine of humanity. Moreover—in effect, though not in intent—the Pope's peace message now asked of these Allied peoples who had been the victims of Germany's iniquities that they should condone the crime, confess to guilt not less great, and put aside all hope of German reparation.

This spelled moral ruin and economic destruction. In substance it denied to the small peoples that liberty the western powers had promised. It perpetuated the Austrian and German rule over subject nationalities. It continued the European anarchy out of which the World War had come. Above all, it continued in power the men, the parties, and the principles which had precipitated the struggle. As a consequence, to listen to the words of the Pope—which were inspired by the same desire to end the conflict, by the same concern for humanity and civilization as those of the President half a year before—was not merely to resign the war itself, but to submit to these very evils against which the Allies had been fighting for three years. It was not merely to betray the future but it was also to abandon those who had died to prevent that which would be established if peace on the Pope's terms should now arrive.

It was fitting, therefore, in view of his own gesture, that Mr. Wilson should make answer for all nations at war against Germany, and his response was in fact adopted by all the Allied governments and chancelleries. On August 27th the President's answer was sent. That response, which was signed by Mr. Lansing, was as follows:

In acknowledgment of the communication of your Holiness to the belligerent peoples, dated August 1, 1917, the President of the United States requests me to transmit the following reply:

Every heart that has not been blinded and hardened by this terrible war must be touched by this moving appeal of his Holiness the Pope, must feel the dignity and force of the humane and generous motives which prompted it, and must fervently wish that we might take the path of peace he so persuasively points out. But it would be folly to take it if it does not in fact lead to the goal he proposes. Our response must be based upon the stern facts, and upon nothing else. It is not a mere cessation of arms he desires; it is a stable and enduring peace. This agony must not be gone through with again, and it must be a matter of very sober judgment what will insure us against it.

His Holiness in substance proposes that we return to the *status quo ante bellum* and that then there be a general condonation, disarmament, and a concert of nations based upon an acceptance of the principle of arbitration; that by a similar concert freedom of the seas be established; and that the territorial claims of France and Italy, the perplexing problems of the Balkan States, and the restitution of Poland be left to such conciliatory adjustments as may be possible in the new temper of such a peace, due regard being paid to the aspirations of the peoples whose political fortunes and affiliations will be involved.

It is manifest that no part of this programme can be successfully carried out unless the restitution of the *status quo ante* furnishes a firm and satisfactory basis for it. The object of this war is to deliver the free peoples of the world from the menace and the actual power of a vast military establishment, controlled by an irresponsible government, which, having secretly planned to dominate the world, proceeded to carry the plan out without regard either to the sacred obligations of treaty or the long-established practices and long-cherished principles of international action and honour; which chose its own time for the war; delivered its blow fiercely and suddenly; stopped at no barrier, either of law or of mercy; swept a whole continent within the tide of blood —not the blood of soldiers only, but the blood of innocent women and children also and of the helpless poor; and now stands balked, but not defeated, the enemy of four-fifths of the world.

This power is not the German people. It is the ruthless master of the German people. It is no business of ours how that great people came under its control or submitted with temporary zest to the domination of its purpose; but it is our business to see to it that the history of the rest of the world is no longer left to its handling.

To deal with such a power by way of peace upon the plan proposed by his Holiness the Pope would, so far as we can see, involve a recuperation of its strength and a renewal of its policy; would make it necessary to create a permanent hostile combination of nations against the German people, who are its instruments; and would result in abandoning the new-born Russia to the intrigue, the manifold subtle interference, and the certain counter-revolution which would be attempted by all the malign influences to which the German Government has of late accustomed the world.

Can peace be based upon a restitution of its power or upon any word of honour it could pledge in a treaty of settlement and accommodation?

Responsible statesmen must now everywhere see, if they never saw before, that no peace can rest securely upon political or economic restrictions meant to benefit some nations and cripple or embarrass others, upon vindictive action of any sort, or any kind of revenge or deliberate injury. The American people have suffered intolerable wrongs at the hands of the Imperial German Government, but they desire no reprisal upon the German people, who have themselves suffered all things in this war, which they did not choose. They believe that peace should rest upon the rights of peoples, not the rights of governments—the rights of peoples, great or small, weak or powerful—their equal right to freedom and security and self-government and to a participation, upon fair terms, in the economic opportunities of the world—the German people, of course, included—if they will accept equality and not seek domination.

The test, therefore, of every plan of peace is this: Is it based upon the faith of all the peoples involved, or merely upon the word of an ambitious and intriguing government on the one hand and of a group of free peoples on the other? This is a test which goes to the root of the matter; and it is the test which must be applied.

The purposes of the United States in this war are known to the whole world—to every people to whom the truth has been permitted to come. They do not need to be stated again. We seek no material advantage of any kind. We believe that the intolerable wrongs done in this war by the furious and brutal power of the Imperial German Government ought to be repaired, but not at the expense of the sovereignty of any people—rather a vindication of the sovereignty both of those that are weak and of those that are strong. Punitive damage, the dismemberment of empires, the establishment of selfish and exclusive economic leagues, we deem inexpedient, and in the end worse than futile, no proper basis for a peace of any kind, least of all for an enduring peace. That must be based upon justice and fairness and the common rights of mankind.

We cannot take the word of the present rulers of Germany as a guarantee of anything that is to endure unless explicitly supported by such conclusive evidence of the will and purpose of the German people themselves as the other peoples of the world would be justified in accepting. Without such guarantees treaties of settlement, agreements for disarmament, covenants to set up arbitration in the place of force, territorial adjustments, reconstitutions of small nations, if made with the German Government, no man. no nation, could now depend on.

We must await some new evidence of the purposes of the great peoples of the Central Powers. God grant it may be given soon and in a way to restore the confidence of all peoples everywhere in the faith of nations and the possibility of a covenanted peace.

ROBERT LANSING.

Thus ended the second of the memorable attempts to restore peace. The Pope had failed as the President had failed before him. Precisely as the President's words were used by German agents and German propagandists, both the words and the fact of the Pope's appeal were employed all over the world in Allied countries and most effectively in Italy to serve Germany. The bitterness of temporary emotions not unnaturally led to the charge that the Pope had himself been a party to German and Austrian intrigue and the charge was sustained by the evidence that his words had been employed effectively to aid the Ger-

man cause.   But the same charge was made on the same basis and with
no less justice when President Wilson had made his proposal.   In-
dubitably the Pope helped Germany and Austria momentarily, as did
the President.   The object of the Pope and the President alike was to
restore peace, and both may perhaps be fairly acquitted of any par-
tisan sympathy to which their words and actions were turned.

V. STOCKHOLM

While the President in December and January and the Pope in
the following August sought to restore peace, a third and hardly less
significant effort was made by socialism.   The Russian Revolution
presented to the various socialist, labour, and radical elements of the
warring countries an opportunity to speak which had long been denied
them.   Socialism itself had temporarily disappeared as a world power
and as an international influence, when, in the first days of the war, the
masses of the peoples of the several nations cast aside all political align-
ments and rallied to the support of their respective governments.
The theory that the mass of French and of German workingmen would
refuse to fire upon each other when war came was instantly disclosed
to be moonshine.   The millions of the various countries demonstrated
that they were Frenchmen, Germans, or Italians, before they were
socialists, and newer political doctrines were submerged in the flood of
secular patriotism.

From this revelation socialism did not recover until that moment
when the failure of governments to procure victory or restore peace
finally led alike to a decline of the governments in prestige and a movement away from the political systems these governments represented.
The Russian Revolution roused socialism all over the world and it became henceforth a dangerous and a potent factor.   It, too, demanded
peace.   It, too, worked for peace, and in Allied countries, where political
liberty was far more firmly established than in Germany, it was able to
do infinite harm to the governments which were conducting the struggle.

The first manifestation that socialism had recognized the new opportunity came in April when a call was issued from The Hague for a

socialist conference at Stockholm. The conference itself, from a relatively unimportant gathering, was transformed to a centre of world interest through the demand of the Russian revolutionary leaders that it should be made something approximating a peace conference; that the representatives of socialist parties and of the masses of the European populations should send to the Swedish capital delegates who were in fact to decide the rights and wrongs of the war itself and thereafter to bring about a restoration of peace. In all this the German hand was patiently disclosed coöperating with the Russian revolutionist.

Socialism in France and Italy, Labour in Great Britain and the United States, divided over the wisdom or folly of sending representatives to Stockholm. Conservative instinct everywhere in Allied countries was against such a course, but largely owing to the influence of Arthur Henderson in Great Britain and Albert Thomas in France—both of whom had been in Russia, both of whom had been impressed by the Russian Revolution and by the gravity of that situation which Russian defection would produce—advocated the sending of representatives to Stockholm.

Henderson represented Labour in the British Cabinet, Albert Thomas was the successor of Jaurès as the leader of the French socialists and was also a cabinet minister. The urgings of both these men, each of whom believed that tactical advantage would be gained by going to Stockholm and presenting the Allied cause, aroused debate, but the Ribot Cabinet refused to permit French socialists to go. The British Ministry refused and then changed its mind, but, after the Cabinet had acquiesced, the British Seamen's and Firemen's Union, having the submarine issue in mind, refused to man ships to carry the delegates.

Still the Stockholm Conference went on. Presently Henderson, finding it impossible to convince the British Cabinet, resigned. Albert Thomas similarly left the French Chamber. Germany, on the contary, sent Scheidemann, and Scheidemann turned to German profit such opportunities as he could find.

The Stockholm Conference, of itself, accomplished nothing of importance. Indirectly, however, it contributed materially to breaking up the union of the socialists and radicals in France, Britain, and the United States with members of the other political parties, all of whom had hitherto been closely associated in the effort to win the war. As a contribution to Germany's campaign to break down the morale of the Allied countries, as a circumstance in the peace offensive, it was successful. A break between the radical and socialist portions of the American, British, and French publics and the rest of the nation was achieved. This break did infinite harm. It was followed by a flood of so-called liberal and progressive utterances and writings which assailed the Allied governments at home, accused them of blundering and of offences similar to those which had been charged against the German Government. It built up a body of suspicion that Allied governments were responsible for the prolongation of the war. It cast doubt upon the sincerity of purpose and the justice of the war aims of the various nations in arms against Germany.

The same division continued after the war had terminated in the Armistice. It reached new heights of denunciation when the terms of the Peace of Versailles were at last presented to the world. This was not mainly, perhaps not largely, a consequence of the struggle over the Stockholm Conference. That was, after all, only an incident. The fact was that three years of war had produced a profound change in all the nations engaged, and that only in Germany—and there solely because of a sudden return of the prospect of victory—was the Government capable of preserving union or preventing discussions, which, however honestly intended, unmistakably contributed to break down the will, not alone for victory, but the will to continue and to escape defeat.

Henceforth, ever growing in numbers and in vehemence, one faction in each of the Allied countries insisted that the Allies should restate their war aims and demanded that a restatement should include an acceptation of the Russian formula of peace without annexations or indemnities. This faction denounced their own governments and ministries as reactionary, imperialistic, Prussian; insisted that peace without victory—"a white peace" following Mr. Wilson's phrase, which the President had now discarded—was the only possible solution of the world conflict which would make peace for the future permanent.

The Russian Revolution became for this group a symbol of democracy and of progress, which the excesses of Lenin and Trotsky and the terrible tragedies of the Revolution were unable to destroy. The Allied course toward Russia was consistently denounced. The feeble and futile efforts of Allied governments to support the elements of order and to restrain the forces of anarchy in the Slav nation were assailed without limit as examples of an effort to restore the Romanoff régime.

The summer and autumn of 1917, then, sees the development of a totally new frame of mind. Many men intellectually and morally prominent in their communities and in their countries now openly and definitively broke with the doctrine that all personal opinions must be laid aside—all independence including that of thought itself must be sacrificed—in the name of national unity and to the end of achieving military victory. This group was largely made up of pacifists and of extreme radicals, to whom nationalism itself was hateful. Within its ranks traitors and cowards found safe intellectual asylum and did infinite harm to the Allied cause. But recognizing these circumstances it is still impossible to dismiss this ferment of 1917 summarily, if only because it exerted great influence thenceforth, during the war and after the war, during the peace negotiations and thereafter endured as a living force.

The majority of the Allied publics continued, though not without some perplexity and hesitation, to support their governments, to stand fast to the belief that unconditional peace was the only possible end of a war with Germany. In no small degree the Germans themselves were responsible for this. Circumstances in Allied countries, the progress of events and of thought in the world, everything combined to give the Germans an opportunity to make a profitable peace in 1917. Their own peace offensive, their use of the Pope's appeal, of the President's note, of the socialist upheaval, cleared the way for precisely this outcome. Fortunately for mankind the German General Staff, the Kaiser and his generals, in the supreme crisis were incapable of laying aside the dream of a complete military victory. The reaction from the Peace of Brest-Litovsk temporarily checked and even silenced the voices that were heard in 1917 with ever-increasing willingness by Allied publics. Liberalism and radicalism were compelled to stand aside once more as they had in the opening days of the war in the presence of Prussianism displaying the old spirit in a new revelation. But the moment the German had lost the war, before even the Allied victory had become absolute, these voices were raised again and have been heard ever since in growing volume.

VI. IN FRANCE

More interesting, and in a sense more significant, since they produced the supremely great war minister of the conflict, were the political disturbances in France in 1917. Before the year had yet begun, the weakness of the Briand Ministry was unmistakable. Briand himself had been a useful factor in the general Allied cause. He was not a man of deep principles or of profound convictions; least of all was he a statesman of the energy or the force of Clemenceau. Like Lloyd George he had been in many camps. He was a clever, adroit politician, a man of personal charm and political instinct, not without patriotic emotion, but beyond all else a politician. He had staked his fortunes in the previous year on the success of Joffre. In many ways his support of the first French Commander-in-Chief was creditable to him. The intrigues directed against the victor of the Marne both by jealous generals and by even more jealous politicians—whose efforts to interfere in military affairs encountered an absolute obstacle at Chantilly—had largely failed through the constancy of Briand's support. Unfortunately, criticism of Joffre was not exclusively due to meaner and baser motives. On the whole, his later course had been a failure, beginning with the terrible costly ventures which he described as "nibbling." At Les Éparges, in Champagne and in Alsace in 1915, Joffre had sacrificed great numbers of French soldiers for insignificant gains. Verdun in 1916 had been a tremendous blow to his remaining prestige and there was necessary a great victory at the Somme to save him. Briand gambled on that victory and lost. He then, after many hesitations, finally consented to the substitution of Nivelle for Joffre, a compromise which avoided bitter assaults from the friends of Joffre, but satisfied neither the nation nor the army. The wrangles in Greece, in which it was felt Briand had shown too great tenderness to the Greek Royal Family, were equally injurious to the Premier.

The truth was that in the winter of 1916-17 the Briand Ministry, from a variety of causes, was sinking. Briand was tired, and not unwilling to go in advance of some event which might preclude a subsequent recall. Accordingly there was little surprise when, on March 17th, as a consequence of a sharp quarrel between General Lyautey and the French Chamber, Briand resigned. Lyautey, as Governor-General of Morocco, had won and held for France a vast empire and revealed himself as the greatest pro-consul in all French history. He had been brought to Paris as Minister of War following Joffre's resignation, but his imperious methods, his unfamiliarity and impatience with politics and politicians had led to one incident after another, and finally to a resignation several times before threatened.

Briand was followed by Ribot, an old man, a notable figure in French politics, a conspicuous member of the Briand Cabinet, but not a man of the force necessary for the situation. He was faced at once by the consequences of the failure of the French offensive at the Aisne, followed almost immediately by an epidemic of strikes, and culminating in that socialist revolt which grew out of his refusal to permit French socialists to go to Stockholm. As domestic disorder increased, as campaigns of treasons and defeatism developed, Ribot more and more showed himself incapable of dealing firmly with mounting perils. As a consequence there was little surprise when, in September, Ribot resigned and President Poincaré called upon M. Paul Painlevé to form a Ministry. Painlevé is one of the interesting figures of the war. He and Henri Poincaré, the President's brother, were the greatest mathematicians of their generation in France. Painlevé had enjoyed a distinguished career as a professor. He was a man of high character and of great intellect. As Minister of Inventions and as Minister of War in the Briand and Ribot cabinets respectively he had rendered great service to

France. Two momentous decisions, one to remove Nivelle and the other to dispose of King Constantine, were due almost exclusively to him.

But on the political side Painlevé was weak precisely where Lloyd George and Briand were strong. Unlike both of them he was a poor speaker. Unlike both of them he was incapable of building up a following in Parliament. He had no dexterity in intrigue or manipulation. Men did not follow him even when they respected him. He was a singularly noble type, rare in the politics of any country. He had courage; his honesty was beyond question; but he could not make friends as could Briand or Lloyd George, nor could he kill his enemies as did Clemenceau.

The result was inevitable. French conditions were approaching a crisis. In a sense the political situation of France was desperate, and Painlevé—with all his honesty, with all his earnestness, with all his great ability in certain directions—was not the man to face the storm. Accordingly, on November 16th, he was succeeded by Clemenceau. The decision of Poincaré to call Clemenceau was interesting. In the Versailles sessions at which Poincaré had been elected President of the French Republic, his most determined enemy had been Clemenceau, who saw in Poincaré a peril to the Republic. In addition to violent opposition in the sessions themselves Clemenceau had finally made a personal appeal, which was in itself almost a menace, to Poincaré to refuse the election. At all times Clemenceau in his newspaper had been a savage critic of the President. Yet there was left to Poincaré no real choice. He had to go to Clemenceau or recognize that the war was lost.

The coming of Clemenceau is one of the great moments of the war. He was the last hope of France, and the measure of his service is not to be found in France alone. This old man, 76 years of age when he took office, had been in the rough-and-tumble of political fights ever since the days when, as a boy, he was sent into exile by the Third Empire. He was one of those who, at Bordeaux, protested against the cession of Alsace-Lorraine. He went through the Commune with all its terrible experiences. Several times in his political career he had been dismissed as finished, notably in the time of the Panama scandal, but it had never been possible to eliminate a man who combined so many of those qualities which the French admire.

As a journalist Clemenceau wielded the deadliest pen in France. All through the war Paris had waited for the publication of his newspaper—frequently interrupted by the Censor—to read the brilliant, fatally caustic phrases of the man who was known to his fellow countrymen as "The Tiger." In politics and in political life he had destroyed one ministry after another by the sheer force of his attack and the fatal exactness of his phrases. He made enemies where most politicians endeavoured to make friends, and then compelled his enemies to do his bidding by the sheer terror which he inspired.

For three years Clemenceau had been regarded as impossible in France because no man could calculate what direction his phrases would take. His criticism of allies might easily be more severe than his denunciation of enemies. His fondness for the perfect phrase frequently led him into excesses which might have fatal effect for the whole French cause in a world crisis. It was always inconceivable that France would appeal to Clemenceau in advance of an ultimate crisis, but that crisis had now come.

Moreover, all through the war Clemenceau's voice had been the one clear note. From the first moment when masses of French reserves arrived in advance of equipment, in the period of inefficient hospital administration, in the days of military failure, Clemenceau had never hesitated to tell the truth. As chairman of the Military Committee of the Senate he had visited every front. The common soldier was known to him in the trenches, and with the passion of an old man, near the end of a great career, his mind turned upon the salvation of his country. Whatever his faults, his limitations, his weaknesses on the human side; whatever his past, Clemenceau in the years of the war has concentrated himself upon the battle and dedicated himself to the winning of the victory.

In the summer of 1917, in the early autumn when treason flourished, when defeatism was rampant in France and out of it, this marvellous

A BAD CORNER ON A MOUNTAIN ROAD

Four camouflaged tractors hauling a monster gun up a rocky pass

ON THE MARNE FRONT
French infantry starting on a raid

EXPLODING AMMUNITION

Beyond this village was an ammunition dump. This was the first of a series of explosions which soon shattered the whole village

THE BATTLE OF MENIN ROAD

Some captured ground on the British front

CYCLE ORDERLIES UNDER FIRE

The enemy's artillery evidently has the range of this road. It seems a poor place to tinker damaged bicycles

LARGE SHELL BURSTING AMONG THE SAND DUNES OF THE BELGIAN COAST

A LIQUID FIRE BARRAGE

The Germans were the first to use this terrible weapon, but the French soon learned to pay them back in their own coin

A LITTLE BIT OF A MODERN BATTLE

It is a German shell which is bursting on the right. The crouching figures on the left are Germans who have been driven within range of their own artillery. A moment ago they yelled "Kamerad." Now they are eagerly awaiting the direction to go back to the Allies' rear

ARTILLERY IN ACTION ON A WOODLAND ROAD

old man day by day thundered his denunciations. France knew that if he became Prime Minister such mistakes as he would make would not be in the direction of caution, compromise, hesitation. Reluctantly, unwillingly, but ineluctably, Poincaré, the French nation—like the commander putting in his last reserves—turned to Clemenceau; and with his coming we enter into one more of those far-shining hours of French history which have meant so much to all mankind.

The achievement of Clemenceau was spiritual before it was material. The army at the front felt, when Clemenceau went to the Quai d'Orsay, that there was no more of weakness and faltering behind it. In fact, in the months that followed, the soldiers in the trenches saw more of the French Premier than did the people in the streets of Paris. Day after day he came to the Chamber with the dust of Champagne or Artois still on his clothes. To every criticism, to every effort to renew discussions as to war issues, peace terms, he returned the single answer: "I make war." "Victory"—he told the French people at the very moment of approximate despair—"belongs to him who lasts through the final quarter of an hour." And the world knew, the French knew, that Clemenceau might die but that he would not surrender. It is impossible to estimate the extent to which this one man transformed the situation. Facing treason at home he sent a former prime minister of France, Caillaux—still the master of the greatest single following in the Chamber—to prison. Malvy, who had been in a dozen cabinets and who possessed enormous political influence, he sent into exile. Bolo Pasha, and smaller men whose guilt was unmistakable, he sent to the firing squad. Sarrail, a political general whose influence in the Chamber had been sufficiently great to save him from the consequences of a dozen intrigues, Clemenceau promptly recalled from Salonica and retired to private life. Of a sudden a clear, strong wind—like that mistral which descends the Rhone Valley—rushed through French political life. France called to Clemenceau and Clemenceau responded with an appeal which the French people could understand and obey.

Nor did Clemenceau merely work at home. From November until April he fought the British to procure that unity of command which was at last achieved after the March disaster, and, by bringing Foch into complete control of Allied armies, first avoided final defeat, and then achieved supreme victory. The energy of this old man is beyond description. He had the physical characteristics of Roosevelt in his most vigorous days. His presence in the Government was almost as valuable as that of Napoleon had been to his armies on the battlefield. He came to power at the most desperate moment in the war. Almost exactly a year later he was able to announce to the French Chamber that the enemy had been beaten, that victory was achieved, and Alsace-Lorraine restored to France. Then France gave to him the title by which he will perhaps be best remembered, that of "Father of Victory."

As a youth Clemenceau had been associated with Gambetta in that despairing resistance of France after Sedan and Gravelotte. He had signed the Bordeaux memorial against the cession of a foot of French soil or a stone of a French fortress. He was almost the sole survivor of that group. Every illusion, every human affection, every dream, save one, had been burned up. A cynical, world-weary old man, his love of his country, his devotion to France, still remained. In war, and in the peace-making that followed war, he had but a single thought. He brushed aside impatiently all those aspirations and theories which were based upon the re-making of the world just as he swept aside all the whisperings and whimperings of those who advocated a "white peace" when he took office. His whole life was dedicated to a single object. Perhaps he would have been more fortunate to have died when the bullet of an assassin reached him in the early days of the Peace Conference. Conceivably he lived too long after the realization of the end he had sought. But no Frenchman in all the long history of the race deserved better of his country than the statesman who, in November, 1917, took into his firm hands the control of that ship of state whose destruction seemed imminent.

VII. IN THE UNITED STATES

America had entered the war in April. Following the arrival at the great decision the country gave evidence of a unity of purpose and of thought as amazing as had been the spectacle of its apparent disunion in the period preceding entrance into the conflict. Of a sudden a single national purpose was disclosed in every branch of life and in the most varied and mutually hostile elements of society. When the war was declared soldiers appeared along the railroads guarding the bridges and tunnels, reproducing a familiar circumstance of Europe at war. Measures were taken to guard against that uprising of German-Americans long forecast and widely feared, but there was neither revolt nor disorder. The very spirit in which the United States entered the war overawed those elements which might have caused trouble. The German-American press became silent. German intrigue went underground. In political life there was only one party and one purpose.

The progress of military preparations belongs to another volume, in which America's campaign will be discussed. On the political side the utterances of the President and the revelation of German intrigue provide the main interest. American missions visited Russia, and Elihu Root, a former Secretary of State, sought, in the Russian capital, to contribute to limiting the extent of anarchy. The mission was a failure. Nor was the American public able then or later to understand the Russian phenomenon. The message which the President sent to Russia might have produced some effect had it been reform rather than peace that Russia sought. As it was, like all other Allied missions, that from America spoke to deaf ears. The Russian offensive began and failed while our representatives were still in Russia, and their return was not unaccompanied by danger.

The President's response to the Pope's note evoked nation-wide approval, and this approval was heightened by the fact that there was published at the same time a German document, henceforth memorable, namely an intercepted despatch from Count Luxburg, the German representative at Buenos Aires to his own government sent through the medium of the Swedish Legation. Argentina at that time was going through a political crisis, partly occasioned by the Government's attitude in the matter of the German submarine campaign. The message in question contained the following sentence: "As regards Argentine steamships I recommend either compelling them to turn back, sinking them without leaving a trace (*spurlos versenkt*), or letting them through.   They are quite small."

"*Spurlos versenkt*" became, thenceforth a characterization of German methods, and the American people found in this example of duplicity and essential violence further proof of the meaning of German procedure which had already been partially disclosed to them in the Zimmermann Note.   There followed a long series of disclosures of a similar character affecting the United States more directly but they were in truth only new appeals to the converted.   The mass of the American people had made up their minds on the German subject.

As a consequence, the political history of the United States during the first year of the war between the declaration and the peace of Brest-Litovsk is merely the history of a nation setting itself resolutely to the unfamiliar task of creating armies, reorganizing its resources, harnessing its gigantic strength for the new task.   Memorable because of its later bearing upon the peace negotiations but notable at the time merely as a statement of America's view of the bases of peace and the President's conception of a League of Nations, was a declaration of Mr. Wilson on January 8th and known thereafter as the Fourteen Points.   These Fourteen Points were as follows:

1. Open covenants of peace and no secret diplomacy in the future.
2. Absolute freedom of navigation in peace and war outside territorial waters, except when seas may be closed by international action.
3. Removal as far as possible of all economic barriers.
4. Adequate guarantees for the reduction of national armaments.
5. An absolutely impartial adjustment of colonial claims, the interests of the peoples concerned having equal weight with the claims of the government whose title is to be determined.
6. All Russian territory to be evacuated, and Russia given full opportunity for self-development, the Powers aiding.
7. Complete restoration of Belgium in full and free sovereignty.
8. All French territory freed, and the wrong done by Prussia in 1871, in the matter of Alsace-Lorraine, righted.
9. Readjustment of Italian frontiers on lines of nationality.
10. Peoples of Austria-Hungary accorded an opportunity of autonomous development.

11. Roumania, Serbia, and Montenegro evacuated; Serbia given access to the sea; and relations of Balkan States settled on lines of allegiance and nationality.

12. Non-Turkish nationalities in the Ottoman Empire assured of autonomous development, and the Dardanelles to be permanently free to all ships.

13. An independent Polish State.

14. A general association of the nations must be formed under specific covenants for the purpose of affording mutual guarantees of political independence and territorial integrity to great and small states alike.

German and Austrian efforts to twist these and succeeding declarations of the President to their own uses failed completely since almost immediately Germany, by her terms of peace imposed upon Russia at Brest-Litovsk, showed her real self and demonstrated how impossible peace on any basis was in advance of German defeat.

The true significance of the Fourteen Points was lost upon the American and Allied publics alike at the moment. The world was at war and had its eyes fixed upon those material issues out of which the war had grown. It did not comprehend, nor could it comprehend, that the President of the United States in his utterance was placing emphasis not upon Alsace-Lorraine, the Trentino, and the liberation of subject peoples, but upon the formation of a league of nations. It did not understand that for him all else was minor and subsidiary; failure to understand had strange consequences a year later, but at the moment, with only the material aspects of the declaration in mind the people of France, Great Britain, and Italy, quite as much as the United States, hailed this speech and, by their very enthusiasm, contributed to convincing Mr. Wilson that his hearers found in a league of nations the same promise which he had there discovered.

CHAPTER FOURTEEN

BREST-LITOVSK—*Conclusion*

I
THE RUSSIAN SURRENDER

It remains now to trace the last phases of the Russian episode so far as it immediately concerns the World War. The domestic circumstances of this supreme catastrophe must await that future time when they may be intelligible to a historian able to deal dispassionately with the complete record. For the western Allies, for the men and women who were giving their best in life and treasure, the Russian defection became immediately and remained an act of treason, not early to be forgiven and not at all to be understood.

We have seen how the collapse of the Russian military power in July had for its consequence the appearance of German reserves in Flanders and at Cambrai in sufficient numbers to defeat the British offensives. We have similarly seen that the arrival of German divisions on the Venetian front precipitated an Italian disaster at Caporetto which only by a narrow margin missed putting Italy out of the war.

In the same fashion, the Russian Revolution had on the political side at one time divided the Allied publics, set in motion domestic protests and rebellion against Allied policy, and destroyed an incipient German movement toward a peace of understanding; thus democracy in Allied countries was weakened, in the Central Powers crushed, Allied military power was checked on the French front and broken on the Italian front: such were the outward circumstances of the Russian Revolution.

In this same time there persisted a total misapprehension in the west as to the purposes of the Russian revolutionists themselves. For the west the supreme concern was to pursue the war to victory. For Russia the sole and overshadowing interest was to achieve peace without delay. The west appealed to Russia to continue in the battle. Russia appealed to the west to lay down its arms.   The truth, long hid from the west, was that Russia was already out of the war, that no Russian statesman or leader was capable of reanimating the Russian spirit.   The Lvov Ministry, which was moderate and liberal, had failed because it endeavoured to preserve Russian faith with the west.   Kerensky was doomed from the beginning because, while he understood conditions better, he lacked the iron necessary to become a dictator and, short of a dictatorship, there was no remedy left.

In July Russian armies had fled a field of victory in Galicia.   Frantic and gallant efforts of Korniloff, the new Russian commander, to rally his broken armies, failed.   In August a great national Congress at Moscow listened to Kerensky and Korniloff, to all that remained of the voice of reason and patriotism, with little enthusiasm and no permanent result.

In early September a new German offensive resulted in the fall of Riga.   This offensive was memorable on the military side as the first appearance of that Hutier tactic which reappeared at Caporetto and Cambrai and then burst forth in deadly menace in the German attacks of 1918.   The fall of Riga was for the Allies final proof of that fact that Russia, in Kerensky's hands, could not help itself or them.   For the enemy Riga was the last detail in Mittel Europa.   The German *ante-bellum* maps, outlining the German place in the sun of Europe, had stretched from Antwerp to Riga, and the fall of the latter city carried with it a death warrant to new German democratic movements.   In addition, it restored German influence in those Baltic Provinces where the Teutonic knights had once ruled and where the German minority still preserved the legend of Prussian return.   The whole pan-German conception was galvanized once more by a victory which, on the military side, was cheaply won and of no greater permanent consequences than the capture of Antwerp three years earlier.

The fall of Riga had immediate consequences in Russia.   Korniloff, seeing his armies slipping from him, military discipline collapsing, conceived that the sole chance now remaining lay in a dictatorship.   His supporters claimed that Kerensky consented to such a solution and agreed to associate himself with such a dictatorship. Kerensky and his friends maintained that no such consent was ever given, but the fact is unmistakable that Korniloff now set out to proclaim a military dictatorship and that in the west he found support among the governments and the military leaders who saw in him the sole chance of keeping Russia in the war. It was at least with the tacit consent of the western governments that Korniloff set out for Petrograd.

But the decay of the army and of the nation had gone too far to leave either the discipline or the patriotism necessary to rally to authority in this critical hour. Russian sentiment mobilized against Korniloff. Kerensky, if he had made any promises, repudiated them and threw himself into the arms of the Bolsheviki, into the arms of the extreme Left. Hitherto he had sought to unite the moderates on both sides. In this impossible task he had failed. Now, called upon to decide between the two, he threw himself at the feet of those who had been his opponents at all times hitherto and now for the moment supported him only because they saw the ruin both of Kerensky and the national cause within their grasp.

Proclaiming himself Commander-in-Chief of the Russian armies and denouncing Korniloff as a traitor, Kerensky now enlisted a force of Red Guards, arrested Korniloff, evicted such patriotic moderates as had hitherto been his associates, and proclaimed Russia to be a Republic.

Meantime, the German armies continued slowly and deliberately to exploit their success at Riga. Seizing the islands of the Baltic and the ports in the Baltic Provinces they menaced Petrograd itself, and on the 19th of October the Russian Government fled to Moscow. Three weeks later, on the 7th of November, the extreme radicals, under the lead of Lenin and Trotsky, seized Petrograd, gained control of the Government itself, and laid hands upon the control of the bleeding body of Russia. Kerensky was a fugitive, and the last remaining chance of orderly reform in Russia was eliminated.

The two men who now gained mastery upon Russian power were singularly unlike. Lenin must remain one of the great figures of his time. In exile, proscribed, subject to every known oppression, he had preserved his ideal, which was to reorganize Russia and then the world on the Marxian doctrine of class warfare, giving to the proletariat supreme control, abolishing national boundaries, and associating the working-men of the world in an international federation.

A great man Lenin was, if only because of the fixity with which he pursued his purpose. Unlike his associate Trotsky, his personal character was above reproach. Unlike Kerensky accession to great power did not turn his head or lead him away from his principles. If Russia as a nation perished, if the whole world system of order was torn to pieces, he was unconcerned so long as there was left to himself the chance of applying his principles. He saw, in the destruction of order in the world, the necessary first step in the direction of that order which he was seeking to establish. He was a narrow-minded, intense fanatic, a visionary, prepared to sacrifice human life without limit, prepared to use force without measure to attain his object. But he was consistent, however insane, and he was faithful to his principles, mad as they were.

Trotsky, on the other hand, was a politician in spirit. He shared Lenin's purposes, but he was ready to compromise, manœuvre, manipulate. He was one of the many revolutionists who had found asylum in America and had slipped back to Russia with the coming of the Revolution. In the United States his reputation had not been of the best and he carried away from that country a hostility to the economic system quite as intense as he had cherished for the Russian governmental system.

The policy of Lenin and Trotsky was simple. They had to do two things to insure a continuation of power and they were prepared to do these two things promptly. These were: first, to destroy the Russian army that there might be no renaissance of national spirit, no military dictatorship such as Korniloff had conceived of, and, second, to conclude peace with Germany. These two things accomplished, Russia was in their hands as completely as a chloroformed patient is helpless under the knife of a surgeon. Thereafter they were free to undertake such experiments as they chose. To gain this freedom they were prepared to pay whatever price was necessary, although they did not perceive in advance how great the German price would be.

Having captured Petrograd on November 7th, and in the following fortnight consolidated their power, Lenin and Trotsky on November 21st, proposed an immediate armistice, and matched this venture in foreign politics by the abolition of private property in the domestic field. Meantime, the destruction of the army was assured by the transfer of the command to an ensign, Krylenko, on December 7th. One of the loyal old generals was assassinated; headquarters were abolished; the military and diplomatic secrets of Russia, including the various treaties with Russia's western Allies, were published, to the supreme delight of the Germans.

II. ARMISTICE AND PEACE NEGOTIATION

Finally, in mid-December, Lenin and Trotsky concluded an armistice with the Germans, which provided for a peace Conference at Brest-Litovsk. This Conference opened its sessions on December 22nd in the presence of representatives of all the Central Powers and of Russia. Russia's allies had in the meantime protested against an armistice which was a clear violation of the treaty of September 5, 1914, between Russia, France, and Great Britain—subsequently signed by Italy—which had pledged all four to make no separate peace. As for Roumania, when the Russian armies had collapsed in Galicia, her own troops, reorganized by a French general, had made a gallant but hopeless stand, and now Roumania, too, was compelled on December 6th to join in the truce. On this same date Trotsky, Commissioner of Foreign Affairs to the Bolshevist Government, invited Russia's allies to define their peace terms and solemnly stated that if they refused, the responsibility for the prolongation of the war must be borne by them. This, too, was playing the German game with a vengeance. When the Brest-Litovsk Conference assembled, Russia, through Trotsky, presented her basis for world peace to a Germany now completely under the domination of the military element, already making preparations for her great western offensive, designed to crush France and England before America could arrive, and enable Germany to dominate the world. The basis of peace was to be the already famous Russian programme of no annexations and no indemnities; subject nationalities were to determine their allegiance by referendum; territories taken in the course of the war were to be restored; armies of occupation withdrawn; all belligerents were to unite in providing for the compensation of the sufferers of the war; colonies were to be restored, and economic boycotts after the war prohibited.

The Germans were of course unwilling to agree that there should be no forcible appropriation of territory, that armies of occupation should be promptly withdrawn, and complete political independence thus be restored to the Belgians, the Poles, and the Serbians, or that the right of self-determination should be conceded to German Poles or Austrian Latins and Slavs. But the opportunity for manœuvre was obvious, and Kuhlmann, who represented Germany with great skill and adroitness, at once seized the opportunity. On Christmas Day Germany and her allies, through the Austrian Foreign Minister, Count Czernin, announced that Germany was prepared to agree to Russian terms, provided Germany's enemies, who had been Russia's allies, would agree to the same terms and associate themselves with the Brest-Litovsk Conference, which now took a recess until January 4th pending a response.

The trick was plain. Germany had not the smallest intention of agreeing to the Russian terms, but for her own purpose, both with respect of the German people, the Russian Revolutionists, and the Allied publics, it was important to place the responsibility for a failure upon the Allied governments. The Allies could not agree to terms such as these without abandoning the war. They knew, moreover, that Germany had no intention of evacuating Belgium or Poland, because in the secret negotiations and exchanges of views which had taken place during the war Germany had at all times declined to give any indication of her future attitude toward Belgium. They were compelled, therefore, to accept the situation which had been created and decline to make answer, notwithstanding the consequences.

Meantime, Germany gave a foretaste of her real purposes on December 28th when she responded to the Russian peace terms with the hypocritical assertion that neither she nor her allies proposed to appropriate any territory by force, but the right of self-determination had already been exercised by the people of Poland, Lithuania, Courland, and portions of Esthonia and Livonia; while General Hoffman, a little later speaking for the military element which was becoming impatient at the farce of Brest, informed the Russians that German High Command, for reasons of its own, was compelled to decline to evacuate Courland, Lithuania, Riga, and the Baltic Islands. while the Polish question was deliberately excluded.

In this situation Trotsky and Lenin sought for a moment to escape the inevitable by a public appeal to the masses of the German people, whom they seemed to believe would rise against their government. Passionate denunciations of the German course were uttered by Trotsky, but the Russian military power had now been completely abolished. Russia was helpless and words had no appeal to the German masses, who now at last saw the age-long Russian menace on the point of disappearance and perceived victory and plunder within their grasp. Moreover, disorder and anarchy were spreading all over the vast Russian Empire. Separatist movements were on foot in a dozen border regions, Finland and the Ukraine were seeking independence with German assistance. In Ukrainia, Bolshevist doctrine found no lodgment and the peasant proprietor turned to the Central Powers as the lesser of two evils, and asked Berlin and Vienna to protect them against Trotsky and Lenin. In Esthonia, Livonia, Lithuania, and Courland similar movements were discovered. Everywhere the elements of order, forced to choose between the German and anarchy, inevitably set their faces toward Berlin, and on February 9th Ukrainia formally made peace with the Central Powers and German and Austrian armies were assigned to the congenial task of protecting the granary of Russia from Bolshevism. Thus at a single stroke Russia was deprived of more than 30,000,000 people of her southern provinces from the Pripet Marshes to the Black Sea, while the Central Powers acquired, through alliance and by occupation, resources in foodstuff and minerals which, could they be made available in time, would once for all defeat the blockade of sea power. The value of the Ukraine was disclosed a few months later when in October, with defeat and even collapse threatening in the west, the German

High Command steadfastly declined to withdraw German divisions and thus surrender Ukrainian food supplies and other contributions.

The separate Treaty with Ukrainia was the death blow to the Lenin-Trotsky policy.   For nearly two months the sessions at Brest-Litovsk had been prolonged by the interminable protests, denunciations, and temporary withdrawals of the Russians.   Germany had endured these delays with complacency because in this time the last semblance of Russian military power was disappearing.   But now the end was in sight.

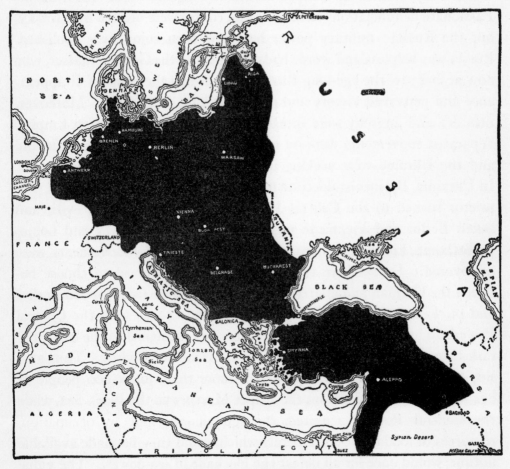

MITTEL-EUROPA IN 1917

The solid black shows the territory occupied by the Central Powers after the fall of Riga and before the capture of Jerusalem.   This is the celebrated war map frequently mentioned by Bethmann-Hollweg and other German statesmen as the basis of Germany's peace claims.

The day after the Peace with Ukrainia was signed Trotsky quit Brest-Litovsk announcing that he would refuse to sign the German peace but that the war was over. He refused to recognize German peace conditions but announced to the whole world, "At to-day's session" [that is February 10th] "the President of the Russian delegation announced that Russia abstains from signing the actual treaty of peace but declares that she considers the state of war with Germany is terminated and has issued the order for the complete demobilization of the Russian armies on all fronts."

But Germany was by no means contented to let the situation rest here, and on February 16th announced a resumption of hostilities. On February 19th German armies were again in motion, while Russian armies fled before them. Appeals from Lenin and Trotsky were of no avail. German armies flowed on toward Petrograd until at last, on Sunday, March 3rd, Russia signed the Treaty of Brest-Litovsk, while Roumania, now completely abandoned, signed an armistice two weeks later and a definitive treaty at Bukharest on March 26th.

So ended the war on the eastern front. Less than three weeks before Ludendorff launched his great offensive Germany at last found herself with her hands free. From the Baltic to the Black Sea the Russian and Roumanian fronts had been abolished, while far beyond the limits of the old firing lines German and Austrian armies advanced at will, occupying Kieff and Odessa and commandeering for their own purposes such provisions and war material as they chose.

III. THE TREATIES OF BREST-LITOVSK

While the settlement of Brest-Litovsk was expressed in three separate treaties—with Ukrainia, with Russia, and with Roumania, they constitute a unit, and can best be examined together. The purposes achieved in the three documents were these: (1) to deprive Russia of all of her western accessions since the time of the period of Peter the Great, and to build up between the Slav mass and Germany a series of states dependent upon Germany and bearing the same relation to her as those

creations of Napoleon on the eastern bank of the Rhine a little more than a century before; (2) to divide what remained of Russia in such fashion as to preclude any reappearance of Russia as a great and menacing neighbour; (3) to place all of what had been Russia, and particularly what was left outside the German sphere of influence, in complete economic subjection to Germany; (4) to foment and encourage differences between the various border tribes, making them mutually hostile and thus incapable of union.

The treaty with Ukrainia defined the boundaries of the new state which included all of Russia extending from the Austrian boundary to the lands of the Don Cossacks and from the Pripet Marshes to the Black Sea including the Crimean Peninsula and the great port of Odessa, while from the old Polish estate there was taken a portion of the province of Cholm, thus perpetuating a feud between the Poles and the Ukrainians. Germany and Austria obtained the right of free transit across the new Ukrainian State and agreed to defend it against the Bolsheviki.

The treaty with Russia abolished Russian control in Poland, the Courland, Lithuania, and the two Baltic provinces of Livonia and Esthonia, whose future condition was to be determined by Austria and by Germany. Russian delegates agreed not merely to evacuate the portion of the Turkish Empire which her troops had occupied as a result of successes in the war, but also to return to Turkey Batoum and Kars and the balance of the territory taken as a result of the successful Russo-Turkish war in the last century. Russia agreed to make peace with Ukrainia, evacuate that country, and also to withdraw from Finland and the Baltic provinces. The economic provisions of the Ukrainian treaty contained a stipulation for a colossal payment of foodstuffs, while the economic provisions of the treaty with Russia went even further. The policy here was obvious. Germany had, by her course in the war, lost her markets among Allied countries and she sought to make good this loss by creating a monopoly in the vast Russian territories.

Finally the Treaty of Bukharest with Roumania complemented and completed those with the Russians and the Ukrainians. This

treaty compelled the cession of the whole of the Dobrudja to Bulgaria, thus depriving Roumania of access to the sea; provided for "rectifications" of the Austro-Roumanian frontier, which gave the Hapsburg Monarchy control of the passes leading into Russia and possession of the Petroseny coal mines; for the demobilization of the Roumanian army under the direction of Germany; for the free passage of troops of the Central Powers across Roumanian frontiers; for the occupation of the Roumanian railroads, a monopoly in the export of wheat, and the control of the oil wells of the kingdom. So far as Roumania was concerned she received, as a sop, possession of certain small areas in the Russian province of Bessarabia, which, with a measure of consent of the Central Powers, was presently stretched to the occupation of the whole of this Russian province.

By the terms of this settlement Russia actually lost 55,000,000 of people. Two states immediately hostile to her, Finland and Ukrainia, were erected on her own soil; the Baltic Provinces, which represent the conquests of Peter the Great, the window of the Slav giving on western Europe, together with Poland, were taken, while the Bolshevist hope of using what remained to them of Russia as a headquarters from which to utter propaganda directed at the German masses, was abolished by a provision in the treaty pledging the Lenin-Trotsky Government to abstain from all such manœuvres. Russia was deprived of all her conquests of 250 years, her unity was shattered, while on the eastern frontiers of Germany and Austria, and of the Mittel Europa that the German had now created, there was sketched a series of helpless states extending from Finland to Roumania, all of them promptly occupied by German and Austrian armies, all of them transformed into economic and military creatures of the Central Powers, and many of them arrayed against each other by skilfully manipulated boundary decisions.

Since Napoleon's Peace of Tilsit, Europe had seen nothing to compare with the Peace of Brest-Litovsk. It upset the balance of power in Europe. It abolished the Russian state. It opened the granaries of Russia and of Roumania, the mines, the railroads, and the rivers to immediate German use and to subsequent exploitation when economic

war succeeded the military operations. Save for the helpless Army of the Orient interned in Salonica, there was nothing left in the east, while the consequences of Caporetto had abolished for Austria the long-standing menace of Italian attack. German mastery of the Continent of Europe, with a subsequent sweep into Asia and even into Africa, was assured if only time were left to organize the victory and perpetuate the system which had been created. Between Germany and the realization of her colossal dream in its fullest extent there now interposed only the British and the French armies, shaken by the disasters and failures of 1917 and sustained largely by the hope of the ultimate arrival of American millions. Freed as it seemed for ever from the eastern danger, the German people were now invited to turn westward and witness the triumphant progress of their armies, swollen by accessions from the eastern front thus abolished. No people in all European history ever looked out upon more alluring prospects of immediate conquest and permanent triumph than had the German people in March of 1918.

The termination of the negotiations at Brest-Litovsk marks the end of one more period in the World War. Once more, as in each of the preceding acts, Allied expectations and hopes had been brought to nothing and now at last Germany had achieved a success which could not be denied or mistaken. If her submarine attack in the west had by a narrow margin failed and was no longer a deadly peril, her military successes in the east had created an even deadlier menace.

Moreover, the last lingering hope that democracy could triumph in Germany, that the war could be ended by negotiations based upon mutual understanding, the final hope that reason and the dictates of civilization might penetrate the German darkness, had vanished.

In the paragraphs of the Brest-Litovsk treaties the world, after momentary hesitations, doubts, self-questionings, saw Germany again as she had been seen in the opening moments of the war, sweeping through Belgium and carrying fire and sword to the gates of Paris—as she had been revealed in the *Lusitania* Massacre, in the horrors of the Great Retreat of the preceding spring. The mass of reasonable men and women in the western nations were now forced to face the truth, to recognize that only by the sword could there be a settlement, that compromise was impossible, that the essentially Prussian spirit, however much it had hidden itself in the spring and summer, in the smooth words of Reichstag debates, no longer even cared to hide itself.

There was no longer a question of attacking this Germany. There was no longer an immediate possibility of depriving her of any portion of the vast booty newly acquired or liberating any of the fresh conquered captives. In their western trenches the Allied armies had now only to await the storm they knew was coming, a storm the extent of which they did not calculate, the fury of which they under-estimated, nor had they long to wait, for the ink upon the treaties of Brest-Litovsk was hardly dry before Ludendorff began his march and the guns between the Oise and the Scarpe announced the opening of the final act in the World War. Having lived through the moral crisis of the war in 1917 the Allies had now to survive the military crisis, which, if briefer, was to prove not less terrible.

MR. SIMONDS'S HISTORY OF THE PROGRESS
OF THE WAR WILL BE CARRIED FOR-
WARD IN THE SUCCEEDING VOLUME.

EDITOR

THE COUNTRY LIFE PRESS
GARDEN CITY, N.Y.

Date Due
